HOW WE GOT TO WHERE WE ARE

How We Got to Where We Are

Modernity, Postmodernism, and Christian Faith

DUANE HIX

Apex Books

Copyright © 2023 by Duane Hix

All rights reserved. No part of this book may be reproduced in any manner whatsoever without written permission except in the case of brief quotations embodied in critical articles and reviews.

First Printing, 2023

A PERSONAL NOTE TO READERS

Dear Reader:

So, how *did* we get to where we are? What has happened over the last 500 years in western culture to make us different from our pre-modern ancestors? And while we're at it, who is the "we" in the book's title? That one is easy enough. On the one hand, it's you and me and all those now living in western civilization who are interested in what ideas have shaped us into who we are. In a narrower sense, it is those among us who have participated in and treasured the Christian faith and want to know how and why our beliefs have changed – or not changed – as time has gone by.

The first question, how we got here, takes longer to answer, which is why I wrote this book. But it all boils down to three gradual shifts in thinking: we now view freedom, history, and happiness (the good life) differently than we did 500 years ago. In the pages that follow, I will explain all this in some detail, maybe more than you want. Along the way, we will get some history lessons, some pages on the interaction of philosophy and theology, a glimpse into how people read the Bible differently, and a few suggestions from me on where we might focus our energy in the decades ahead.

I invite you to join me on this journey. You will probably disagree with me on some points, and that is fine. I'm only part way through the journey myself. I have tried hard to make the book worth your while, but I don't promise it will be easy.

~ Rev. Dr. Duane Hix

ACKNOWLEDGMENTS

Anyone who has written a book eventually discovers that finishing a first draft is only half the job. If the author is not wise enough to submit that early work to a wide range of secondary examiners, critics and copyeditors, he or she is doing a disservice to eventual readers of the finished product. However satisfactory a first draft appears to the author's eyes, enough humility to seek other opinions will serve him or her well. The suggestions, corrections, and questions from those outside examiners will improve the book's focus and clarity immensely. Such has been my experience, at least, and I owe that debt to the following people.

First, I thank those who read early versions of this work and offered their criticisms and encouragement: former seminary colleagues Reverend R.C. Smith and Reverend Bill Getman, plus theologically astute laity from Cary Presbyterian Church, Tom Van Scoyoc and John Page. Their comments prompted me to include a summary Postscript. Dr. George Stroup, former Green Professor of Theology at Columbia Theological Seminary, was most helpful in the book's early stages and supportive of my effort to publish.

I appreciate deeply my wife Medora's ongoing support throughout this process, as well as her comments on many pages and her suggestion to include the appendix of theologians and philosophers. Mike Boyd, another church friend, contributed his professional copyediting skills to the final stages of this work. My daughter Emmie offered her own book publishing experience, and daughter-in-law Kate was especially valuable in the formatting procedure. To all these, I am deeply grateful.

Though the contributions of these people have improved my work, I am, of course, ultimately responsible for all inadequacies, factual mistakes or misleading assumptions. I welcome comments from readers to improve any further edition of the book that might eventuate.

~ Rev. Dr. Duane Hix

TABLE OF CONTENTS

A Personal Note to Readers v
Acknowledgements vii

Introduction and Prospectus 1

PART ONE: MODERNITY

Chapter One:
The Elements of Modernity; Setting and Overview 6
    The Elements of Modernity 7
        Late Medieval Era, the Renaissance, and the Reformation 7
        The Development of Modern Science 16
        A New Sense of Freedom 16
        History as Progressive Development 24
    Summary 29

Chapter Two:
Knowing God: Protestant Theology in Modernity 31
    Introduction: The Task of Theology 31
    Reason, Revelation, and the Knowledge of God 34
        The Reformation 36
        Cartesian Rationalism 41
        Newton, Locke, and the Rise of Natural Religion 45
        The Challenges to Rationalism 53
        Hegel and the Progress of History 63
        Schleiermacher and the Beginning of Theological Liberalism 69

Optimism's Pause:
Barth and Niebuhr; the Critique of Theological Liberalism 79

Chapter Three:
Modernity and Its Challenge to the Church 93
    Western Christianity: An Apprehension of Irrelevance 93
    The Reinterpretation of Freedom 97
        Prominent Images of Freedom in Christian Scripture and Doctrine 99
        Civil Liberty and the Social Contract Theory of Government 104
        Kant's Categorical Imperative and Freedom as Autonomy 106
        Free Trade, Self-Interest, and Personal Identity 110
        Criticisms of Capitalist Consumerism 115
    History as Fact and Progress 121
        History and Interpretation within Scripture 121
        Roots of Historical Critical Method 130
        Comparing the Two Views 135
    The Good Life 143
        Philosophical Idealism 145
        From Custom and Tradition to Education and Innovation 148
        From Superstition to Science 155
        From Hierarchical Authority to Liberty and Equality 166
        Reconsidering Mill's Conclusions 170

Chapter Four:
Christian Faith as Counterpoint 177
    Central Christian Beliefs 183

PART TWO: POSTMODERNISM
Chapter Five:
Overview and Setting; Five Central Themes of Postmodernism 194
    A Century of Background 195
    Dimensions of Postmodernism 198
    Central Themes of Postmodernism 200
        The Complexity of Meaning 200
        Language and Mediated Knowledge 204

Constructivism and Freedom 207
The Immanence of Norms 211
Analysis of Privileged Power 215
Conclusion 221

Chapter Six:
Christian Faith and the Postmodern World 223
New Space for Faith 224
Obstacles to Cooperation 230
Epistemological Relativism: Clarity is Elusive 231
Suspicion of the Past: History Is Misleading 235
Humanly Constructed Knowledge: No External Standards 240
Recent Theological Responses to Postmodernism 246
Death of God Theology 247
Narrative Theology 252
Process Theology 257
Liberation Theology 265
Dietrich Bonhoeffer's "Nonreligious Christianity" 272

Chapter Seven:
Prospects for Cooperation 283
Deconstructing Cultural "Isms" 283
Cultural-Linguistic Interpretation 293
Returning to Dialogue: Science, Nature, and Technology 303
Returning to Dialogue 304
A Theology of Nature 307
Re-examining Technology 312

A Concluding Postscript 317

Appendix: Philosophers and Theologians 325
Works Cited 331
Index 343

Introduction and Prospectus

This book considers the interplay between knowledge of God and knowledge of oneself in the modern and postmodern eras of western civilization.

Given that opening sentence, it is appropriate to begin this introduction with a quotation from John Calvin. On the first pages of the first chapter in Calvin's *Institutes of the Christian Religion*, he says, "Without knowledge of self there is no knowledge of God" and "Without knowledge of God there is no knowledge of self" (35&37). Calvin introduces these blunt statements with the following, "Nearly all the wisdom we possess...consists of two parts: knowledge of God and of ourselves. But, while joined by many bonds, which one precedes and brings forth the other is not easy to discern." He elaborates on how awareness of our own situation can lead to appreciation of God's presence in our life. Concomitantly, he explains how we never achieve a clear picture of ourselves unless we have "first looked upon God's face." Simply stated, we can increase our knowledge of God as we gain true knowledge of our own situation and personality, but we only accurately gain that personal knowledge when we enter into daily dialogue with God. The two should not and cannot be separated for real wisdom to emerge.

Many modern Christians have recognized Calvin's twofold emphasis in a well-known quotation from Karl Barth that he tries to begin every day "with the Bible in one hand and the morning newspaper in the other". In what follows, however, we will expand Barth's classic statement. It is not enough to have just the Bible in one hand; we need also multiple books on the doctrines and core beliefs of the Christian church. It is not enough to have just a newspaper in the other hand: we need deeper analyses of worldly events that reveal the underlying philosophical theories and scientific discoveries that have shaped wide cultural trends and practices. Attempting to obtain and juggle these two mountains of knowledge is a prodigious task, one that has humbled this writer repeatedly and may potentially overwhelm many readers.

This introduction intends to clarify the task by explaining some of the **presuppositions** that underlie this effort and by granting a preliminary insight into the sequence of what follows.

First, with a few exceptions, this volume is **not an empirical sociological study** of society with facts and figures pertaining to how people lived in different centuries of the modern era. We are more concerned here with ideas, with the philosophical systems and theological doctrines that shape thought and faith. While it is certain that unexpected historical events and emerging cultural practices can shape later ideas, our focus will be on the reverse, how ideas shape behavior, often in unrecognized ways. We will look at how, for example, prior emerging ideas first influenced Adam Smith's theories about the free market, and then how his new theories affected the later spread of capitalist practices. By extension, then, the process followed below often states a philosophical or scientific theory that has gained prominence, and then treats the theological responses that incorporate or criticize those ideas.

A **second presupposition** follows from the first. Many of the current public debates about the role of religion in society merely brush the surface of the real dilemmas and possibilities posed by modern and postmodern ideas. Magazine articles and newspaper editorials in both the secular and sacred press seem more concerned with the latest political elections or manifestations of unrest than with underlying causes and long-term prospects. Such works engage in too much repetitious hacking at the outer branches of an issue rather than offering a deep analysis of its roots. Therefore, we will not pay the substantial attention to popular topics that some readers might appreciate. It is to be hoped, however, that those readers can draw implications from the broader treatments of ideas displayed in the pages below as they consider current issues.

Intended Audience: A well-trained university philosopher will find this volume short on details and full of general statements that do not examine the ongoing academic debates about a particular thinker. In most cases, my interpretation of a particular theory arises from observation of the long-term impact of the idea and avoids involvement in more professional disagreements within the academy. That focus may not be satisfactory to those who have deeply immersed themselves in the study of a particular figure or theme.

At the other end of the spectrum, I suspect that many prospective readers will find the philosophical treatments too abstract or unfamiliar and decide that the reward of finishing the book will not be worth the effort of untangling theoretical concepts. This category of readers might benefit by reading the concluding postscript first; it traces the outline of themes in summary fashion. They will also find the appendix to be useful. It lists brief biographical data about prominent philosophers and theologians.

Those who might best appreciate the work likely are pastors or seminary students who have an abiding interest in theology, and well-informed laity who are not afraid of striving for a wider intellectual grasp of what ideas inform and shape their daily faith.

Descriptive, not Prescriptive: A further presupposition deserves mention. Throughout, this book attempts to be descriptive rather than prescriptive. It is a sufficiently difficult task to simply understand the wide array of themes in these pages, let alone try to judge which are beneficial and which we should repudiate. Doubtless, my attempt at restraining personal preferences (or even prejudices) will fail at times. Still, the primary intention is to state what I, and the more capable authorities whom I quote, have observed about past and present trends. Only in the final sections of each part do I venture to offer a few recommendations and warnings.

Reinforcing Central Ideas: The specific intended audience noted above (not academic professionals, but dedicated laity and students in seminary or upper-level university) bears implications for one tactic in the book's composition. As readers work their way through these pages, they will notice that central ideas receive repeated treatment in different contexts. The overall impression might be that the author could have avoided the circularity, especially in Part One. However, repetition can be a useful pedagogical tool to acquaint and re-acquaint novices in these fields with difficult philosophical and theological themes. Thus in some cases I have repeated aspects of an idea simply as reminders to the reader after many pages had intervened. More to the point, though, the context each time is important.

Chapter One intends to be an overall short summary of the themes that have influenced modern thought. Consider it a sketch whose details will be filled in later. Chapter Two addresses the same themes but from an ongoing historical perspective, tracing their interaction with theology, especially re: how we know God. Chapter Three reintroduces many of the earlier themes but interprets them in terms of the challenges they pose to traditional views of Christian beliefs and practices. Therefore, Sketch, Interaction, Challenge – that is the sequence of settings in which themes emerge and re-emerge. Part Two covers postmodernism. It considers a shorter time span and utilizes a similar but less extensive scheme.

Inclusive Language: The majority of authors quoted and discussed in this book lived in earlier centuries, eons before anyone adequately considered inclusive language. This presents an awkward pinch for modern commentators on the late authors' work, as their insistent use of masculine pronouns for God, exclusively, and for humanity, predominantly, seems an affront to modern readers, male and female. It is often tempting to correct their quotations to bring them up to date. Despite feeling twinges of guilt, I have resisted that update. I simply do not believe that I have the authority to alter history to salve even rightly troubled consciences. I trust the maturity of all readers to allow with good grace these now anachronistic references. If I am found to be personally guilty of using the same anachronisms, I hope readers will readily hold me accountable, as they should.

Some years ago, I discovered a Thomas Carlyle poem that captures the range of emotions, both pure and sullied, which Christian writers may feel as they share their ideas with the public. The poem's insights are a good way to acknowledge my shortcomings, end this introduction, and send the reader with my thanks into the pages that follow. The poem is titled "Expositor" and from Carlyle's collection *Mistaken Identity*.

> On Christ's behalf, I am not the first nor last to speak.
> In my own bag are many trinkets.
> Some are labeled wisdom;
> Some I should discard, considering they fail to fit the facts.
> I love to hear my voice composing arias of arid philosophy in beautiful cadenzas.
> The applause I give myself is devastating.

PART ONE

MODERNITY

| one |

The Elements of Modernity; Setting and Overview

Let us embark on an admittedly difficult errand. We intend, in the two parts of this volume, to examine the central doctrines of Christian faith in light of historic changes to western philosophy and public practice over the last 500 years. This will include studying the interaction of those changes with Christian theology, and the challenges they raise to the Christian church's continued existence. This chapter is preliminary. It valiantly tries to condense into a few pages the dominant ideas and developments that constitute the historical era commonly called *Modernity*. It presents a broad-stroke sketch to provide an introductory framework for themes that will resurface in subsequent chapters.

To clarify, we use the term "modernity" instead of "modernism" because the former conveys a broader scope of years and topics. "Modernism" more commonly refers to a movement in art, literature, architecture, and social science in the late 19th and early 20th century. It includes developments like stream-of-consciousness fiction, abstract art, 12-tone music composition, and functional architecture. It actually connects more to postmodernism than to the Enlightenment themes that appeared centuries earlier.

As this brief overview of modernity proceeds, please remember the sociological concept of "cultural lag". Ideas launched in elevated academic and scientific circles can take centuries before their impact manifests itself in everyday societal practices. Remember also that ideas attributed to one revolutionary thinker are invariably the result of many small, anonymous contributions both before and after the announcement of a new theory or startling breakthrough.

The Elements of Modernity

Pinpointing the beginning of an era is fraught with difficulties. Most commentators would list the early 17th century mechanical theory of Galileo or Francis Bacon's *Novum Organum* as the triggers for modern thought. Jonathan Swift, however, in his satirical essay "The Battle of the Books", lists two 13th c. Scholastics, Thomas Aquinas and Duns Scotus, among the lieutenants of the modern forces (156). Though most scholarship does not support such an early starting point, let us honor Swift's insight enough to begin this rough chronological tracing with a brief review of ideas from the late Middle Ages, the Renaissance, and the Reformation.

Late Medieval Era, the Renaissance, and the Reformation

In the 14th and 15th centuries, a once-scattered population in Italy began to congregate in urban areas, prompted by a land crunch and post-plague population growth. With this revival of urban life, the feudal system tottered. The new merchant class brought with it a better banking system, providing portable money rather than bartered goods. A rise in upward mobility began, hitherto regarded as impossible under strict feudal divisions and land-based wealth. Literacy increased in townspeople, and basic understanding of math and economic principles spread. The circle of trade widened from ports such as Venice, broadening awareness of different cultures, as goods from the Middle East and Far East enhanced daily life and expanded horizons. The medical schools of Bologna and Salerno made significant advances in surgical practices as early as 1300. The 14th c. poetry of Petrarch and Boccaccio rediscovered the ideals of Greece, initiating a new humanism that blossomed in the mid-15th century Florentine artistic explosion supported by the Medici. The abilities of gifted humans replaced the glory of God as the primary source of inspiration. Gutenberg's 1461 movable-type press rapidly promoted widespread literacy.

The last decades of the medieval era brought forth ideas that resurfaced in following centuries. Examples include:

Scientifically, the theory of impetus (or motion) that gained credence later under Galileo, was already breaking ground in the 14th and 15th centuries, as Herbert Butterfield has shown in his classic *The Origins of Modern Science...* (19-20). **Philosophically**, the system called *Nominalism* gained ascendancy. Only individual things are real, it says; there are no universals, no separate eternal realities underlying the specific names that we have created to describe groups of things. This debate cast doubts on the entrenched scholasticism of previous centuries. Later postmodern theories will draw upon this viewpoint. **Religiously**, the writings of John Wycliffe raised many of the same issues in the 14th century that Luther raised later, from criticism of a corrupt church to translating the Bible into common languages. **Politically**, remember that the

Magna Carta and its revolutionary challenge to the absolute right of kings occurred as early as 1215. Machiavelli's *The Prince* in 1513 condoned a gap between personal morality and political expediency that regrettably describes politics even today.

Granted, these early signs of a new era arose in isolation from one another. No wide spirit of change united them into a defined movement. Nevertheless, we will do well not to forget that early ideas foreshadow later developments, even if those ideas arise in centuries we are tempted to consign to insignificance.

The transition from the Renaissance to the era of the Protestant Reformation was recognized only in retrospect. But a definite new direction did begin in Germany, Switzerland, and England in the early 16th century. Therefore that movement, how it started and what it portended, occupies the next paragraphs.

In one respect, the Protestant Reformers were still trying to answer the same question that troubled their late medieval Roman Catholic predecessors: How does a sinful human being become justified, righteous, in the eyes of God? Yet, the answers given to that question, and the emerging political and cultural environment surrounding those answers, prompted another component in the irreversible movement toward the modern world. Foremost in this religious revolution are two complex factors:

- The challenge to established authority and the resultant emphasis on individual interpretation
- The further fracturing of a stable political structure in Europe that shifted the locus of influence and power from the Mediterranean basin toward northern Europe

Challenging Established Authority: Whether or not Martin Luther actually bravely stated "Here I stand; I can do no other" when he refused to recant at the Diet of Worms in 1521, that act of defiance against papal power has a rightful place among the specific events that changed the way people regard authority. It is one thing to disagree with papal pronouncements and the resolutions of church councils. Other loyal priests had done as much. Luther stepped across an invisible line and granted permission for others to challenge established power by denying the authority of the pope and his representatives, claiming that the plain meaning of scripture contradicted the papal decree on indulgences, and refusing to back down when threatened with excommunication.

We misinterpret Luther's action if we think his intention was to unleash bald personal freedom and purely autonomous will over against papal authority. He would still affirm an authority higher than an individual's opinions, and that authority would be scripture, the Word of God in the Holy Bible. Only because this monk turned biblical scholar had discovered verses that revealed a more gracious source of righteousness did he trust in the rightness of his cause. Nonetheless, it was his own personal interpretation of such passages - over against the collective wisdom of papal theologians - that marked the difference between acquiescence and refusal. The locus of authority to interpret scripture moved from the halls of the Vatican to a quiet space in the home of anyone who could read the Bible with understanding. Neither Luther nor his adversaries could adequately imagine what this challenge to religious authority would mean to other cultural and political institutions. However, within days after Worms, Luther got a hint of the future, as he escaped to the Wartburg castle under protection of the Elector of Saxony.

Fracturing of a Stable Political Structure: A wide variety of disputes inside and outside of Roman Catholicism added fuel to the fire of the Reformation. The divided papacy in the late 14th century, the misuse of clerical power to avoid punishment for public malfeasance, resentment that vast properties belonging to monasteries or bishoprics were exempt from taxes - all of these and more fed the growing desire of local princes far from Rome to have greater control over their own territories. Therefore, when Frederick III of Saxony provided Luther secret protection from persecution in the Wartburg castle, his motives were both political and religious.

Other German states and Swiss independent cities soon joined the movement, including Huldreich Zwingli in Zurich and Calvin and William Farel in Geneva. Although growth of the Protestant spirit in the Netherlands and Flanders was slow due to the military resistance of Holy Roman Emperor Charles V, Protestantism still gained a foothold there, and then spread upward into the Scandinavian countries. Less than 10 years after Luther's death, the German princes and their allies in the Schmalkaldic League had forced a truce upon the emperor by 1555. In the Treaty of Augsburg, these princes gained acceptance of the principle that the region in which a person lives determines the form of Christianity that person practices (*cuius regio, eius religio*). If one adds to this the Henrician (i.e., Henry VIII) Reformation in England in the 1530s, then the seemingly universal Christendom of 14th century Europe would, two centuries later, lay divided into distinct political and religious regions. The influence that Protestant countries would have upon future education, commerce, and politics would slowly shift power away from the Mediterranean toward the Baltic and North seas. These religious and political changes helped mark the beginning of the modern era, and these changes led into the less visible, but even more revolutionary developments below.

The Development of Modern Science

Although the word "science" has Latin and Greek roots, it did not enter everyday parlance until the early 19th century. Until an 18th century split developed between rationalist reflection and empirical investigation, the profound thinkers and experimenters who revolutionized our approach to the world called themselves "natural philosophers". The change in terminology is significant, because aspects of this development ultimately drove a wedge between investigation of nature and philosophical reflection upon it. Risking blanket generalizations, let us seek to explain key features of the new science and show the effect upon the common understanding of God's role in the universe.

Francis Bacon, Rene Descartes, and Galilei Galileo were contemporaries in the early 17th century. Their respective theories further upended the Aristotelian view of natural philosophy imbedded in Scholastic theology that had dominated prior centuries. Aristotle marvelously categorized living and non-living things through investigation of and reflection upon their "natures" (their innate tendencies or aspirations, their "souls", if you will). It was a *qualitative* form of science. For example, he claimed it was the natural aspiration of all heavy things to fall toward the center of the universe (which at his time meant the middle of the earth). Aristotle's view, later reinforced by Ptolemaic astronomy, also postulated a division between two realms, the distant heavens and the "sub-lunar" regions, and declared that in the heavens there is beautiful, dependable order, while all things below the moon were subject to change, decay and chaos. Finally, his view of motion or impetus depended on God as an ever-present unmoved mover, a steady force propelling things forward through perpetual contact.

Francis Bacon's 1620 work called the *Novum Organum* ("New Instrument") challenged this framework of Aristotle's science, insisting that true knowledge of an object requires close observation of the object's physical properties, not its supposed spiritual tendencies. This inductive practice works best when you break apart a complex whole into its smaller parts, detail how each works, and then add knowledge of the parts back into a composite knowledge of the whole. Bacon believed this freed the search for knowledge from theological presuppositions and provided more reliable information. Since then, Bacon's method has been the primary model for scientific research. It turns the spotlight on physical properties rather than philosophical deductions. You must burrow through the details long before you can gaze toward the wider horizon. Bacon is famous for the memorable quotation "Knowledge is Power", which conveys his desire for more useable information about an object. The goal and purpose of science is utility.

Rene Descartes' contribution to the new science began at the other end of the spectrum. Although Descartes was equally committed to a practical application of knowledge for "the general amelioration and increase of human life", he believed there was a more significant preliminary question to answer. Influenced toward skepticism by Montaigne's *Essays…*, Descartes desperately wanted to begin his quest for knowledge from a standpoint of absolute certainty. Steeped in mathematics and on the cusp of inventing analytical geometry, he believed that these tools were the criteria by which knowledge could be verified. In his *Meditations*, he had concluded

> …not indeed that arithmetic and geometry are the only sciences to be studied, but merely that in our search for the direct road to truth we should busy ourselves with no object about which we

cannot attain a certainty equal to that of the demonstrations of arithmetic and geometry. (76)

Thus, (as described by a translator and editor of his works, Arthur Wollaston) Descartes' aim was

> to compose a philosophy in the likeness of mathematics, to exhibit all varieties of knowledge as the consequence of a set of ultimate principles of final simplicity which would be universally accepted like mathematical axioms. (*Discourse on Method*, 8)

All that one examines in the world must be submitted to such rational categories, and any subject matter not meeting the criteria of such "clear and distinct" ideas will be regarded with less confidence and afforded less authority.

Descartes' method included the presupposition that there is a division between the soul, or thought, and the body, or matter. Rational thought, soul, is indivisible and eternal. A body is divisible into parts and recognized through its extension in three spatial dimensions (height, depth, breadth). The soul, though, has no extension in space. It observes matter from the perspective of clear and distinct ideas and finds that matter provides only provisional, clouded knowledge. Matter is worthy of investigation but takes a distant second place on the scale of reliability and certainty to purely rational investigation. This dualism has affected philosophy since Descartes' time, but it lies at the heart of his metaphysics, which provided great confidence to those who seek a sure and certain rational starting point for knowledge.

Galileo's discoveries prompted the turn toward the modern in two ways. His astronomical observations with a "new and improved" telescope provided proof of the Copernican theory of our solar system, *viz.* that the sun, not the earth, stands at the center. Resistance to this discovery arose promptly from both religious and other scientific authorities. The latter objections concerned the shape of the orbits of the planets and Galileo's explanation of tides. The church objected because of the potential dismantling of a secure system that emphasized the unchanging, heavenly perfection of God's mind. Remember the former Aristotelian belief that the heavens are stable and reliable but the earth and sub-lunar regions are subject to decay. However, if earth's orbit is governed by the same laws as other planets, and "the heavens" are both above and below earth, then the distinction between the two realms is overthrown. The settled scholastic Aristotelian worldview is in trouble, and the church recoils from the prospect of having to rethink about 4 centuries of its theology and 1600 years of astronomy.

Although Galileo is famous mostly for his debate with the church on the heliocentric system, it is his theory of motion, *impetus*, which had perhaps greater effect upon how people viewed God. Imagine how your conception of God would change if you for centuries believed with Aristotle that God accompanied a moving object all along its path, providing the constant force behind its motion, and then Galileo demonstrates that things acquire impetus simply because they have been set in motion, that they do not require the original mover to maintain contact. What is more, you can measure this movement through space mathematically, thus predicting its future course, its rate of fall, etc. No knowledge of its "aspiration" or "natural tendency" is required. One no longer looks upon the universe as if it were filled with spiritual natures, but with the eyes of mathematically measurable mechanics. Science is now *quantitative*, not qualitative.

Furthermore, Aristotle had posited four causes to any event or object: the *material* cause (e.g., the wood for a boat) and the *instrumental* cause (the boatwright and his tools), to be sure, but also, and more significantly, the *formal* cause (a mental picture of the finished product) and the *final* cause (to travel safely on water). On the other hand, inductive, quantitative science downplays the third cause and essentially disregards the last one, concentrating instead on what is physically measurable.

The result of these challenges by Galileo, and the church's resistance, led him (and Bacon) to argue for greater separation between theological speculation about God's place in the physical universe and specific scientific examinations of that universe. They criticized the use of the Bible as a science textbook and lamented the imprisonment of Christian philosophy within Aristotelian chains. (We return in more detail to Galileo's quarrel with the church in Chapter Three.)

A complete picture would explore many more discoveries of the 17th century, from Harvey's discovery of the circulation of blood to Newton's brilliant *Mathematical Principles of Natural Philosophy*. However, the work of Bacon, Descartes, and Galileo provided the core principles of the scientific revolution that would blossom into practical improvements: inductive experimental investigation, restricting research to what meets standards of geometric certainty, mathematically measured motion, and less attention to final causes.

A New Sense of Freedom

Freedom conveys a variety of meanings and begets an even wider variety of inferences. Out of that breadth of options, let us focus here on three key developments that contributed to a new conception of this word that is such a central feature of the modern world. They are the challenge to established authority, the social contract theory, which revised how nation states begin, and an epistemological theory that sees the human mind as the shaper of reality rather than its recipient. Later, we will add one further component: economic choice.

The Challenge to Authority: Luther's defiance of the pope's established sway, mentioned above, is but one example. Throughout the 16th to 19th centuries, there runs a consistent series of challenges to pope, emperor, king, and nobility. These were in some part occasioned by the contradictory blunders of the authorities themselves. In the 14th century, there is not one pope, but two: one in Rome and one in Avignon. In one decade, the Holy Roman Emperor and the pope are allies; in the next decade, the pope is the emperor's prisoner. For one brief period in the 1500s, the English crown and the French are allies against the emperor, yet earlier the English conspired with the emperor against the French. No one looking upon this political chaos could be uninfluenced. Revolutions both mild and violent erupted. In 1649, King Charles I of England is executed; in 1792, Louis the XVI of France meets the same fate. In 1776, American patriots write the Declaration of Independence and launch war against England. In 1789, Parisian citizens, supported by rebel troops from the militia, storm the Bastille and declare the Rights of Man.

Behind and beneath this revolutionary fervor lies a rejection of the traditional reasons for government by the few over the many. Ancient societies of Greece and Rome and later feudal societies of Europe clearly differentiated among classes, assigning greater privileges to those of higher rank. Both Plato and Aristotle argued that the absolute rule of a wise king is the political ideal. Fullness of liberty and equality is not the primary measure of good government. Justice is. Justice means "giving to everyone their due", and not everyone is due the same, since not everyone contributes equally to the society. Gifted citizens from traditional high-ranking families who bear the burden of leadership simply deserve more rights and liberties than a tenant laborer. To think otherwise would be to violate both the "organic" view of society based on nature's own hierarchy of creatures and also the ancient theory of moral virtue that maintains lasting justice and order. Yet, the modern world forthrightly rejected this explanation. Perhaps writings like John Locke's *Second Treatise* on Government (1690), which explicitly challenged the absolute power of a monarch, were the source of the change. However, it is equally likely that Locke's writing simply articulated and redirected a multi-sourced humanist spirit that was already spreading through the countries of Europe.

Social Contract Theory: The second theme also springs from Locke's writings. He initiates the vision that would soon replace the authority of king or queen. His *Second Treatise...* most clearly expresses the Social Contract theory of government. Primacy of place goes to Locke, although it was Thomas Hobbes a generation earlier that first published the theory in England. The theory is a thought experiment, as neither author claimed that any current nation was historically founded this way, but it describes an underlying dynamic that could be, and was, put into practice in the future. Simply put, the social contract theory hypothesizes that a group of people live near one another in what is termed a primitive "state of nature". Each individual possesses a kind of raw freedom, since no authoritative government hovers over him or her. Each can do what one wants. Nonetheless, because of scarcity and inherent egotistic perspective, the competition among them is fierce and limiting. So these free people rightly recognize that they will be better off ultimately if they form a mutually binding contract and surrender a portion of their freedom to a higher entity. For Hobbes that could be a king. For Locke, the better arrangement will be a republic, but in either case, the citizens could replace the sovereign if needed. That sovereign entity keeps order, punishes breaches of the contract, and ultimately enhances the social betterment of all.

Although it might seem that the contract actually requires a surrender of individual freedom, the initial freedom existed only in isolation. In proximity to others, it was severely limited. In Hobbes' words from *Leviathan* (9), the state of nature means that human life is "solitary, poor, nasty, brutish, and short". The new arrangement means three things:

- The contract could not exist unless free people chose voluntarily to develop it.
- Every person in the contract has equal rights in the eyes of the law.
- The total amount of freedom increases for all because of the order provided by the sovereign state.

The benefits of this type of government over one based on the divine right of kings gradually dawned upon the general public.

The social contract theory strode with long legs into the future. Its adoption by most Enlightenment philosophers expanded its implications. John Stuart Mill states one set of those implications in his little book, *On Liberty*, 150 years after Locke. Note these statements from *On Liberty* and the way that they are ensconced in western societies today. The statements reveal how the social contract theory helps define modern freedom.

1. Limits on freedom: "The sole end for which mankind are warranted in interfering with the liberty of any of their number, is self-protection. The only purpose for which power can be rightfully exercised over any member of a civilized community, against his will, is to prevent harm to others. His own good, either physical or moral, is not a sufficient warrant." (9)
2. Freedom of speech: "All silencing of discussion is an assumption of infallibility." And "If the teachers of mankind are to be cognizant of all that they ought to know, everything must be free to be written and published without restraint." (17,38)
3. Diversity as a means to truth: "Those who have never thrown themselves into the mental position of people who think differently from them...do not, in any proper sense of the word, know the doctrine which they themselves profess." He also quotes another author: "the two prerequisites for full human development are freedom, and a variety of situations." (36,57)
4. The progress of knowledge: "As mankind improve, the number of doctrines which are no longer disputed or doubted will be constantly on the increase; and the well-being of mankind may almost be measured by the number and gravity of the truths which have reached the point of being uncontested." (43)
5. Self-development and self-expression: "Where not the person's own character but the traditions or customs of other people are the rule of conduct, there is wanting one of the principal ingredients of human happiness, and quite the chief ingredient of individual and social progress." Mill also writes: "He who lets the world choose his plan of life for him, has no

need of any other faculty than the ape-like one of imitation." (56,58)

"From Hierarchical Authority to Liberty and Equality in Chapter Three" goes into more detail on these implications.

The Mind as the Shaper of Reality: To describe the third factor in a new understanding of freedom, it is necessary to shift temporarily from the political arena into the deep waters of epistemology, the theory of how we know. For most philosophers until the 18th century, the human mind is a kind of blank tablet upon which sense impressions from the outside world register themselves. The objects of that external world bear characteristics that determine human perception of them.

The Scottish philosopher David Hume, among others, challenged this theory in the mid-1700s, insisting that we cannot base knowledge of the external world upon our sensory experience of it, since what we actually know is only our own impressions. We do not study the thing itself; we study only "the psychology of our beliefs" about the thing. This skeptical viewpoint combines with a second premise of his thought, that we cannot have logically necessary truths, that is, things knowable prior to sense experience. (The only things we can know outside of experience are pre-set definitions; e.g., bachelors are unmarried males, or 1+1=2.) Hume's premise would upend many common assumptions. For example, if all we know are sense impressions, then when we see one event following another event, all we know is that it usually follows the first event. We cannot logically and necessarily say that the first event causes the second. Based on sense impressions only, past actions cannot reliably predict future results; hence, we cannot rationally affirm the idea of causation.

Hume goes so far as to end his *Inquiry Concerning Human Understanding* with this bold statement:

> If we take in our hand any volume (of a library)...let us ask: Does it contain any abstract reasoning concerning quantity or number? NO. Does it contain any experimental reasoning concerning matter of fact or existence? NO. Commit it then to the flames, for it can contain nothing but sophistry and illusion. (173)

Hume's assault on the theory of knowledge leaves a very shaky foundation for confident trust in the conclusions of research.

This greatly troubled Immanuel Kant, the German philosopher who represents both the height of Enlightenment philosophy and the door through which later thinkers will exit it. He writes the famous *Critique of Pure Reason*, primarily to counter Hume and instill confidence back into experimental research. In the process, he changes the whole relationship between the external world and the human mind. His basic premise in this respect is that hitherto philosophers had assumed that "our knowledge must conform to objects" (like the blank slate etched by the object's impressions). But Hume has called that into question, so Kant thinks we will have more success if we suppose "that objects must conform to knowledge". Within the mind itself are pre-existing categories of organization, ideas like causation, time, space, or substance. These shape the sense impressions that encounter them. The mind has a structure (a grid, a set of ideas) which provides reliability. This theory he calls Transcendental Idealism, or Critical Idealism. There are two stages in the act of learning: sensibility and understanding. "Through the former, objects are given to us; through the latter, they are thought" (92). Kant believes this process rescues rational concepts like causality.

He would agree with Hume that these concepts do not exist in the external world that we sense, but he has confidence that they do exist in the mind, and because of them we can depend on sense experience and trust inductive reasoning.

Kant's "rescue" was welcomed and accepted. There were, however, some perhaps unforeseen implications, and it is here that we return to the theme of freedom. If the human mind has such a huge role in constructing what we make of sense impressions, if it is not a blank slate passively receiving sense impressions and is instead the active shaper of them, this is a major shift in our relationship to the outside world. The external world becomes a series of malleable impressions. Objects do not carry their own meaning to the mind. They are shaped by it, given meaning according to its categories. The ideas define what we know, or to put it more bluntly, the human mind constructs reality. In one respect, the human being has the freedom, constrained only by the categories of one's own mind, to shape reality rather than being shaped by it.

In his later writings on history and political matters, Immanuel Kant reveals some of what this freedom implies. In the essay *What Is Enlightenment?* he begins:

> Enlightenment is man's release from his self-incurred tutelage. Tutelage is man's inability to make use of his understanding without direction from another. Self-incurred is this tutelage when its cause lies not in lack of reason but in lack of resolution and courage to use it without direction from another. *Sapere aude!* (Dare to know!).... that is the motto of enlightenment. (*On History*, 3)

In the essay "Idea for a Universal History...", the third thesis reads:

> Nature has willed that man should, by himself, produce everything that goes beyond the mechanical ordering of his animal existence, and that he should partake of no other happiness or perfection than that which he himself, independently of instinct, has created by his own reason. (13)

In both quotations, Kant clearly regards this epistemological freedom as the servant of reason. We are free so we can exercise our reason for the betterment of our own situation and society. It is an open question, however, what would happen if such freedom cared little for the constraints of reason. Would that freedom become merely unrestrained Titanism? As we will see in upcoming pages, some of Kant's followers answered that question in a manner he might not have approved.

The combination of the challenge to established authority, the social contract theory of government, and this reversal of the relationship between the human mind and external objects have combined to offer a radical new freedom to citizens of the modern world. This new view of freedom is one of the most significant and longest-lasting features of modernity.

History as Progressive Development

One final factor that distinguishes the modern era from the ancient world is its view of history. Over the last 400 years, for a combination of reasons, we have come to regard the events of history as a development toward a goal. It is as if Reason, or God, were moving through historical events to accomplish a plan that will benefit humanity.

Certainly, this concept of providential activity is not entirely absent from the ancient world. Central to the Jewish and Christian religions is the belief that creation, though broken, can be restored, that God guides our decisions providentially, and that the Messiah will bring about the end of time. This straight-line movement of events toward an end contrasts with Greek, Egyptian and far eastern interpretations of time as cyclical. Herbert Butterfield clarifies this in *The Origins of Modern Science*:

> ...the modern idea of progress owes something to the fact that Christianity had provided a meaning for history and a grand purpose to which the whole of creation moved. In other words, the idea of progress represented the secularization of an attitude, initially religious, which looked to a final fulfilment in some future far-off event and saw history, therefore, as definitely leading to something (225).

However, the grip of the Greeks remained strong through the centuries, and the idea of a Golden Age of the past, from which humanity has retrogressed, still dominated even through the medieval era. The Christian doctrines of original sin and the fall from grace presented stubborn obstacles to any who would look upon history as progress. (It is noteworthy that many Enlightenment thinkers, including Kant and Georg Wilhelm Friedrich Hegel, interpreted the early chapters of Genesis as though Adam and Eve's sin were a "fall upward" toward greater freedom and use of personal reason.) In addition, St. Augustine's sketch of earthly history in *The City of God* conveyed to the medieval world that there were two parallel realms of life, but the good fortune that came to those who sought the way of God was largely reserved to another world and did not manifest itself much in the amelioration of life on this earth.

For people to believe that the future will be better than the past, that time will develop toward a positive conclusion, and that humanity will be the primary shaper of history, attitudes would have to change. J.B. Bury, in his masterful study on *The Idea of Progress*, noticed such positive tendencies as early as the writings of Jean Bodin in the mid-16th century (37ff). To believe that history is progress, society must reject the theory of degeneration from an earlier Golden Age of virtue. This is happening, says Bodin, because people are beginning to believe that their own age is at least equal to, and in some respects superior to, the age of classical antiquity in the fields of science and art. As horizons enlarge through navigation to a distant city and even toward other continents, people begin to look beyond their own personal situation and see how the common interest of all people could benefit from the universal movement of history toward a better day. The advances in health, science and freedom of the 16th through 18th centuries slowly turned all of these tendencies into observable reality. As the 19th century begins, humanity is ready to express optimism about its future. The grand vision of Hegel carries that optimism to dizzying heights.

The Impact of Hegel: G.W.F. Hegel starts in the philosophical camp of Immanuel Kant's idealism and then keeps going. In between Kant and Hegel, three important philosophic developments arose. Johann Fichte had pushed Kant's idealism to its implicit conclusion, that all reality is determined by the actions of the self and its mind. Fichte also first coined the terms "thesis, antithesis and synthesis" that Hegel would occasionally use. Friedrich Schelling postulated a kind of romantic pantheism that draws all things into one mind and sees it developing. In religious terms, this implies that God evolves into ever newer states. Other writers, like Johann Herder, were increasingly emphasizing the idea of history, tracing civilizations to their roots and arguing that their behavior can best be explained by their particular cultural and temporal context. Hegel takes these three developments, adds to them a keen appreciation for freedom that had arisen in the American and French revolutions, and blends this all into his comprehensive grand system.

To Hegel, there is ultimately only one actor in life. It is one Being, which incorporates all lesser beings into itself, while allowing those beings to have their own consciousness of themselves. This being he calls Mind, or Spirit (*Geist* in German; we will use all three words interchangeably). The goal of that Being, that Mind, is to reach a point where it totally comprehends and totally expresses itself, where it becomes Absolute Self-Consciousness. All of history, every fact and action, is part of the process by which that goal is accomplished, as Mind manifests itself in specific situations, working its way toward perfection, i.e., toward its absolute state of reconciliation between what is possible and what is actual.

Hegel calls this historical process the dialectic, a word that commonly meant the give and take of argument. What happens is something like this: *Mind* takes one form in, say, a political system, and people begin to live out that system. The people, and Mind through them, realize the shortcomings of that system and move toward something quite different. That eventually appears too radical a shift, and the two sides move on to a new idea that incorporates the best of both: thesis, antithesis, synthesis. The synthesis then becomes the next thesis, for Mind is not yet finished. What is going on in these cycles is the self-positing of Mind away from itself, a free act of discovery, but then there is a realization of estrangement and a yearning for resolution. Each completion of the cycle is progress toward what Mind wants eventually to be, fully realized, yet not outside of history in some supernatural sphere, but in and through history and all of its contingencies. These cycles can occur in many different arenas, in art, science, politics, religion, or philosophy. (Hegel taught courses to his students in Berlin on most of these topics, relating how their particular developments manifested the overall movement of Spirit. That was the breadth of his knowledge.) Time is moving toward that ultimate self-realization of Spirit, when the dialectic will stop and all will be resolved.

This seems like a completely abstract and ethereal plan, but the implications of Hegel's view of a universal mind developing in history toward a comprehensive goal are immensely significant. First, despite occasional setbacks, it is now widely held that the Golden Age will be in the future, and any former splendor of the past will surely be eclipsed. We could almost say that progress is inevitable, as the dialectic moves with a power that envelops minor interference. Second, *Conflict* is good; it is necessary for progress and leads to the self-realization of both individuals and Mind. If there were no independent positing of a new direction, and no pushback against that from an opposite standpoint, there would be no ultimate resolution into the better situation. Third, the nature of Truth changes. Nothing can be finally understood to be true or false until the end is reached; all things are only partially true because they are yearning for their opposite to complete them. Hegel utilizes what we would call a theory of "coherence", in which truth is determined by ultimate relationship to the whole, rather than the more common theory, which states that ideas about an event should clearly "correspond" to the facts of that particular event. Hegel's dialectical system helps cement into place the usually unconscious modern assumption that we are inevitably moving toward better conditions in the future, that history is progress.

Summary

In this chapter, we have described settings and themes that coalesce to shape the modern world. In late Medieval and Renaissance ideas and trends, we see incipient, isolated factors that later re-emerge in a more receptive era. We can look upon these as early indications of what lay ahead, but which came too soon to be properly received. The Protestant Reformation, albeit unintentionally, became as much a political as religious force, which harnessed the vision of personal interpretation of scripture to early trends in populism and nationalism. The snowballing effect of breakthroughs in science facilitated the burgeoning hope in using new discoveries to change daily life, and edged theology out of any role in experimental investigation. Excitement about political and personal freedom challenged authority, sparked revolutions and reversed the way we regard the external world of sense impressions. Finally, learning to regard history as a development toward progress launched a spirit of optimism that would carry all the way through the 19th century. (In the second part of this work, we will ask what has become of that optimism in the 20th and 21st centuries, and how it culminated in the era we now call Postmodernism.)

A final word reiterating the role of this initial overview: Throughout the pages to follow, our intention is to elaborate substantially on the themes and developments noted above. That elaboration will include an historical tracing of how these themes affected the Christian church and its theology. It will then reorganize some of the themes according to particular challenges posed to the church by modernity. Lest these closer examinations may obscure the larger picture, this condensed introduction has allowed readers from the start to sense the wide sweep of elements that have combined to shape the modern world. Readers will benefit, I hope, from this broad view and will maintain a general awareness of the roots and direction of modern thought as we proceed.

| two |

Knowing God: Protestant Theology in Modernity

Introduction: The Task of Theology

As the 21st century approached, respected Yale theologian Jaroslav Pelikan reviewed the predominant images of Christ over the 2000-year history of Christian church and culture. *Jesus Through the Centuries* allocated roughly 100 years to each of 18 pictures. Examples included "Jesus the Rabbi" to the writers of the gospels, "King of Kings" as Constantine's Rome embraced Christ, "The Monk who Ruled the World" as Benedictine monasticism influenced Medieval society, and "The Teacher of Common Sense" in the natural theology of the 18th century.

Pelikan's review prompts the question, Why does Christianity across the centuries have so many different conceptions of Jesus Christ, the central figure of our faith? Does not the apostle James testify that God "has no variation or shadow due to change?" Does not the Epistle of Hebrews declare, "Jesus Christ is the same yesterday, today, and forever?" What then encourages and assists successive generations of the church to reframe the message of the Messiah so that he might speak persuasively to changing cultures? In essence, we are asking the question, "What is theology?"

The predominant understanding of theology within Protestantism, and perhaps in all Christian thought, affirms that the primary role of theological reflection is to assist believers in discovering a transforming knowledge of God's person and ways. It accomplishes this purpose by recognizing that God acts in and through events in time, recorded both in biblical history and in the history of subsequent eras. In addition, if Jesus Christ is resurrected and living among us, and if the Holy Spirit is the divine companion who speaks to generations of apostles on behalf of Christ and the Creator, then the church, the body of Christ, will always have divine guides helping it discover the eternal, transforming presence of God in an ever-changing landscape of culture.

This reality has led some theologians to regard the Christian church, especially Protestantism, as an ongoing "historical community" (Dillenberger and Welch, 307). According to these historians, Protestant Christians, despite their differences, share a history of change, a self-understanding shaped as they reflect on the dynamic presence of God in surrounding cultures. Therefore, Protestant theology has less hesitation than Catholicism or Orthodoxy about reinterpreting God's presence for new circumstances. Branches of Protestantism vary in their attempt to accomplish that. For example, the Presbyterian Church (USA) utilizes a *Book of Confessions*, a collection of creeds, confessions, and catechisms that span the history of the church. Declarations of faith from the Apostles' Creed through the Reformation and into the 21st century relate the resilient gospel of Jesus Christ to pertinent issues of different eras, whether that issue be the classic definition of the Trinity, the practice of usury, or combatting the specter of nuclear war. This collection of these creeds and statements of faith is one denomination's reflection of that historical community through centuries of change, but every denomination will find its own way to understand God's eternal word amid the fleeting movement of time.

The philosophical label for this effort at understanding is *epistemology*; i.e., how we know what we know, or alternatively, how we believe what we believe. This next chapter presents epistemological questions through an historical approach. It follows movements within European and American church thought on the relationship between reason and revelation, or faith and certainty, as this has long been the fulcrum around which Christians define how we know God. Readers will thus be able to trace the development of Protestant theology on this topic of Christian epistemology as it has responded to changes brought on by Modernity over the last 500 years.

As this chapter unfolds, you will notice a particular organizational framework. Gerald Cragg, in *The Church and the Age of Reason*, groups new developments across these centuries in wide but discernible trends, as follows:

- The 16th century sees the rise of Protestantism as a challenge and alternative to Catholic Medieval Christianity.
- The 17th century Enlightenment emphasis on rationalism and empiricism then challenges both Protestant and Catholic strands of Christian thought.
- As the 18th century dawns, questions and challenges to the Enlightenment itself emerge with Hume, Rousseau, and Pietism.

- With Hegel and Schleiermacher in the 19th century, progressive Romanticism overtakes and transforms reason still further, leading to theological liberalism.
- In addition to these earlier categories noted by Cragg, the trend continues into the 20th century, for the optimistic sense of progress receives challenges of its own. "Neo-Orthodoxy" reclaims some ground, and other ground lies plowed and ready for the seeds of Postmodernism.

This rough sketch of movement helps organize the new insights that awaken the church to its role in the modern age.

Before we begin, note this caveat: Lest we feel that these historical trends are hard and fast categories, it is wise to remember that in Christian theology the Holy Spirit has its own timetable. Many groups and beliefs arise that do not fit any neat schedule. These "outliers", as we may call them, are plentiful. For instance, the Quakers' emphasis on the inner light from God began in the 17th century rather than waiting for Schleiermacher's *Speeches...On Religion* as the Enlightenment waned. The Italian Renaissance humanist Lorenzo Valla began an analysis of the origins of New Testament texts long before that enterprise gathered momentum in the 19th century. Throughout church history, early prophetic predecessors spark later, well-developed theological movements. Accepted doctrine often emerges through subsequent reflection upon a much earlier cry of the heart. Our topic will proceed historically, but God's Spirit is not limited to that framework.

Reason, Revelation, and the Knowledge of God

To begin our account of Christian responses to epistemological issues in the last few centuries, let us establish a base. A useful place to start is the predominant view on faith and certainty, reason and revelation, in the late medieval Roman Catholic Church. In the 12th century, Hugh of St. Victor proposed a definition of faith that influenced Aquinas and is especially apropos for our current study. Faith, he contends, is the will to assent to things unseen with a certitude greater than that of opinion and less than that of direct knowledge. The importance of this interpretation is its awareness that there is a range of certainty in our knowledge. While Hugh might not have used the word, he acknowledges that we "doubt" some observations more than others, and if we are going to trust that which we cannot fully prove, we will do so on grounds that are not self-evident to any random observer. Using Hugh's definition as a center point, we will see how subsequent theories shift along its spectrum.

A century later, Thomas Aquinas expands Hugh's definition with slightly different terms, *viz*. the relation between reason and revelation. Aquinas' resolution of this prevailed up to the Reformation. Building on St. Augustine's understanding of the two books of God (the book of nature and the book of scripture), Aquinas cautiously incorporated the insights of Aristotle and decided that while reason and revelation occupy somewhat distinct realms, they intersect at many places, and their findings will not ultimately contradict one another. The carefully investigated findings of reason and the gracious insights of revelation both come from God. Reason generally employs sensory observations, and it does have the dual ability to enhance general knowledge and lead people toward belief in God. Yet only revelation - transcending though not contradicting reason – can plumb the depths of God's being and God's will for humanity. The two gifts work together to provide the fullest range of wisdom.

Obviously, late medieval Christian thought cannot be adequately summarized in a few theological categories, and doubtless, some trends, like mysticism, nominalism and Renaissance humanism already existed that could pull asunder the unified church. Still, Dillenberger and Welch, as they begin their esteemed account of Protestantism, have observed that in the medieval religious tradition: "The nature of God, the structure of the world and the order of the church formed part of a single whole in which the church completed and fulfilled the natural order." "It is no wonder that the culture was characterized as the *Corpus Christianum*, the body of Christendom" (4). Let this be a stable place from which to mark the changes that followed.

The Reformation

Within the wide parameters of Reformation theology, these present observations concern the stated theme of epistemology, how one knows God and God's relation to the world. Let us then consider the stances of the two primary reformers, Martin Luther and Jean Calvin, on the meaning of faith and the relation between reason and revelation. Although the predominant theme of Protestant theology, justification by grace through faith, may appear to be a different type of issue, it repeatedly responds to and illuminates epistemological issues of how we know and come to believe in God.

Neither of the two primary Reformers would stray far from Hugh of St. Victor's definition of faith. Although both would clarify their agreement by reminding that faith is a grateful response to God's revealed gracious presence, and not a steely act of autonomous will, they would nonetheless both agree that faith lies somewhere between direct, indisputable knowledge and mere opinion. Luther interpreted Christ through a theology of the cross rather than a theology of glory in the Heidelberg Disputation: "The 'theologian of glory' calls the bad good and the good bad. The 'theologian of the cross' says what a thing is"(Tappert, 79). This meant that we apprehend God through suffering and brokenness rather than through the exalted acts of a successful church in the world. We grasp the full reality of Christ by believing in spite of conventional wisdom and logical reasoning. He rejected the idea that the Pope in Rome cannot err in matters of faith, that the magisterium (the teaching office of the papacy) alone can rightly interpret scripture and then declare its interpretation incontestable. Faith to Luther is an act of trust that arises out of the struggle of the soul. He is willing to place individual conscience over against the full weight of tradition, as long as scripture informs that conscience.

Calvin, like Luther, claimed a deep conviction arising from a sudden conversion in which God gripped and redirected him. This gave him assurance of faith. But assurance is not the same thing as proof. It would be easy to misunderstand the confidence Calvin places in faith. In book 3, chapter two of his *Institutes*, and indeed throughout his writings, Calvin regularly claims that faith is sure and certain. Section 15, "Faith Implies Certainty", gives the impression that a faithful Christian does possess indisputable evidence for what he or she believes. That is not, however, exactly what Calvin means by his confidence in the certainty of faith. In section six of the same chapter, he offers his definition of faith and notes what must precede it: "now, therefore, we hold faith to be a knowledge of God's will toward us, perceived from his Word. But the foundation of this is a preconceived conviction of God's truth" (549). Once one has taken that step of trust in God, the "preconceived conviction", then, guided by God's Word, one develops the surety that is so valuable in the life of faith.

In addition, although we might feel God's presence strongly, and know aspects of God's will, God remains mysterious. We can know who God is to us, and that prompts our obedience, but what God is in metaphysical terms is one of the questions Calvin left unsolved. J.T. McNeill elaborates in his *The History and Character of Calvinism*: "While we dwell upon the divine attributes, we are not called upon to penetrate the mystery of the divine essence" (210). This too recognizes the limits of human understanding, and places any believer's attitude in between mere opinion and direct, incontrovertible knowledge. Despite the confidence and clarity both Luther and Calvin had in their relationships with a personal God, for them "The total dimension of faith includes both the mercy of God, rooted in God's activity, and trust in God when he is not experienced." (Dillenberger and Welch, p. 33) We emphasize here this need for an attitude of trust to demonstrate their difference from the hyper-confident rationalism that would arise a century after the Reformation.

On the second theme, the relationship between reason and revelation, the reformers are reticent to embrace Aquinas' full interpretation. Certainly, Calvin, to a lesser extent Luther, and the Protestant tradition that they launched, believed there is both general revelation and special revelation. According to general revelation, one may find hints of God in nature, the joys of daily life, or in moral principles that cross cultures. In such general revelation, natural reason cooperates. Luther actually ventures only to the edge of this direction. He speaks little about natural reason except to criticize its consistent attempts to justify a theology of works righteousness. However, in his famous defiant protestations at Augsburg and at Worms, he claims that unless he can be disproved by the scriptures or by "right reason" he must stand his ground and not recant. It is doubtful that he means reason is a ground of his faith, but he does allow some role for reasonable consistency and clarity in debate.

Calvin goes further in his acceptance of general revelation. For example, in book 1, chapter III of his Institutes, he declares in its first line "There is within the human mind, and indeed by natural instinct, an awareness of divinity" (43). Calvin's support for general revelation included a special appreciation of the liberal arts and their ability to highlight God's presence in the world of culture.

Despite sympathy for an alliance between reason and revelation in some areas, the reformers' insistence on total depravity, i.e., the complete distortion of all human faculties in the original fall from grace, reduces their confidence in the power of reason to understand the ways of God. Though Calvin may have agreed on the possibility of a general knowledge of God in Chapter III, immediately in chapter IV he emphasizes that such knowledge is smothered and corrupted by ignorance and malice. Thomistic Roman Catholic doctrine, alternatively, left reason largely untouched by the sin of Adam. This aspect of the image of God imprinted upon humans at creation stayed intact despite the fall, and is a significant tool for the recovery of virtue. In his *Summa Theologica*, Thomas argues: "Now the reason why man inclines to virtue is that he is rational. It is because he is rational that he acts in accordance with reason, and this is to act virtuously. But a man would not be able to sin without his rational nature. Sin cannot then deprive him of it altogether" (Q. 85, art. 2).

In stark contrast, Calvin states forcefully in Book 2, Chapter I of his *Institutes* that "sin overturns the whole man". Referring to Paul's Letter to the Romans, Calvin is clear:

> As if Paul were indicating that only a part of the soul, and not its entire nature, is opposed to supernatural grace! Paul removes all doubt when he teaches that corruption subsists not in one part

only, but that none of the soul remains pure and untouched....
Paul especially contends the mind is given over to blindness and
the heart to depravity. (252-253)

Luther is even blunter about the limits of reason. In the commentary on Galatians, he calls reason "... the fountain and headspring of all mischiefs. For reason feareth not God, it loveth not God, it trusteth not in God, but proudly contemneth him." In the last paragraph of *The Freedom of a Christian*, he summarizes his disdain: "... human nature and natural reason... are by nature superstitious and ready to imagine that righteousness must be obtained through laws and works" (85).

To summarize, there were similarities and differences between Reformation theologians and their medieval predecessors. Both responded to the same question of how one can be justified before a righteous and merciful God, though their responses obviously varied. Likewise, Reformation theologians and their predecessors maintained that faith dwells in the middle ground between opinion and self-evident knowledge, as Hugh had proposed. Nonetheless, a rift appeared regarding the preeminent means of knowing God and God's ways in the world. This issue dominated the philosophy and theology of later centuries. The comfortable connection between reason and revelation crafted by Aquinas lost ground to the new insights of the reformers. Revelation ascended, natural reason retreated, in the quest to know the person and will of God. Protestant Christians would enter the next century confident in the sovereign God but intent on using scripture first and reason only second as the means of knowing such a Lord. As we will see in later sections, this movement bears implications for the rationalism of the 17th century and also the focus on the historical Jesus discovered through critical examination of scripture.

Cartesian Rationalism

Rene Descartes (1596-1650) was, like the Protestant reformers, a bridge from an old world to a new. His early faith was solidly Catholic in solidly Catholic France. His philosophy presumed the Aristotelian concept of eternal substance as well as the Scholastic notion of eternal ideas in the mind. Belief in God was central to his system. Yet, he regarded himself as the one thinker able to remove the shackles of Aristotelian Scholasticism from philosophy. His new method created a form of knowledge that reduced thought to mathematical, rational categories. This, as we will see shortly, inevitably edged tradition, intuition, and revelation toward the sidelines, regarded as unreliable sources of truth.

The wide destructive effect of the 30 Years War (1618-1648), fed by religious and dynastic competition, spurred philosophers in all nations to seek less contentious means of defending what is true and right. As a young soldier himself during those decades (a "gentleman volunteer" as such were known), Descartes would have gained personal motivation for finding a less violent means of establishing truth. That method arose from his aptitude for mathematical and geometric reasoning. Surely, a mathematical model of problem solving could become a universal method of solving the other problems that challenge humanity also. Clear and distinct innate ideas, like the pure principles of geometry, should be the highest authority in the human mind for reasoning.

It is this underlying belief that led Descartes, while still a young man, to the process of discovery variously described in his two later publications, the *Meditations and the Discourse on Method.* Sitting (eyes closed, perhaps) in a quiet room, Descartes conducts a thought experiment, needing no added evidence from observation of the external world. He begins by asking if there is anything that cannot be doubted, anything self-evidently clear and distinctly real. The result of this thought experiment is that neither the testimony of the senses nor the logic of self-contradiction can eliminate his conviction that "I think, therefore I am." We know that we exist because no matter what might challenge our existence, we have a clear and distinct perception of ourselves thinking about that challenge. From that irrefutable starting point, he argues similarly for the existence of God, as a necessary first cause of anyone who thinks, and the existence of a real world that extends into time and space. These three conclusions are the foundation of Descartes' metaphysical, purely rational method of knowing.

What, then, does Descartes' method portend for a Christian's attempt to know God and the world God created? Although in the course of his thought experiment, Descartes included both ontological and design "proofs" for the existence of God, his primary motivation was to gain clear and distinct ideas about the physical world, so that like Galileo and Bacon, knowledge could be useful for the betterment of society. Yet, this method profoundly affected the quests of subsequent centuries to understand God, in three ways: his use of doubt, his restrictions upon what is clear and distinct knowledge, and a resultant inevitable dualism between body and soul.

Descartes' attitude toward doubt is intriguing: doubt is the primary means of investigation, and yet the goal of that investigation is to eliminate doubt. Gerald Cragg describes one part of this dynamic in *The Church and the Age of Reason*. Descartes "... recognized the fact of doubt and assigned it a regulative place in human thought; so far from being the final sin it became the primary virtue" (38). It appears that the more we are willing to doubt, the more we will learn. To the Protestant Reformers, doubt was indeed a tool when questioning human institutions, but it was mostly an unwelcome obstacle to full faith in God. It was never a primary virtue to pursue, for it makes the human mind the determiner of truth, forcing God to justify the divine ways to the limited breadth of human understanding. Faith gradually overcomes doubt, through an ongoing experience of God's presence and mercy, but the Reformers' faith neither begins with overt skepticism nor creates a metaphysical system intent on eliminating doubt and granting absolute, irrefutable knowledge.

From the start, opposition arose to Descartes' quest to know only the clear and distinct ideas based on geometry, logic, and mathematics. Blaise Pascal, Descartes' contemporary and his equal in mathematical and scientific ability, insisted that the Cartesian system eliminated from consideration a wide arena of other ways of knowing and other things to know. In a famous phrase from his *Pensees*, Pascal testifies, "The heart has reasons that reason knows not" (59). Reason as conceived by Descartes purports to contain both the fundamental truths of religion and the best method for science. But Pascal rebelled against the premise that God's existence is simply a necessary logical conclusion of thought. God will not be bound by human ideas. Pascal believed that reason is a neutral force influenced by the will toward either good or bad. He thinks Descartes and others deceive themselves by thinking that their inherent rational attitudes can create a harmonious world. Grace must enter in from outside the circle of human reasoning to purify the will and guide reason in the right direction.

Later commentators also decried the limits imposed by Cartesian reason. Two Russian giants of literature were among them. Leo Tolstoy, in Ch. IX of *A Confession*, insists that Descartes set the stage for how modern scientific thought is unable to reach anything but its own presupposed identity. If knowledge via methods like faith and intuition are not admissible, and everything is built up within the mind's own rational framework, how can it see anything ultimately but itself? Fyodor Dostoevsky in *The Brothers Karamazov* testifies that when the human mind is enclosed in Euclidean three-dimensional geometry, it can never comprehend problems and answers not measurable in this world; i.e., it can never understand God. We will also see in a later examination of Postmodernism that Descartes' view of mathematically restricted reason comes under fire more recently. Thus, the 20th c. Roman Catholic philosopher and historian Christopher Dawson, in *Progress and Religion*, clearly faults Descartes for restricting the arena of knowledge:

> From the 17th century onwards the modern scientific movement has been based on the mechanistic view of nature, which regards the world as a closed material order moved by purely mechanical and mathematical laws. All other aspects of reality... were treated as mere subjective impressions of the human mind.... (170)

The third of Descartes' dubious bequests to later philosophy is the radical dualism between soul and body. The definitions of soul and body that Descartes employed make any integration or interplay highly unlikely. Soul is essentially Mind. Mind has no extension. It does not exist within measurable time and space. Body, or Matter, on the other hand, is explicitly defined by its extension, its dimensions of height, width, and depth. In his introduction to Descartes' *Discourse on Method*, translator and editor Arthur Wollaston concludes that these two distinct ideas are necessarily separate: "It follows that, as the idea of the soul or mind contains nothing pertaining to a body, the soul itself is radically separate from the body, on the principle that distinct ideas are representative of distinct existences" (24).

If these perimeters remain intact, subsequent research divides into opposite directions. Metaphysicians would follow Descartes' rationalist route through the soul/mind, largely neglecting the effect that physical circumstances and bodily needs could have upon one's reasoning. Empiricists could search for physical facts, sort them into categories, and experiment with them without ever considering the larger questions of their nature or purpose. Descartes certainly did not initiate his meditations with the belief that science and philosophy were two different disciplines, but as his dualism filtered through a few decades, the rift began to widen. Christians, indeed all citizens, would eventually find themselves living in two different worlds, one of physical facts and one of spiritual values, unable to link one to the other.

Newton, Locke, and the Rise of Natural Religion

The final paragraphs in the treatment of Descartes above have emphasized some dubious aspects of his legacy, especially concerning our understanding of God. Yet, it would be a mistake to forget the immense debt owed to Descartes by subsequent centuries of science. His insistence on the reasonable, mathematical regularity and reliability of laws governing the material world replaced ecclesiastical and political authority or superstitious impressions as criteria for understanding how the world works. Like Galileo and Kepler before him, he insisted that mathematics could describe basic structures of the universe and advance human learning by disciplined mental examination of many unwarranted presuppositions. He contributed the practice of rational deduction to an investigative process later refined into the scientific method. The blessings of that method are readily visible in the many medical and industrial advances of later centuries.

This confidence in the rational regularity of the universe continued in the profound cosmological system of Isaac Newton. Ever since Galileo and Kepler confirmed the Copernican interpretation of the solar system, one thorny question remained, *viz.* what caused the planets to move in such an orderly fashion around the sun? Newton's *Principia Mathematica* in 1687 answered the question permanently with his theory of universal gravitation. The planets, indeed all physical objects, relate to one another through mutual attraction, or gravity. Moreover, this attraction's strength follows a simple mathematical formula based on the distance between two objects. The heavens above can be measured! Add to this pivotal law of physics three more laws of motion that Newton defined, and the philosophical world marveled at the geometrical beauty of creation. In contrast to Descartes, however, Newton realized that to make his formulas useful, the scientist could not just depend on isolated reason. Someone had to do the careful work of measuring accurately the distance between the objects or the amount of energy expended by moving an object. Experiments, observations, and investigation re-entered the total scientific project, placing Francis Bacon's inductive, hands-on approach alongside Descartes' deductive reasoning. Science gains a full complement of tools and the 17th century's scientific revolution is nearly complete.

Newton was a committed Christian believer (although he stepped back from fully embracing the mystery of the Trinity). In addition, he viewed his scientific work in physics as testimony to the wonder of the Creator. "This most beautiful system of sun, planets and comets could only proceed from the counsel and dominion of an intelligent and powerful Being", he writes in the *Principia*, book 3. Like most early scientists (natural philosophers), Newton believed that by studying nature we could come to a better understanding of the creator of that natural world. Science and religion are not adversaries; indeed, they support one another, and even though it appears that God created a mechanical, clock-like world, Newton himself believes the first cause of this world is a personal God, not a machine.

It is problematic for future generations, however, that Newton seems to use God as a supernatural explanation for unknown gaps in his interpretation of the universe. Certain irregular phenomena in the skies, like the passage of a comet, he explained as an occasional intervention by the divine hand. Even his tracing of the original source of gravity back to God leaves his system vulnerable when later explanations of gravity do not seem to require an external first mover. Newton was neither the first nor the last to use God when a persistent dilemma needed unraveling. Too often, religious apologists, trying to find a place for God in science, insert God into a system as the "gap-closer", an explanation for what is currently inexplicable, only to be trapped, forced to retract that option when a better explanation comes along. Ancient Greek dramatists used to call this a *deus ex machina*, a god in a machine lowered onto the stage from heaven to extricate a hero from a tricky situation.

Newton's defense of God's omnipotent plan for the physical universe prompted enormous excitement in universities, parlors and pulpits in England, and later on the European continent. In England especially, John Locke doubled its influence and its intensity when he completed his *Essay Concerning Human Understanding* in 1690 and *The Reasonableness of Christianity* five years later. This philosopher, whose political writings had such an impact on the American Revolution, also had much to say about the knowledge of God. In the *Essay...*, (Bk. 4, Ch.'s 17-19) he agrees with Descartes that rational deduction leads us inevitably to the existence of God: "The existence of a God reason clearly makes known to us."

The next step in his argument is crucial, however, and portends a new direction. Even the theological tenets that others might claim are known by faith alone, Locke says must be regulated by reason. Again from the *Essay...*: "Faith is nothing but a firm assent of the mind; which if it be regulated, which is our duty, cannot be afforded to anything but upon good reason." In other words, what to some might be a special revelation from God will not be acceptable to Locke unless it also conforms to reason, which he defines as "deductions made from ideas which one has got by the use of one's natural faculties." Later in the *Essay...* Locke is even clearer, saying that no one can rightly claim to be inspired by God or receive a revelation if "...the proposition he utters is contradictory to our clear intuitive knowledge." and again: "Reason must be our last judge and guide in everything" (Cragg, 75-77).

Therefore, when Locke writes *On the Reasonableness of Christianity*, he might intend to pay a compliment to the religion, while also ridding it of superstition and rash authoritarian pronouncements, but he ultimately accepts things like miracles, prophecies, and revelations only insofar as they conform to reasonable limits. Such events do point to the power of the God who performs them, and their credibility is enhanced if the healings and ideas they include prove lasting and useful, so Locke here is not denying their possibility. Still, he is intent on reining in speculative and mysterious forces in the Christian faith, and that is the most prominent conclusion of the essay. Certainly, Locke and others had great cause to provide an alternative to the religious infighting that decapitated a king and spawned civil war in England. But what remains of biblical Christianity in his treatment hardly resembles what the Reformers knew. Under Locke's influence, Thomas Jefferson in America produced his own version of the New Testament that edited out any miraculous event and restricted the Christian scriptures to only what seemed reasonable and profitable for ethical behavior.

It is uncertain if either Newton or Locke could have foretold such use of their principles in subsequent decades, but as explained by Gerald Cragg in his historical assessment of this era, the inner logic of their thought emerged more strongly than their original intentions.

> Locke's successors made explicit what is latent in his thought. The role of reason is magnified, that of revelation was depressed..... In this struggle lies the perennial interest of this period. At the outset, the new thought was cordially disposed toward the Christian faith. Gradually the balance shifted from what God has revealed to what man has discovered. In due course the sufficiency of reason was confidently affirmed, and the whole content of Biblical theology was relegated to a marginal status of comparative insignificance. (Cragg, *The Church and the Age of Reason,* p. 13)

Belief in Natural Religion leapt into this fertile intellectual environment as the 18th century began.

Natural Religion and Deism: The concept of Natural Religion bears a wide range of meaning and implication. Like Newton himself, it promotes greater openness by the church to scientific discovery to some; preachers and divines across England saw Newton's system as reinforcement of faith and enhancement of God's wonder. To the *philosophes* of France, it offered the opposite: a way to eliminate mystic superstition and priestly dominance without surrendering a moral compass. Many welcomed natural religion as a relief from the petty bickering of 17th century Protestant Orthodoxy over minute doctrinal differences. Furthermore, as the bounds of geographical exploration widened, and cultures in Asia and the Americas became familiar, advocates of natural religion recognized common trends in worship and cultic practice among all peoples.

Inevitably, the rational framework behind natural religion shifted public opinion about where to appeal for solutions to daily problems. At the beginning of the 17th century, farmers might consult a priest about a worrisome anomaly in the weather, but by the end of that century, they would instead ask what the Royal Society of philosophers and scientists would recommend. For our purposes now, however, we will focus on the rise of deism and the gradual trend to replace a supernatural yet personal God with an impersonal deified Nature as the governor of the universe and the basis for ethics.

The logic of natural religion is this: God created the natural world according to mathematical laws that work with a mechanical regularity. Those laws are universal, the same everywhere, and everyone everywhere can know those laws by careful observation and rational thought. Therefore, can we not know the intention of God better by studying the laws themselves, rather than needing a personal relationship with God? Is not the Nature that God created a more certain source of knowledge than the confusing book of scripture, some parts of which apparently violate those very laws of nature, or than personal mystic experience, which cannot be verified by an external observer? It is hardly an exaggeration to emphasize that this logic and its conclusions continue to influence western Christianity profoundly to this day.

As the 18th century progressed, that logic worked its way from obscurity to dominance, with deism as its ultimate result. We have already noted how Locke's writings influence the direction of this logic; many others expanded on his foundation. Reviewing the works of English writers in this time period, Dillenberger and Welch in *Protestant Christianity...* (127-129) trace three phases of this unfolding of natural religion. The first retains the supernatural character of Christian revelation, but declares, like Locke, that it is fully agreeable to reason. Prophecy and miracle provide evidence for the sublime yet reasonable truth of Christianity, which remains pre-eminent over all other religions. John Toland's 1696 publication *Christianity Not Mysterious* exemplifies this. All requisite conditions for religion being intelligible and reasonable are present in Christianity. In the second phase, Christianity is regarded as an instance of the natural religion of all humankind. Matthew Tindal's book *Christianity as Old as Creation* (1730) insists that since the beginning of time people have accepted the same fundamental religious tenets that Christianity exhibits so well.

With the third phase, deism appears more explicitly. Those who insist on the strict rationality of religion cannot accept the miracles and prophesies of scripture, which exhibit supernaturalism and challenge natural laws. God may be necessary as a first cause, a prime mover who set the inexorable laws in motion, but after that, it is much wiser to explore the mind of God in those laws rather than in the muddle of scripture and sacraments.

The prescient forerunner of English Deism was Edward, Lord Herbert of Cherbury, whose work *De Religione Gentilium* (published posthumously in 1663) already sees five universal ideas that define a moderate form of natural religion. They include:

- There is a God.
- We ought to worship this God.

- The best way to worship is by practicing virtue.
- It is a duty to repent our sin.
- There is a life beyond this one, with rewards and punishment for our actions.

Nothing is included in Lord Herbert's summary about miracles, sacraments, knowledge of scripture, or even prayer. It is a heavily rational, moral interpretation of the faith and reinforced by one quasi-supernatural element of life after death, intended primarily to reinforce the moral code.

A similar set of essential tenets of rational faith persisted in France, despite attempts by the *philosophes* to edge even further toward outright atheism. Ultimately, though, they retained a kind of tamed, naturalized God who would keep order. We will not investigate this turn of events in France in detail, but there is an illuminating quotation in Gerald Cragg's *The Church and the Age of Reason*, (237). Speaking of Voltaire, Diderot, and others, he explains:

> The idea of a disordered universe was abhorrent to them. Hence, for convenience sake, they retained the idea of God that Deism… could countenance. He was scaled down and domesticated.…. He was abstract and remote; he was no longer inconvenient because he no longer encountered man with an exacting personal demand.… The God they retained inevitably faded into the abstraction of a first cause. This was the natural consequence of their glorification of the Newtonian revolution; having "deified nature", they "denatured God".

It is this prevalent conception of God that Christians across Europe had to reject or reconcile with their Bible and their faith as the 18th century moved across its landscape of change. In that struggle, dissatisfaction with natural religion began to percolate upward, and help came from three, perhaps unexpected, sources.

The Challenges to Rationalism

The first challenge: The first source demonstrates again the historical twist that sometimes, even before a dominant idea has gained deep roots and clear momentum in an age, criticisms and challenges to it are already emerging. Indeed, at times an effective response will have been at hand for decades, and only needs revival and reinterpretation for a new context. Hence, it is indeed accurate to claim that Natural Religion evoked enthusiastic acceptance in philosophic and theological circles. Moreover, it is true that the systems of Descartes, Newton, and Locke irrevocably influenced the public attitude toward nature and reason. Nevertheless, it is equally accurate to remember that a broad swath of believers in England, France, and Germany was unconvinced that deism and the "reasonableness" of Christianity could adequately represent what they believed and experienced about God.

Decades before Locke's essay "Concerning Human Understanding", Lutheran pastor Philipp Jakob Spener had gathered parishioners and neighbors into small groups for prayer and sharing of their experience of God. These *Collegia Pietatis* reflected the dissatisfaction in Germany with the entrenched scholastic orthodoxy that had dominated Lutheranism for a century. Vitriolic debates and accusations of heresy had disrupted the church over minor theological sub-doctrines. Cultivation of a personal spiritual life had given way to doctrinal conformity in Protestant orthodoxy (which in its own way was an earlier form of rationalistic religion). In 1675 Spener published *Pia Desideria* as his testament to the experiential dimension of Christian faith. Over the next years, his ministries in Frankfurt, Dresden, and Berlin launched a wave of devotional emphasis known as Pietism.

As deism and natural religion gained ground in mid-18th century England, another preacher reacted against doctrinal aridity and intellectualism. John Wesley, with his brother Charles, started a groundswell of revival, again organizing small groups of believers who held one another accountable for their spiritual conformity to Christ. The parishes of high church Anglicanism spurned Wesley when he sought to proclaim his new approach from their pulpits. Undeterred, he gathered crowds in outdoor public spaces. His preaching tours across England beginning around 1740 galvanized the forgotten public, called them to repentance, and granted them an experience of the personal presence of God.

One could claim that providence guided John Wesley, for he had met Moravian missionaries earlier on his voyage back from a disappointing mission endeavor of his own in America. Those Moravians, in turn, had gained instruction and purpose from the Pietism of Spener practiced in their collective community on Herrnhut, the estate of Count von Zinzendorf in Saxony. The Moravians prompted Wesley's recovery from failure and toward clarity about his faith. One of the Moravians counseled John in England after the voyage. One night in May of 1738, Wesley experienced the famous conversion on Aldersgate Street in London while listening to a reading from Luther's commentary on Romans. In that event, Wesley felt the full assurance of salvation. Shortly thereafter, his preaching ministry began, guided at first by the more seasoned preacher George Whitefield. By measurable standards, his ministry proved a success. Estimates tally that he traveled a quarter of a million miles over his lifetime and preached to crowds as large as twenty or thirty thousand.

The preaching of John Wesley, the hymns of Charles Wesley, and the eloquence of George Whitefield spread their transformative gospel so capably that it altered the landscape of both social and religious institutions, first in England and Wales, then soon in America. Many attribute the eventual abolition of slavery to the prior religious revival of conscience in men like William Wilberforce. One other example of the change such personal faith can bring to an individual, noted by Cragg in *The Church in an Age of Reason*, is Hannah More. She was a prominent literary and social figure who, inspired by her awakening, combated ignorance and squalor in rural England. She and her sister built schools for children and adults and alleviated poverty in the area, despite the intransigence of traditional farmers and the apathy of the established church. Such popular appeal and visible results of Methodism, as it came to be known, counteracted the "natural religion" that in various forms still enthralled the scientific and intellectual communities of Britain.

The second challenge: From another direction entirely, skepticism about the logic of rationalism challenged the foundations of Locke's epistemology and cut at the roots of natural religion. These were the reluctant but perceptive conclusions of the Scottish philosopher David Hume. The word "reluctant" is apt, because Hume often gives the impression that he would be more comfortable should his critique of rational categories be unnecessary. Early in his career, as his first attempt to explain his position reached publication, he acknowledged that its woeful public reception was "more the result of manner than of matter". In other words, he stated his radical premise with little recognition of how much it threatened, and was unprepared for the stark negative response. In addition, he intentionally withheld until on his deathbed the instructions for publication of his last critique of natural religion, because of the likelihood that it would prompt charges of atheism. Throughout that work (the *Dialogues*...) he cautiously hides his full criticism until the very end, and even then offers readers a possible alternative opinion about the debate's resolution. His reputation eventually recovered from its early depths, and through his well-traveled career, Hume's writings covered a spectrum of controversial topics, but our current purposes limit this review to how his skepticism affects a believer's attempt to know God and God's intentions for the creation.

Two conclusions of Hume cast serious doubt that natural religion, and the rationalist approach to knowledge it employs, stand on solid ground logically or methodologically. The first of these comes from Hume's *Inquiry Concerning Human Understanding* (1749); the second he elaborates in *Dialogues Concerning Natural Religion* (1779, posthumously).

One of the fundamental modes of reasoning involves seeing an effect in the world and seeking the cause for it. Hume recognizes that this method is absolutely crucial for establishing facts and their connections, whether in history, science or philosophy. In other words, this is how people "understand". In *An Inquiry Concerning Human Understanding*, (26-30) however, Hume states his skepticism about the logic of that common process. He agrees with John Locke that people know only their perceptions of an object rather than the object in itself, but Hume then takes these distinctions one step further. There is also a separation between the perceptions (he prefers the term "impressions") and the ideas we form about them. Hume is convinced that sense impressions come first, before ideas. They "arise immediately from nature"; they are "antecedently felt" and "take the precedence of the ideas". The ideas thus derive from the impressions.

Causation, the connection of cause to effect, is one of those ideas. Hume, though, (72-89) disputes that there is a necessary, indisputable relationship between an observed effect and what we assume is the cause of it. There is at best a recurring regular "conjunction" between them. Like with the common example of one billiard ball hitting another and moving it, we observe repeatedly that when one ball hits another with adequate force the other will move. But we have no necessary, *a priori* basis for knowing that it will happen the next time. We can of course base our practical knowledge upon previous experience, but that is not the same as an indisputable, logical relationship between the first ball and the second. Causation is just an idea based on a series of observations.

What does Hume's explanation portend for science and philosophy? It introduces an element of skepticism, a slight hesitation to conclude resolutely that what has happened regularly can become a law that governs those actions irrevocably. Hume would state it this way, that there is a "conception" of causation, but not a "demonstration" of its validity. He continues by explaining that these conceptions of ideas are guided by customs, by beliefs, that take likely results and presume they are hard and fast laws. To Hume, no experience of past events can become an infallible predictor of future events. We suppose that the uniformity of nature will dictate that what happened before will happen again, but that is a custom, a belief, not a truth on the level of mathematical or geometric certainty, which Newton and Locke had presumed. Hume has therefore challenged the reliability of their process of rational understanding. This in turn undermines the assumption in natural religion that we can trust the laws of nature to reveal the mind of God.

Hume's conclusions in his *An Inquiry Concerning Human Understanding* carry over to his decades-later composition *Dialogues Concerning Natural Religion* and his second objection. An integral premise in natural religion is that the wondrous design of the universe revealed in Newton's laws testifies to a designer God. Although commentators on these *Dialogues...* earlier disagreed about which of the three main debaters in the text represents Hume's own opinions, it is now firmly agreed that the one called Philo comes closest to Hume's views expressed elsewhere, and Philo presents a clear rebuttal to a Newtonian argument from design. The substance of his challenge is in Part VIII, where he again insists that ideas arise from perceptions and impressions, not the other way around.

> Let us once more put it (the argument from design) to trial. In all instances which we have ever seen, ideas are copied from real objects.... You reverse this order, and give thought the precedence. In all instances which we have ever seen, thought has no influence upon matter.....(186)

His point (directed to Cleanthes, the defender of design) is that people have an idea in their mind that there must be a perfect God, and then regard their impressions of the world's activities according to that presupposition, finding an orderly, regular universe. But when Philo (Hume) carefully observes the animal kingdom (including human animals), for instance, he sees far more disorder than order, far more violence than cooperation, far more tragedy than happiness. If there is so much unhappiness, so much conflict, so much suffering in the world, how can those perfect metaphysical laws of Newton rightly promote the view that a benevolent God designed a benevolent universe? Like Epicurus in ancient Greece, Hume raises the problem of evil as a counterweight to those who argue for the existence of a benevolent God. This too presents a formidable challenge to rationalism's complacent assurance that the human mind can resolve all problems by conforming observations to reasonable principles and consulting the laws of God revealed in the starry heavens above.

Before leaving this brief commentary on Hume, it is useful to register his effect on Immanuel Kant. We will hear more from Kant later as we evaluate his impact on a "structuralist" interpretation of freedom and in his effect on Schleiermacher, but one aspect of his epistemology, as detailed in Kant's *Critique of Pure Reason*, has had enormous impact on the limits of knowledge about God. Responding to Hume, Kant analyzes human reasoning (Kant's word "critique" denotes analysis, not criticism in the negative sense) and separates knowledge into 'phenomenal' and 'noumenal' realms. Phenomena are material sensations supplied by observation of the external world, what philosophers call *a posteriori* facts. These physical observations provide substantial information about physical objects, but are restricted in their usefulness until they are structured into categories that give them context and relationship. That is the role of the noumenal realm; this realm includes categories such as time and space, immortality, and God. We cannot, however, approach and understand this realm with the same senses and tactics used in the phenomenal realm. Indeed, one cannot know these a priori categories with certainty. They are postulates, metaphysical entities beyond the realm of technical reason. Using this distinction, Kant appears able to disprove all the traditional rational arguments for the existence of God. We cannot know ultimate realities like God; at best, we can only have faith that God exists. This is not a loss in Kant's eyes, but ultimately a gain. Thus, he can say, "I have therefore found it necessary to deny knowledge in order to leave room for faith" (29). For better or worse, since Kant, theologians have placed far less confidence in proofs for the existence of God, and Christians have struggled to link their "phenomenological" religious experiences to a God they cannot approach with their reason, for this God dwells in a noumenal realm beyond empirical examination.

The third challenge: The third hint of dissatisfaction with rationalism's optimism centered in France, right in the midst of the *philosophes'* revolutionary fervor to eliminate superstition and priestly oppression in favor of the goddess of reason. This minority opinion came from the voice of Jean Jacques Rousseau. In contesting the general trend, Rousseau introduced both a new romanticism and what some would later call naturalism. From his earliest public writings – *Discourse on the Arts and Sciences* (1749) and the *Discourse on the Origins of Inequality* (1755) to his later publications like *Emile* (1762) – Rousseau argued that progress gained through rational investigation was overvalued.

An honest examination of history, Rousseau contends in the first *Discourse...,* proves that rational progress did not satisfy the human heart, that it led us away from the practice of natural virtues, and that it promoted deterioration of original well-being. By his interpretation of ancient cultures like Egypt, Greece, and Rome, and his assessment of "primitive" societies like Native Americans, Rousseau concluded that moral decay accompanies cultural progress. The more cultivated and advanced a society, the more prone it is to laziness, boredom, and multiple schemes to demonstrate one's superiority over others through wealth, art, or status. Progress satisfies only artificial needs and desires, not the natural needs inherent to all human beings. Luxury, vanity, and decadence are the real fruits of advanced culture.

In the second *Discourse...*, Rousseau wonders openly whether inequality is natural or created. He paints a picture of an original state of nature in which primitive, prehistorical human interrelationships were more cooperative and limited in violence than Thomas Hobbes had painted in *Leviathan* a century earlier. Following natural passions would have led to far less turmoil and oppression than what results from political structures that concentrate power. Societies created by science and material progress inevitably become more repressive, as greed displaces natural harmony and those who have more wealth must protect it from those whom they perceive will try to steal it. As property ownership, division of labor, and accumulation of wealth advance, Rousseau sees increasing inequality, arbitrary power, and alienation from our original, more satisfying beginnings. In a revealing statement from the second Discourse..., Rousseau affirms, "...he would have to be accounted most virtuous, who put least check on the pure impulses of nature" (180). We are, however, beyond that ideal natural state. What, then?

Years later, Rousseau realistically acknowledged that despite all his protests against society's inequality, against the progress of art and science, nonetheless the world is as it is, influenced by and entrenched in the very customs he deplores. How then to live according to native virtues and natural strengths in the midst of a depraved and lax culture? He proposes a system of education based on the ways of nature and writes *Emile*, a lengthy, story-filled novel about his tutelage of a young boy from early childhood to full maturity and marriage. The naturalism of his earlier writings blends with a romantic picture of learning as the child gains both physical strength and a keen, curious intellect. From the start, Rousseau rails against certain unnatural customs forced upon infants, such as the tight swaddling in cloths that makes the infant easier to control but restricts its ability to breathe deeply, or the practice of aristocratic women who hire a wet-nurse to suckle their own children rather than personally, maternally nursing them.

As Emile grows, the tutor's prime intent is to avoid rote memorization or even books, and allow the child to grow according to the inbred guidance of natural impulses. The child responds with genuine interest when observing the ways of nature in animals and forests. The youth gains a sense of social interaction by observing relationships of adults, and learns morality by considering the natural consequences of indolence or pride in both domestic animals and overly domesticated humans. Along the way, Rousseau offers an insight into his own faith, a combination of deism and romanticism, and then explains why instruction in religion must wait until Emile is ready to ask the right questions and doubt easy answers.

The end result of Emile's education is an admirable, capable, healthy young man who discovers the joys of romance as he falls in love with Sophy, becomes a father himself, and then turns to the tutor for advice on how to raise the new child. This is how one can at least faintly resemble the "noble savage" in a surrounding culture of questionable progress.

Whether in the winsome account of Emile's education or in his earlier polemical discourses, Rousseau's inventiveness and conviction challenged the optimistic rationalism of the 17th and early 18th century. While it may be accurate to say that his philosophic peers complimented his imagination, they also largely ignored his warning. Therefore only in retrospect can we recognize his lasting influence. The nativist ideas in the *Emile* have filtered down in educational theory and influenced educational reformers like Maria Montessori. The Romanticism of the 19th century and the "back to nature" sentiment of mid-20th century communalism clearly draw inspiration from Rousseau's sense that the empirical analysis and rationalism in materialistic societies fail to encompass the full range of emotions in the human spirit. His implication that the natural tendencies of a person's psyche provide adequate guidance for one's moral and emotional development also quickened an ideology of individualism that has grown in the 250 years since his death. As the church of the 21st century tries to find alternatives to cybernetic dominance and the often-hollow satisfaction of technological progress, it can remember this earlier voice of protest. However, it will also probably question whether Rousseau's romantic naturalism is the best source of inspiration.

Hegel and the Progress of History

With the background of deistic natural religion in England, revolutionary fervor against church and monarchy in France, and a moribund Catholicism in Spain and Italy, it fell to the philosophers and theologians of Germany to begin a reconstruction of Christian beliefs and doctrines as the 19th century dawned. On the theological side of the effort, Friedrich Schleiermacher responded to Immanuel Kant with a religion based on self-consciousness of dependence. We will treat his interpretation shortly, but his contemporary at the University of Berlin, George Wilhelm Friedrich Hegel, developed a more influential philosophical system that requires our attention first.

A previous chapter related key themes in Hegel's philosophy; they bear repeating here, albeit briefly. His central accomplishment was to elevate the concept of history. The scientific achievements of the 17th and 18th centuries had prompted people to regard their own recent era as superior to previous centuries. Then in 1800,

Johann Herder published a philosophy of history explaining how it is dynamic and grows organically. Hegel combined the general cultural optimism with Herder's insights and articulated a belief in history as progress. It moves toward a goal; it is not static, and the golden era for humanity is not in the past but in the future. Secondly, drawing upon the romanticism of Friedrich Schelling and the earlier work of Benedict Spinoza, Hegel interpreted all of reality as if it were one, a grand mind or spirit. His system is monistic and idealist, which means that all sentient things - from green plants to chimerical dreams, and including both human individuals and God - are part of the same single spiritual reality. As this spirit, this mind (the German word is *Geist,* which we use interchangeably with Mind and Spirit), moves toward its goal of perfect self-realization, it creates a dynamic dialectic, a dialogue with itself. It achieves a state of being, then posits its opposite, and then incorporates both of those into a synthesized, better state. Yet, this new being is not yet complete, and begins the dialectic over again, as mind marches onward. Only when the Spirit at some glorious future day achieves full self-realization, will history, and all that is in it, finally end.

Although all of Hegel's publications express these general themes, posterity regards his 1807 publication, *The Phenomenology of Mind,* as his most comprehensive work. It is a formidable and often obtuse book, reflecting Hegel's highly abstract, all-inclusive system. These central ideas of Hegel's system ultimately developed at other people's hands into Marxism, Darwinian evolution, and a doctrine of inevitable progress. They also posed two substantial new options for how to understand the being of God and God's presence in the world. Explaining those alternatives is the task at hand.

The first new option is multi-faceted. If all reality is one, without lasting separation or distinction, as Hegel's monistic philosophy supposes, then the relationship within God's own being, the relationship between God and humanity, and even God's relation to all physical creation, must be radically reinterpreted. Taking the last of these three first, the predominant Christian doctrine of creation states that God placed the physical world outside Godself, that creation is not an emanation of divine radiance but a distinct act of separation, allowing contingency and freedom in the created world. God enters the world again in specific acts of incarnation and revelation, as in the birth of Jesus Christ, the salvific activity of sacraments, or in the Holy Spirit's special acts of illumination. Nonetheless, even in these moments of immanence, God paradoxically remains truly transcendent, not merely apparently so. In contrast with Hegel's conception of *Geist's* ultimate indistinguishable unity with the world, our understanding of God's action in creation changes substantially. Transcendence and immanence blend into one, and creation is not distinct from God, i.e. Absolute Mind *(Geist)*. Creation's contingency is not lasting, and freedom is not genuinely free. It is conditioned by the process.

Hegel's interpretation of the Holy Trinity also does not allow distinct personhood for each member of that triune relationship. In his *Lectures on the Philosophy of Religion*, Hegel interprets the movement of the Absolute Mind in a threefold manner, where God the Creator/Father is Mind's universal manifestation, the Son is its particularity, its individuality, and the Holy Spirit, expressed in worship, is the way Mind overcomes that differentiation and reconciles itself again. While this schema may exhibit some similarity to the complementary activity of the Trinity in customary Christian theology, in Hegel's system the three persons of God are swallowed up in something larger than God. They are simply phases in the movement of a rational Mind that operates through these ultimately inadequate symbolic religious representations of itself.

Yet another facet of his alternative view arises because Hegel's system implies that human beings seeking a relationship with God should adopt a new perspective on how such a God acts. Hegel diminishes, indeed ultimately removes, the separation between a transcendent God and the world that God created. Whether this be a true picture of God or not, it nonetheless shifts the focus to the activity of God within and through the created world rather than outside of it. If God, as a manifestation of the Absolute Mind, works in and through the visible world to arrive at a full realization of the divine purpose, then that very natural, physical reality is where one must search for knowledge of God, rather than in other-worldly, transcendent realms of mystical experience, prayer, or revelation in scripture. Thus, in the wake of Hegel it seems that God's design for creation, and God's providential guidance, is discerned better within the movement of the visible world toward an eventual goal rather than in the mathematical laws of nature set in place by a deistic God in an original act of creation before time. Stated simplistically, should our religion be more this-worldly and less otherworldly to understand God's intentional activity?

In this regard, it is possible - without committing to the truth or falsity of Hegel's vision - that he offers the church a legitimate response to what followed in the next decades, *viz.* Darwinian evolution's challenge to traditional pictures of God's transcendent design. An immanent God, working in and through evolutionary changes, could still provide an ongoing, adaptive, sense of intention and order to creation, even if the picture of a transcendent, pre-existent designer appears now outmoded. At this point, such a conclusion is a speculative supposition rather than a recommended change of course, but even as Darwin's evolutionary scheme gained philosophical footing from Hegel's progressive movement of history, so might there also be a response to natural selection hidden in Hegel's emphasis on the immanent activity of God.

The second option by which Hegel's system overturns traditional ways of understanding God concerns his shift away from a theory of truth based on correspondence to an external reality, and toward a theory of truth based on coherence to a complete, moving system. In pre-modern times, the predominant epistemology often called "naïve realism" explained that we know what is true by examining the relationship of our perception of something to the object itself. You presume that a particular stone drawn from a moving stream will be hard and smooth. To determine if your expectation is true, you look carefully at the stone and evaluate the correspondence of your expectation to the thing in itself. However, the skepticism of Locke and Hume about the accuracy of our sense perception casts doubt on the reliability of the correspondence theory. After all, when you look at a stick in the same stream, it appears bent at the water line. Our senses can mislead us. In addition, Kant's insistence that many "things-in-themselves" are unverifiable by sense perception means that the correspondence theory is inapplicable to many important ideas, like God or causation.

Most of us in our daily lives will continue to determine truth or falsity through a correspondence theory of truth. (Is the dishwasher on or off? Listen for the rushing water and check the lights on the panel.) Nonetheless, Hegel's dynamic understanding of history and his dialectic unfolding of ultimate reality mean that our most important current concepts of science, morality, religion, and philosophy are incomplete. At any one time, a concept like the structure of the atom, or economic equality, is only a temporary manifestation of how Absolute Spirit moves through that realm of investigation on its way to a more complete realization of itself. As time continues, these concepts will be outmoded by the next phase of the dialectic. All conclusions must be tentative. Nothing will summon up lasting conviction and commitment, because we will always be waiting for the next change to come that will reveal a better understanding of how Mind is revealing itself. The correspondence of our expectations to a stable reality gives way to a theory of truth in which the more an idea reflects, coheres to, the ultimate result of a dynamic system, the truer it is. Yet, that ultimate result will always be in the future, and all one can say is that something appears to reveal the next dimension of what the final truth might be.

The value of this coherence theory of truth is its reminder that no human concept is ever complete or adequate, that there will always be a greater, more complex, more satisfactory interpretation of what we are studying. Probing of the atom first revealed protons, neutrons, and electrons, then the movement of electrons, then quarks, and the quest continues, perhaps endlessly. Tolerance, patience, and further investigation become the greatest virtues. Stated religiously, humanity must always remember that it cannot attain to complete knowledge of God's ways, unless that comes at the Parousia, the final curtain of history.

Yet, one wonders whether this coherence theory is equally valuable for moral questions that require definitive answers. Even things that we now regard as inexcusable, evil, horrible, might just be the second stage of Mind's dynamic as it posits an opposing idea, which will be blended into a more perfect finished product. Should we restrict and oppose those actions now labeled evil, or do we simply monitor them until we see their ultimate result in the final revelation of Mind? That 10 Commandments would be true forever, or that one historical manifestation of God on earth in Jesus Christ could redeem the whole of humankind, are faith claims that require conviction and lasting commitment. In a theory of truth based on coherence to a dynamic progressive system of history, it is hard to see the grounds for such conviction.

Hegel's idealistic influence on modernity remains profound, even though most philosophers repudiate his pure monistic idealism. The view that life is moving forward toward some splendid culmination is entrenched in economic and political thinking. Yet, Christian commentators remain concerned that Hegel's system misrepresents the central doctrines of the faith. Historian Alec Vidler, in his *The Church in an Age of Revolution*, summarizes those concerns:

> Hegel's intention was to enable Christianity to understand itself, but it is a question whether he did not change it into something else. In his system God is subordinated to the Absolute, Christ is a logical construction and not a living person, evil is raw material on the way to becoming good or spirit, redemption is not an event in time but an eternal truth, the resurrection and ascension of Christ mean that the universal which became particular returns to itself. (30)

Schleiermacher and the Beginning of Theological Liberalism

In the realm of philosophy, Hegel's grand system was clearly the most significant development in the 19th century, but theologically, that century marks the birth and predominance of liberalism. Today, the word "liberalism" sounds vague notes in the political arena of progressivism and radical equality, but in the church of the 1800s, it meant a combination of three trends. One was the historical consciousness roused by Herder, Hegel, and biblical criticism. A second was Kant's restriction of religion away from metaphysics but toward practical morality. The third was the wind of Romanticism that accentuated the individual's unique faculties for experience.

The person who began the integration of these trends was Friedrich Schleiermacher, rightly called the "father of modern theology". It is indicative of his foundational role in the century that his first book, *On Religion: Speeches to its Cultured Despisers*, appeared in 1799, his *Soliloquies* in 1800, and the most complete statement of his theology, *The Christian Faith*, emerged before the first quarter ended. As the new century arrived, Schleiermacher greeted Kant's restrictions on metaphysics with approval and even relief. He was convinced that a watershed in theology was at hand, prompted by the Enlightenment. The old dependence on rational proofs of God and exacting precision in doctrine was gone, and for him, gone without lament. The question now was what new form of faith would replace it. Schleiermacher believed he would find the answer in the profound religious experience of Christian believers, what we might refer to as the existential dimension of their knowledge of God.

As with other pivotal Christian leaders like John Wesley, the Moravian strand of pietism influenced Schleiermacher. His father, an army chaplain, wished his children to breathe in this vibrant personal religion of the heart. This imprint of personal devotion and religious experience was indelible, though for a time it hid in the shadows when, as a student, Friedrich absorbed the stiff doctrines of Protestant Orthodoxy and read Kant. His move to Berlin in his late twenties cast him into a vibrant intellectual culture, but one in which a young pastor found little support for Christianity. This challenge from these "cultured despisers" prompted him to draft his *Speeches...*, defending his faith and explaining the value of religious sentiment and religious community. He begins by redefining the meaning of religion. It is not a series of doctrines, a set of moral rules, or an attempt to "analyze the nature of an incomprehensible Being". Religion instead is a "pious exaltation of the mind" when "the whole soul is dissolved in the immediate feeling of the Infinite and Eternal." (cf. *The Christian Faith*, 51-57.) We know God not by thinking, as in metaphysics, and not by acting, as in ethics, but in feeling, a direct apprehension of God's presence. Religion is thus a form of "affection, a revelation of the Infinite in the finite." It provides an intuitive contact with reality, thus outflanking the rationalistic restrictions on what we can know that had held sway since Descartes.

This theme from his early work would gain clarity and depth in subsequent decades. In *The Christian Faith*, Schleiermacher explicitly defines religion as an immediate self-consciousness that includes a feeling of "absolute dependence" upon God. That particular phrase received ridicule from Hegel, who quipped that "absolute dependence" sounds like the emotion a dog feels for its master. The criticism, however, misses the point of Schleiermacher's more extended explanation. In religious experience, we have an awareness of the inexplicable "givenness" of our existence in the world, as though we are a gift amidst a greater gift. In a famous paragraph from *The Christian Faith* (16), Schleiermacher points to this feeling of "givenness" and says that the source of and reason for that feeling, the "whence" of such an immediate existential relationship, is what we mean by God. This sense of absolute dependence does not eliminate freedom and responsibility but connects them in a self-conscious relationship to the source of gracious existence.

Schleiermacher employs this basic definition of religion to develop new interpretations of specific Christian doctrines. Four of the most important re-interpretations are on the nature of the church, the identity of Jesus Christ, the meaning of sin and the authority of the Bible.

Although specific religious experiences in themselves are isolated and infrequent, they culminate in an increased God-consciousness as a person lives faithfully. As one dwells in this God-consciousness, religious beliefs, doctrines and convictions arise, both individually and in the collective reflections of the church. This leads to his insistence that the church's creeds and practices do not so much create genuine relationship to God as the other way around. First come the experiences of religion, defined according to his sense of absolute dependence, and then come the institutions appropriate to the context of those experiences. The implication of this view, which Schleiermacher accepts, leaves no clear distinction between Christianity and other religions. If it is in the very nature of humanity to experience this feeling of absolute dependence, this "givenness" of existence, then the Christian expression of this feeling ranges right alongside the other world religions. From this perspective, the Christian church cannot claim uniqueness because of its dogmas, its origin, or its moral superiority. It is one institution among many trying to provide adequate structure and context for the growth of God-consciousness among its adherents.

What, if anything, does give clarity and distinction to the Christian religion? It is the centrality of Jesus Christ. Schleiermacher's way of describing Jesus the Messiah is to claim that he enters the world with a perfect God-consciousness. His whole being is infused with awareness of God's gracious activity in and beyond the world. God so fully indwells Jesus that he remains sinless and completely united to God. Nonetheless, his humanity also is real. He is "tempted as we are". His consciousness of God is matched by an equally developed consciousness of humanity, which brings sympathy and identification to Christ's person. This twofold identity allows reconciliation between a broken humanity and a gracious God, and illustrates why the Christian religion centers on the redemption won by Jesus of Nazareth. He is neither a mere teacher of morality – as he had become in natural religion – nor a mere manifestation of a larger spirit, as in Hegel. He is the fountainhead of forgiveness and the path to union with God. The goal of his followers is to attain the same level of God-consciousness as their savior.

However, sin stands in the way of complete God-consciousness. Sin, to Schleiermacher, is the incompleteness of one's consciousness of God. In turn, original sin is not some pre-existent, lingering effect of Adam and Eve's first act of disobedience. It is instead the factual assertion that all of humanity is separated from God, inadequately conscious of God, and thus in need of redemption. The human separation from God arises due to the resistance of all finite things to the infinite. In *The Christian Faith*, he says that sin is "a positive antagonism of the flesh against the spirit" (271). Sin arises as the flesh takes dominance over the spirit, arresting the God-consciousness by dwelling on sensual self-consciousness. (This stance becomes an object of later criticism, that his view of sin is gnostic.) Sin is not so much a willful rebellion against God as an incompleteness awaiting its completeness in Christ. It is individual and collective, personal and social. It is so strong and pervasive that one cannot overcome it by dint of will and effort. Salvation from sin requires the redemptive work of God. Indeed, we understand sin best when we regard it as part of the dynamic of redemption. As Schleiermacher puts it, sin is "God's strange work intended to drive us into his arms" (330-338).

Schleiermacher also revealed a new attitude toward the Bible and its authority. Because religion is a type of affection, an attitude created by the experience of God and the "givenness" of life, this living experience of Christians claims ultimate authority and normative power. No external authority, neither creed nor scripture passage, determines the meaning and truth of a religious belief. To Schleiermacher, the Bible is not an external, objective revelation delivered from on high by the transcendent God. Scripture, rightly understood, records the religious experiences of the people of God. Its authority comes from the stories it tells of God's interactions with both righteous and unrighteous people. By communicating these experiences to later generations, the Bible provides a link to earlier works of God and testimony to the transformative power of Christ. The result of this attitude toward scripture is a freedom from worry about contradictions between texts, historical inaccuracies, and alternative interpretations of events. The Bible can be a human book that nonetheless reveals divine sovereignty.

It would be easy, given the personal nature of religious feeling, to accuse Schleiermacher of creating a thoroughly individualistic form of faith. But throughout his writings and in his personal life he emphasizes that God works in and through human communities. Religious consciousness requires a tradition, a supportive fellowship, and a regular practice of communal worship. One both teaches and learns within the community and within the surrounding culture. There is to be no anti-institutionalism or isolationism in religion, no separated perfectionist commune. Schleiermacher's prominent position as both professor at the University of Berlin and preacher at Trinity Church in the city afforded him an influential voice in political issues such as the Prussian treaty with Napoleon and liberal social reforms for the still backward feudal society of King Friedrich Wilhelm III. He was instrumental in shaping the eventual union of Reformed and Lutheran denominations in 1822. He relished dialogues between church and state and church and individual Christians. Society is not the enemy of faith. God works in it as well as in the church; so should dedicated Christians.

A review of liberal Protestant theology in the 19th century, and the still strong echoes of that viewpoint today, will confirm how appropriate it is to call Schleiermacher the father of modern liberal theology. In the final pages of an introductory book simply titled *Friedrich Schleiermacher*, C.W. Christian summarizes the legacy of this seminal theologian that shaped the integral principles of liberalism. From the start, Schleiermacher recognized that the world, and theology, had changed substantially in the 17th and 18th centuries, which called for a new dialogue, a dialogue that reflected a more positive attitude toward society. He knew that the rise of an historical consciousness challenged traditional sources of authority and cleared the way for a new, more experiential approach to religion. As metaphysical emphasis declined, a more confessional and pragmatic approach to truth emerged in Christianity, held together by personal knowledge of a personal Christ. All these characterize the dominant theology of the 19th century. All these are central themes for Schleiermacher. Nevertheless, liberalism grew bigger than Friedrich Schleiermacher alone, so let us consider further dimensions of that growth, especially the direction taken by Albrecht Ritschl.

Albrecht Ritschl, a Second Theological Liberal: In the decades after Schleiermacher published *The Christian Faith*, five strands of liberal theology developed as parallel companions. One was the greater openness to science, including reconciliation with Darwinian evolution and hope in the ability of science to improve society. A second was the anti-metaphysical, historical emphasis of Adolf Harnack, who insisted that Greek speculative philosophy had infected the purity of the original biblical gospel, which had emphasized a simple human brotherhood. Next was the insistence of the American Horace Bushnell on the immanence of God within culture and thus the key role of *Christian Nurture* (the title of his seminal book) in faith formation. Fourth, Walter Rauschenbusch and Washington Gladden, also in America, launched the social gospel movement with its goal of transforming society into the kingdom of God. Finally, gradual acceptance of the historical-critical method of biblical interpretation provided more reliable information about the person of Jesus Christ. If these tendencies were not already evident in Schleiermacher, they leapt into visibility in the work of Albrecht Ritschl 50 years later.

Ritschl commanded wide knowledge of his topic. He knew both the church and the Bible from the inside out. His father was a pastor for decades, then bishop of the Prussian Church of the Union (the former Lutheran and Reformed branches that Schleiermacher helped reunite). As Albrecht began his academic career, he delved into biblical theology and used the tools of historical criticism to investigate the Jesus of the Gospels. In two early publications, he first rejected and then accepted the chronological primacy of the Gospel of Mark. Armed with that twofold knowledge of church and scripture, he later turned his attention to the broader disciplines of systematic theology. In 1870, he published the massive three-volume *The Christian Doctrine of Justification and Reconciliation*, in which he expounded his central beliefs. A short delineation of those beliefs should illuminate how Ritschl promoted and intensified what Schleiermacher had begun.

First, Ritschl shared Schleiermacher's experiential approach to religion. Under Kant's influence, Ritschl insists that faith is beyond the scope of empirical reason to analyze it. He also rejects the metaphysical view of religion, saying we should base our understanding of God not on abstract proof and rational process but on the living experience of Christ's work for us and in us. Experience of Christ, the pivotal figure around which faith revolves, will enhance one's moral awareness and inspire action. Religious knowledge is essentially a string of judgments, decisions about the value and significance of Christ's effect upon us. For example, we understand the divinity of Jesus Christ not as an historical statement of fact or a speculative doctrine about his nature but as an expression of how much Christ's presence enhances the moral and spiritual growth of those who believe in him. Later, many criticized this view of faith, which seems to contribute to the separation between facts and values and the dualism it implies.

Next, he believes Kant was also right in his emphasis on human freedom and fulfilment of human potential. To Ritschl, this is the innermost intention of the gospel. From creation through the exodus and on to redemption in Christ, scripture shows that God wishes people to be free of oppressive structures and forces. The goal of religion is to affirm the worth of the individual human person, who is God's child and image. As one commentator on Ritschl puts it, "Christianity, as indispensable means and form, accords with the end and self-fulfillment of humanity itself." (Foster, 53) Like Schleiermacher, however, this is not an individualistic, autonomous freedom, but is born in and conditioned by the community. When Ritschl considers issues of sin and redemption, he introduces his belief that God's activity in overcoming sin is to restore and strengthen God's human family, which has been broken by alienation from God and one another. Redemption has little meaning outside of community.

Two other interconnected components of Ritschl's theology even more directly show his influence on later liberalism. He, more than Schleiermacher, insisted that God is not primarily holy, not primarily sovereign, not primarily lawgiver, but that God is love. Love is not just an attribute of God; love is God's essence, inmost being and nature. Therefore, God could not ever eternally damn any creature for the sake of divine righteousness. Double predestination violates the very nature of God. God's loving, redemptive activity will not cease until all have been gathered into a fellowship of redeemed persons. This will be 'the kingdom of God', a title in the gospels that Ritschl believes is the central goal of Jesus' ministry. God lovingly reconciles the world through Christ not merely to right a past wrong but to initiate "the organization of humanity through action inspired by love" (Dillenberger, 199). God grants deliverance over the bondage of nature, victory over sin, so the redeemed may work for moral improvement and social enhancement in the world.

This outward transformational focus, this desire to "change the world" in modern parlance, broke early ground in the Reformation in places like Calvin's Geneva, but it assumes a permanent central place with Ritschl's contribution to theological liberalism. From his day onward, church leaders will repeatedly promote the idea of a perfect future kingdom of God as the pre-eminent goal of church mission and ministry. Whether this is actually what the New Testament implies by the idea of the kingdom is another matter. Ritschl receives plenty of criticism on this point. Still, if the embrace of his sense of the kingdom by over a century of Christian leaders is any indication, he has sounded an attractive, lasting call toward discipleship in social and political arenas. Along with Schleiermacher, Albrecht Ritschl expressed the pre-eminent theological ideas that shaped recent Protestant thought and articulated a theological version of the optimistic 19th century societal attitude, inspiring Christians in the local church and the worldwide mission field.

Optimism's Pause: Barth and Niebuhr; the Critique of Theological Liberalism

It is wise to remember, as this next section begins on what we are calling the critique of theological liberalism, that such a critique arose within a larger cultural disillusionment about the inherent goodness of humanity and the nobility of its accomplishments. A devastating world war, the rise of fascism, and an international economic depression provided more than enough fodder for a serious reevaluation of 19th century optimism. Part of the impetus for a new theological direction may have come from that cultural context, which laid bare the illusions of progress. Yet, the souls of some young pastors in Europe and America had already grown dissatisfied with 19th c. liberalism, and were yearning for a less defensive basis for their proclamation of God's Word. A whole theological movement launched as World War I concluded, incorporating over the next 50 years often disparate thinkers named Thurneysen, Tillich, Bultmann, Gogarten, Brunner, and Bonhoeffer, but the two whom we consider here as most representative are Karl Barth and Reinhold Niebuhr.

Karl Barth was a pastor in the town of Safenwil in the Swiss Alps from 1911 to 1921. Toward the end of that pastorate, as the guns of war subsided on the other side of the mountains, he wrote a commentary on St. Paul's Epistle to the Romans. Published late in 1918, and greatly amended in a 1921 edition, Barth described how this Pauline proclamation led him – as Luther before him – into a challenging new perspective on the Bible. The liberalism of Schleiermacher, Ritschl, Adolph Harnack, and Wilhelm Herrmann had trained Barth to seek God through knowledge of the human experience of that God and to emphasize mostly the moral dimension of Christ's teachings. As Barth puts it, his teachers implied that we could speak about God just by speaking about man in a loud voice. Moreover, they seemed to shy away from the "scandal" of scripture passages that could not be rationally explained.

In contrast, Paul wrote about an authoritative Word that came from outside human consciousness, about the lasting freedom of grace rather than the tenuous human freedom in social progress, and how what God thinks about us is more important than what we think about God. Barth expressed this insight a few years later.

> The Bible tells not how we should talk with God but what he says to us; not how we find the way to him, but that he has sought and found the way to us; not the right relation in which we must place ourselves to him, but the covenant which he has made with all who are Abraham's spiritual children.... (*The Word of God and the Word of Man*, 43)

Struggling to proclaim a transforming word to his congregation and dissatisfied with 19th century liberalism, Barth grasped this rope handed him by Romans. Only later did he discover, in his words, that the rope connected to a steeple bell, which rang out a new message eagerly awaited by the next generation.

Barth continued writing prolifically (one commentator jokes that even a popular mystery writer like Erle Stanley Gardner wrote fewer words). His readers in turn variously attempted to label his theology. Neo-Orthodoxy, Dialectical Theology, Crisis Theology, and even just Barthianism, gained relative popularity. Barth was unsatisfied with any such label, especially the last-mentioned option.

His own suggestion was *Evangelical Theology*, which he then used as the title of a very helpful series of lectures toward the end of his career. Those first three options above, however, can provide respective insights into his thought. Let us use them to offer a too-brief summary.

Neo-Orthodoxy: Barth's followers might be excused for thinking that the term Neo-Orthodoxy best described his work. It definitely hearkened back to the Reformation, to Luther and Calvin especially, and their splendid reaffirmations of justification by grace through faith, the centrality of the scriptures, and the sovereignty of God. Regarding justification by grace, Barth insists not only that grace is unmerited, that God alone offers grace, but also that God will even prepare the human recipient with the faithful ability to receive it. Regarding the centrality of the scriptures, Barth proclaims that we will find God only in Jesus Christ, and that the best way to know Christ is through scripture, not through religious self-consciousness. God's revelation as declared in the Bible must always control the church's proclamation. Regarding the sovereignty of God, Barth's whole theological method, seen especially in the multi-volume *Church Dogmatics*, resists encapsulating God into a particular system. Others might have called this massive output a systematic theology, but Barth explicitly rejected that title because it would imply he had systematized God, had defined and limited the God whose Word remains free and ever new. God takes the initiative in all things. Barth will allow no philosophy, no ideology, and no theology, even his own, to restrict the height, breadth or depth of divine sovereignty.

Still, this is a *Neo*-Orthodoxy. It is far from the 17th century Lutheran or Reformed Orthodoxy that hardened the Reformation into narrow, defensive dogma. Nor does it merely repeat uncritically the full positions of the reformers. Barth challenges Calvin on a misinterpretation of election and its result of double predestination. He substantially revises Calvin's explanation of the Trinity. He does not emulate Luther's resolute separation of spheres into spiritual and temporal. Likewise, Barth's criticism of Schleiermacher's emphasis on religious self-consciousness does not preclude a certain admiration for his adversary's awareness that the Enlightenment changed how the modern world regards Christian truth. Therefore Barth, for example, does not reject the historical critical exegetical method out of hand, as fundamentalists would. His theology is not an entrenched, comfortable resistance to anything new. God's sovereign freedom in revelation implies that one must always search the horizon for what God will do next.

Dialectical: Other Barthian followers have attached the term Dialectical to his work, with some justification, for his writings exhibit a running dialogue between variant perspectives on the divine activity. This is explicitly not a Hegelian three-part dialectic, which pushes ahead the progress of Geist. Instead, it is an interplay that causes us to stop, to consider, pausing before we assume we understand God's intentions. There will always be a "yes" hidden in God's "no" to us, and a "no" hidden in the "yes". The positive response may ring more loudly than the negative, but both will always be present. The cross always connects to the resurrection; they cannot be separated. One cannot speak about justification without immediately introducing sanctification. We cannot have grace without faith, nor faith without grace.

In a later essay titled "The Humanity of God", Barth offers an extended example of such connections. He acknowledges that the urgency of the moment, when he wrote his commentary on Romans, led him to emphasize only the sovereign transcendence of

God. As he turned later to emphasize the immanent dimension of God, however, he insisted that his earlier mistake was simply not carrying through sufficiently the idea of God's deity. The inevitable outcome of true deity will be God's accompanying presence. The deity of Christ leads us to the humanity of Christ, and then the humanity points back to deity. Repeatedly, Barth expresses this dialectical tendency in his theology, using it as a protection against abstract categories that would freeze God in one dimension. The Servant is always the Lord. God's free grace for us becomes our free gratitude to God. God's freedom allows the Lord to exist not only in and for Godself, but also in and for us. All of these paradoxes, these dualities that hang together, express Barth's insistence that revelation is a dynamic, existential event. Understanding that dynamic event better leads us on to the third label given to his thought.

A **Theology of Crisis** (*krisis* in German) accentuates the situation one faces when he or she comes face to face with God. One of the reasons Barth opposed attempts to explain God's activities and presence in terms of an ascendant contemporary philosophy was his concern that precisely such explanations reduced the crisis God presents to the believer. Schleiermacher's embrace of Kant, Bultmann's use of Heidegger, and all other attempts to interpret the Christian experience within an external philosophy explain away the problems, reduce the scandal of the moment, and diminish the seriousness of the decision that God sets before us. In order to hear the full Word of God, we must follow the summons into a situation where we feel that our whole existence is called into question, where we sense that God is examining us rather than us examining God.

Here is where observers see the influence of Soren Kierkegaard on Barth. Were Kierkegaard an ordinary philosopher, Barth's use of his work would violate the very principle just noted, but Kierkegaard clearly criticized the philosophy of his time and the culture it fostered. He insisted that Christianity proclaims an "infinite qualitative distinction between time and eternity" (*Concluding Unscientific Postscript*, 169ff.) a gulf which one can cross only by taking a "qualitative leap". Standing on the edge of that decision, we see the radical demand of Christ to love our neighbor, the insistence that we surrender all forms of self-justification, and the awareness that we will never understand the paradoxes of faith, yet we are led to embrace them anyway. At this moment, at this time of declaring our faith, the revelation of God in Christ captures us and transforms our relationship to God and the world. This event in the midst of time links us somehow to eternity. We do not become Christian by growing up in a Christian environment or culture. We become a Christian when God claims us in the moments of revelation to which we have submitted.

One spinoff of Kierkegaard's influence is Barth's questioning of the value of "religion". Barth certainly is not an individualist; his emphasis on the community of the church protects against this. Still, Barth was keenly aware of how the church can substitute religiosity for faith. As one clever modern phrase expresses it, the church gives us just enough religion to inoculate us against the real thing, which is faith. Barth worries that cultural Christianity compromises the deepest meaning of God's revelation in Christ, and allows a substitute to appear as an easy alternative. Dietrich Bonhoeffer extended this theme of Barth in his suggestion that the future will require a "nonreligious" Christianity. (Barth later criticized Bonhoeffer's interpretation of that concept.)

Karl Barth definitely led the way into a reevaluation of theological liberalism, and his resistance to the rise of Nazism, including authoring The Barmen Declaration in 1934 for the Confessing Church in Germany, solidified his reputation as the foremost Christian leader of the mid-20th century. But others also sensed the gravity of the situation and responded with memorable, penetrating analyses of modern culture and faith. In America, Reinhold Niebuhr deservedly received the attention of both academic and public spheres.

A Second Critique: Like Barth, Reinhold Niebuhr began his theological career as a parish pastor in an era of rapid social transformation. Born in 1892, Reinhold grew up in the pietistic Midwest environment of the German Evangelical Synod of North America. (It is worth noting here that both his sister Hulda, in Christian education, and his brother Helmut Richard, in theology, also made significant contributions to American Protestant thought. Imagine the dinner table conversations!) To his parents' delight, Reinhold from his early years seemed destined for the ministry, first attending the small denomination's Eden Seminary in St. Louis, and then Yale Divinity School, distinguishing himself at both.

Barely out of graduate school, Niebuhr in 1915 assumed the pastorate of a very German, very small mission charge, Bethel Evangelical Church, in Detroit, on a bare subsistence salary. His first battle was with the Synod's German nationalist tendencies during World War I, as he sought to Americanize the church and draw it into a more progressive understanding of the social situation. Moderately successful with that, a still greater battle awaited, as the automotive industry's rapid mechanization radically altered the economic and cultural landscape of Detroit and indeed the whole country. Like all of Detroit, Bethel saw substantial growth in the late teens and early 1920s. Niebuhr's fearless preaching was the main draw, reminding his parish that material progress was an illusory victory, that

Christ's message was clear: "Those who seek their life will lose it. Those who lose their life will find it." Niebuhr discerned that Henry Ford's production lines and strict capitalism benefitted the few and upended the lives of the workers. He temporarily joined the socialist party and publicly supported unions, stances that troubled some in the congregation but enhanced his reputation as an emerging voice among young religious leaders. His first book, *Does Civilization Need Religion?* in 1927, prompted an invitation to Union Theological Seminary in New York City, where he taught and frequently preached for more than 30 years.

During that span of time, especially until 1952, when a series of strokes substantially limited his frenetic travel schedule and voluminous publications, Niebuhr stood in the whirlwind of international theological debate and American political upheaval in World War II and the Cold War. He would never cease trying to explain how Christian truth could illuminate struggles in the political and social arenas. *Moral Man and Immoral Society* vaulted him into the forefront of theological circles in 1932. *An Interpretation of Christian Ethics* solidified that standing in 1935. *The Children of Light and the Children of Darkness* in 1944, *Faith and History* in 1949, and *The Irony of American History* in 1952, along with almost weekly preaching at college campuses and regular consultations with highly placed government officials, exhibit why Time magazine placed Niebuhr on its front cover in March 1948.

All of these significant publications, and even his less frequent writings after the strokes, center around the theology Niebuhr articulated in his Gifford Lectures at Edinburgh in 1939, published in two volumes in 1941 and 1943 as *The Nature and Destiny of Man.* There, in a grand sweep of human history and thought, he laid out the pivotal principles of his beliefs. Admittedly, the following summary of the Gifford lectures does not do justice to Niebuhr's capacious knowledge.

Niebuhr sees that the fundamental conflict in human beings, both individually and in society, plays itself out century after century and across all geographical and cultural boundaries. We are both physical creatures and reasonable creatures, hence Aristotle's definition of a human being as a "rational animal". (Niebuhr will offer an important variation on Aristotle, insisting that we are spiritual, not just rational, animals.) Some philosophies insist that since we are a child of nature, we should not pretend otherwise, but allow that physical, natural tendency to shape our decisions and goals. Opposing philosophies point to our rational faculties as proof of our ability to suppress the body's material inclinations and rise above the limits of nature. In classical Greek and Roman thought, this dualism prompted the idealist philosophy of Plato, Aristotle and the Stoics. It regards the body, human finiteness, as the source of evil, requiring regulation by the purely rational, divine dimension in humanity. Of course, this rationalism was reacting against an earlier naturalism promoted by Democritus and Epicurus; *viz.* that one's reason is merely a manifestation of natural tendencies away from pain and toward pleasure, so humanity does not stand above nature but remains within it.

Lest modern culture assume it has progressed well beyond the ancients, in the early pages of *Nature and Destiny...* (23,24) Niebuhr portrays this same opposition now. "If modern culture conceives man primarily in terms of the uniqueness of his rational faculties, it finds the root of his evil in his involvement in natural impulses and natural necessities from which it hopes to free him by the increase of his rational faculties." And alternatively, if a philosophy conceives of humanity "...primarily in terms of his relation to nature, it hopes to rescue man from the demonic chaos in which his spiritual life is involved by beguiling him back to the harmony, serenity, and harmless unity of nature." Not just classical and modern systems maintain this opposition. Niebuhr traces aspects of it throughout western thought, sometimes moderated, sometimes extreme. It could emerge in the Dominican against the Franciscan, Descartes versus Rousseau, or technological mastery contra the flower children of the 1960s. Both options in this debate remain alongside one another, ascendant in one era and recessive in the next. Neither grasps the whole picture; neither admits a possible integration into a larger truth. Humanity leaps back and forth from one inadequate worldview to another.

Progressing through the two volumes, Niebuhr articulates the central beliefs of the Christian faith as a way beyond the impasse, beliefs like God as creator, sin as self-centeredness, Jesus Christ as the only true liberator, and the Parousia as both the end of history and its goal. If God is good and God is the one creator, this implies a unity of body and soul. The mind is not divine; it is neither essentially good nor eternal. The body is not essentially evil either, as it is the product of a benevolent creator God. Finitude is not the source of sin, and mind, though invisible, is no less subject to misuse than visible matter. If sin, then, is not due to human frailty and finitude, what causes it? It is the inevitable human tendency toward egoism, which places oneself at the center of, and regards oneself as the source of, one's life. Thus, sin and evil are "at the very center of human personality: in the will" (16). Whether one embraces rationalism, naturalism, or neither, the human tendency to self-centeredness corrupts our perspective and poisons our relationships. Neither body nor mind is immune. Only the "foolishness" of Christ's sacrificial love can rescue humanity from our self-centered, self-enclosed dilemma. This agape love, revealed upon the cross, expresses the essential reality, the character, of God. "The self... cannot understand itself except as it is understood from beyond itself and the world" (14). Therefore, the revelation of God is not an increasing God-consciousness in the human soul, as in Schleiermacher and theological liberalism; it is divine grace, which enters history from outside.

Niebuhr does introduce here, however, a distinctive idea that sets him apart from the Augustinian-Calvinist-Barthian mainstream Reformation view of grace. He contends that one gift from God's initial creation of humanity remains: the *image* of God, which original sin does not completely obliterate. This is not just reason; it is instead a persistent sense of self-transcendence. The residual divine spirit within us has the ability to recognize that our sinfulness is not the state God intends for us. "Some memory of a previous condition of blessedness seems to linger in his soul; some echo of the law which he has violated seems to resound in his conscience" (265). These words, from the final chapter of the first volume, imply that in the image of God an original righteousness remains, which informs our personal choice to accept the offer of grace when offered. This is the single point of contact maintained by the spirit of God so that humanity can respond freely to the offer of grace. It sustains the full paradox that both irresistible divine initiative and human freedom coalesce in the event of justification.

As Niebuhr moves from the first volume on human nature to *Volume II, Human Destiny*, he accentuates the role and meaning of history. There is a clear movement of history in scripture, from creation, through the Messiah's victory on earth, and toward his second coming. From the Renaissance onward, however, and especially in the 18th and 19th centuries, the understanding of history changed significantly. Modern thought too often collapsed eternity into history. It did not conceive how the fulfillment of history could come from outside itself, transcending history and therefore bringing it to an end. Thus the belief in history as inevitable progress arose, which influenced (consciously or unconsciously) the liberalism of Ritschl and the social gospel's work to bring in the future kingdom of God. Niebuhr emphasizes instead the Reformation suspicion of any possible realization of the kingdom within history. The Christian understands that the final coming of Christ, the Parousia, is both the end as *finis*, the termination point of history, and also its end as *telos*, its goal (II,299).

Certainly it is clear that history is dynamic; it moves toward an endpoint in some sense. Niebuhr writes that humanity has grown "… towards more inclusive ends, towards more complex human relations, towards the technical enhancement of human powers and the accumulation of knowledge" (II, 315). However, the cataclysmic events of the 20th century have shown that such growth does not necessarily imply moral and spiritual progress. Such historical growth has no moral connotation. It is not good in itself but only if and when God intervenes in its events. The biblical doctrine of the Parousia shows that the consummation of history is *supratemporal*, outside of time. History does not end because humanity has perfected it. The last judgment refutes "…all conceptions of history, according to which… it is able by its process of growth and development, to emancipate man from the guilt and sin of this existence , and to free him from judgment" (II, 293). God still judges the good and the evil, an eternal arbiter who stands outside of time and evaluates it. History is at best an interim period between the disclosure of its meaning in Christ's first coming and the fulfillment of its meaning in the Parousia, his second.

Those who have worked through Niebuhr's two volumes on *The Nature and Destiny of Man* recognize his realism, his skeptical assessment of human accomplishments, his awareness of the irony embedded in history, and his suspicion of all who launch grand schemes to lead us back to nature or on to the full use of our technological capabilities. Still, on the final page of *The Nature and Destiny of Man*, he summarizes the ultimate reason for his hope, his realism, and their basis in the Christian faith:

> Thus wisdom about our destiny is dependent upon a humble recognition of the limits of our knowledge and our power. Our most reliable understanding is the fruit of "grace" in which faith completes our ignorance without pretending to possess its certainties as knowledge; and in which contrition mitigates our pride without destroying our hope. (321)

In effect, Reinhold Niebuhr would answer the underlying question of this chapter, "How do we best know God and ourselves?" by stating that the revelation of God in Jesus Christ and the fundamental doctrines of the church provide humanity with the humility and perspective essential for such knowledge. That was his goal in the pivotal Gifford Lectures and in the political contributions of his public life. Combining this with Karl Barth's emphasis on the sovereignty of God in the face of multiple attempts to replace it with human schemes of meaning, we have heard two strong voices who encouraged Christians to pause and reevaluate the optimism of theological liberalism.

The effort of theology to draw people toward a transformative relationship with God has obviously continued to the present day.

It did start in a new direction, however, with the emergence of postmodern philosophy in the mid-20th century. This next era of theological reflection will raise a thorough challenge to the very idea of theological language and the presuppositions that undergird religion of any form. However, before we enter that revolutionary arena, we will examine the lasting effects of modernity on key concepts of the previous five centuries of Christian faith. Chapter Three, Modernity and Its Challenge to the Church, builds on the forgoing review of Christian epistemology by considering a modern believer's relationship to society in three specific (and familiar) categories:

- Our understanding of freedom
- Changing views of history, including its effect on interpretation of scripture
- The moral principles that guide our pursuit of happiness or "the good life"

In the upcoming chapter, we hope to present a balanced view of the many blessings of modernity along with the distinct challenges it brings to a Christ-centered life.

| three |

Modernity and Its Challenge to the Church

Western Christianity: An Apprehension of Irrelevance

North American visitors to the splendid cathedrals of Europe often remark that, apart from gawking tourists, the buildings appear empty, symbols of the demise of organized Christianity in places it once flourished. The criticism slightly exaggerates, as many cathedral chapters still provide multiple worship opportunities and tend a diminished but faithful flock. Nonetheless, the contrast between the vitality of both Roman Catholicism and Protestantism in Western Europe today and their vigor three or four centuries ago is striking. Moreover, the strength of North American Christianity over the last two centuries, once an exception to the trend, is now also fading, to the point that denominations are combining seminaries, slashing mission budgets and closing small congregations daily. Decades ago, evangelical conservative churches provided a counterpoint to that trend, but that is no longer true.

It is of course wise to resist blunt generalizations. Worldwide, the Christian religion still grows and prospers, especially in Asia, South America and Africa. Many vibrant American congregations are expanding their mission, their staff and even their nurseries. Also, let us not forget that at the dawn of the American nation, prior to the Great Awakenings, fewer than 1 in 10 citizens were active in a church. However, today's trends do not favor the long-term health of North American Christianity. Recent surveys from the Pew Research Trust, Gallup and Barna polls and the Lilly Foundation all point to reduced church membership, influence, and public respect, as younger generations especially find alternatives for community, service, and intellectual growth. The church of Jesus Christ is amazingly resilient, but the challenge ahead is formidable.

What has happened? What changes in thought and culture prompted sociologist Peter Berger to recognize, over 50 years ago in *The Sacred Canopy*, that "...the fundamental problem of the religious institutions is how to keep going in a milieu that no longer takes for granted their definitions of reality" (127). What were those "definitions of reality" possessed by Western Christianity in, say, the 17th century that no longer appear accurate and helpful to an increasing number of modern and postmodern people? Building upon the historical development of theology in the preceding chapter, the following pages attempt to answer that question, at least within the perimeters of what society once called "mainline" American Protestantism, with which I am most familiar. If the conclusions offered also help Roman Catholic, Pentecostal, and other leaders of the Christian religion address the philosophic and cultural trends that keep them awake with worry at night, then the Holy Spirit has seen fit to extend its wisdom into arenas of which I have little experience.

Certainly, over previous decades wise philosophers and theologians have already responded to Berger's observation about the changed definitions of reality. A brief recounting of four such reflections provides a starting point for our own response.

Carl Becker, in *The Heavenly City of the Eighteenth Century Philosophers* (102f.), characterizes the Enlightenment as a kind of religion in its own right, though one whose doctrines clash with traditional Christianity. He cites the following aspects of what he calls the "creed" of the Enlightenment, a creed that encouraged modern societies to overcome the backward religious burdens of the past.

> 1. Man is not natively depraved; 2. The end of life is life itself, the good life on earth instead of the beatific life after death; 3. Man is capable, guided solely by the light of reason and experience, of perfecting the good life on earth; and 4. The essential condition of the good life on earth is the freeing of men's minds from the bonds of ignorance and superstition....

Langdon Gilkey, writing in *Theology Today*, likewise identifies four traits that characterize the modern ethos, each of which corrodes the acknowledgement of and submission to claims by an external authority, which religion requires. The four traits are:

> a sense of contingency that doubts overarching purposiveness; a relativism that renders everything transient and prevents the past from making claims on the present; a temporality that claims human knowledge and understanding have been evolving over time, so that we're further along the road to human maturity than people in the past; and an autonomy that claims nothing can or will come from outside to help us. (378)

Roman Catholic Cardinal Avery Dulles, in *Models of Revelation*, also acknowledges that trends within the last 400 years challenge the external authority of revelation, God's word from outside the normal sphere of human knowledge. He includes eight factors, including the philosophic agnosticism fostered by Immanuel Kant, modern epistemology's insistence that all knowledge is limited by the conditions of the learner, biblical criticism, with its emphasis on the heavily mediated writing of scripture, and the deconstructionism in critical sociology, which interprets revelation as just another form of ideological preservation of power. Dulles seeks to show how someone might trust a revealed truth despite such intellectual constraints (6-8).

Finally, the Princeton philosopher/theologian Diogenes Allen writes in *Spiritual Theology* (47), that belief in the Christian religion is vulnerable today due to a thoroughly secular understanding of life normative in modern times. "Two main forces have contributed to this secular worldview: the conviction that morals and society do not need a religious foundation, and the overriding drive toward material progress." Hence (48), "What developed was a type of humanism that saw itself both as alternative to and incompatible with Christianity."

These authors represent a sampling of centuries-long debates on how the Christian Church can recognize the challenge presented by the ideas and culture of modernity. Summarizing many such discerning observations, the following pages will try to present an accessible interpretation of this very complicated subject. There will be three sections of the chapter, expanding the three themes first noted in an earlier chapter: the modern reinterpretation of freedom, the new understanding of history, including its effect on scriptural interpretation, and the redefinition of happiness (or "the good life") made possible by modern science and education.

In anticipation of these topics, one more caveat is in order. The reader should not assume that this author regards challenges to previous theology and practice of the Christian church as unwelcome. If God's truth is ultimately one, then the Holy Spirit of God works through all realms of thought to reveal new dimensions of God's majesty and plan. We can welcome these social, scientific, and philosophical developments as prompts and messengers urging us to review, refine, and articulate clearer visions of God's work. The dialogue between tradition and challenge will reveal both lasting relevance and mistaken assumptions in the differing definitions of reality that have set the modern world and the Christian church in conflict. However, it is naïve to think that new conceptions of freedom, history, and the good life do not unsettle, and at times upend, traditional views. There inevitably will be substantial challenge, some "pinch" that squeezes the church to decide how far it can accept, reject, or adapt to these changes. That is what this current chapter examines.

The Reinterpretation of Freedom

To speak the word "freedom" is to open a wide spectrum of variations in meaning. Mortimer Adler's article on Liberty in his *Great Ideas* acknowledges this variety and quotes Leo Tolstoy's words to that effect.

> What is sin, the conception of which arises from the consciousness of man's freedom? That is a question for theology.... What is man's responsibility to society, the conception of which results

from the conception of freedom? That is a question for jurisprudence.... What is conscience and the perception of right and wrong in actions that follow from the consciousness of freedom? That is a question for ethics.... How should the past life of nations and humanity be regarded – as the result of the free, or as the result of the constrained, activity of man? That is a question for history. (425)

A comprehensive look at all these aspects of freedom could carry us well beyond the scope of this work. It is obvious that the varieties of freedom intermingle and interrelate. That is largely unavoidable and will be apparent as we proceed. Nonetheless, it is also possible to distinguish one from another, so for the sake of clarity, let us use slightly different labels for each. For example, the abstract question of freedom's metaphysical possibility requires a stance on free will vs. necessity. The ethical debate on how freedom operates in the deliberation between good and bad might best use the term free choice. The political issue about the relation of natural rights to governmental oversight will be clearer if it employs the term liberties. What we might call an ideological dimension, which defines an individual's identity in terms of freedom from imposed limits, is a quest for more autonomy. Finally, the religious yearning for freedom from powers of sin and death is best understood as a desire for deliverance, or in broader terms, redemption. The following pages will concentrate on the last three of these categories, although as noted the discussion also intrudes upon others. We begin by explaining central biblical interpretations of freedom.

Prominent Images of Freedom in Christian Scripture and Doctrine

The Christian scriptures employ two related ways of depicting freedom, as deliverance, rescue, often by the action of God, and as a state of free choice. The first emphasizes the action of the deliverer: the second emphasizes an accomplished status of liberty.

Freedom as Deliverance: In the Old Testament, multiple Hebrew roots receive in translation some sense of the English verb "deliver", including various meanings ranging from a rescue out of bondage to handing over an item to another. The term used most often to describe the liberation from Pharaoh at the Exodus implies a "snatching away" from danger. With the same verb, the Psalmist earnestly seeks rescue of one's soul from both one's enemies and one's own sins. A different root describes God as delivering the Canaanites into the hands of Israel. The Old Testament word translated "redeemer", *gaol*, can also signify in Hebrew a deliverer. The New Testament also utilizes the idea of deliverance, and in the same two senses: to rescue, and to hand over a person or item. In the Lord's Prayer, Matthew and Luke write, "Lead us not into temptation, but deliver us from evil." The passion stories of the Gospels, alternatively, regularly describe Jesus as delivered into the hands of his accusers. Indeed, the New Revised Standard Version explicitly translates the verb there as "to hand over".

Freedom as a State of Liberty: Both Old and New Testaments, however, also use words that imply a more abstract, lasting status in which one receives liberty to decide for oneself. Whether in the ceremony to release an indentured servant or in the year of jubilee, the Hebrew word transliterated *chophshi* describes an achieved state of free decision-making. Likewise, the Greek word *eleutheria* implies the freedom to go where one wants. When released from slavery, one becomes a freeman or freewoman, no longer under the commands of a master. In Galatians 5:13, Paul speaks of freedom as a new state of being, a liberation, with enough free will and free choice to do what you want unless you choose to be constrained by the law of love. In the Greek-speaking world of the New Testament, the word conveys political or social freedom, independence, or liberty.

What unites the two primary definitions in scripture, whether the activity of deliverance or the more abstract state of free choice, is that one's freedom, one's liberation, begins with God. Although scripture does generally recognize that people have some ability to make choices, its predominant emphasis is on an external force liberating one from some type of bondage. In Exodus, the bondage is from pharaoh, but deliverance comes through the active intervention of God. In the return from Babylonian exile, the Lord who acts in history summons a third party, Persia, to liberate. In the gospels, disease and shame crush the human spirit, but Christ's compassion restores to health and wholeness. In Galatians, the burden is an overextended law that imprisons the will; the redemption is through divine grace. It is not by one's own power or expertise that freedom arises, even though Moses does wield the staff that parts the sea or the blind man must go wash in the pool of Siloam. Human participation is always secondary to the originating force of divine redemption.

Obedience and Freedom: Consistently in both the Old Testament and New Testament, liberation from a destructive bondage also initiates a constructive relationship to a new master. When Israel escapes Egyptian tyranny, it follows the fire and cloud of a new guide, and arrives at a mountain where God establishes a new covenant based on specific laws. David arises from obscurity not so he may establish an empire through his own military expertise, but through obedience to the Lord who called him. When he disobeys, a prophet of God calls him to account. Matthew the tax collector responds to Jesus' invitation and leaves behind a despised occupation, but thereby embarks upon the rough road of discipleship in the footsteps of the Messiah. Paul in Romans rejoices that those who once were slaves to sin have now become slaves to righteousness. Therefore, the state of freedom implied in the Hebrew word *chophshi* and the Greek *eleutheria* is not an isolated, autonomous opportunity to determine one's own norms, but deliverance from a destructive allegiance and into a constructive one.

Nonetheless, this relationship of obedience to a new, divine master does not curtail the free actions of a Christian, but paradoxically enhances them. St. Paul, in Romans 7 and 8, voices this dynamic. He struggles with his inability to do what he knows he should. "I do not understand my own actions. For I do not do what I want, but I do the very thing I hate." Something, his sin, keeps him from exercising his free choice in the way he wants. He feels powerless to overcome the force of sin by himself, and in forceful language bemoans his fate. "Wretched man that I am! Who will rescue me from this body of death?" His answer, to himself and to all who ask the same question, is this: "The law of the Spirit of life in Christ Jesus has set you free from the law of sin and of death. For God has done what the law, weakened by the flesh, could not do...." Upon this background, Paul repeatedly celebrates the ability of one who lives by the Spirit of Christ, in obedience to Christ, to accomplish what one is unable to do on the sole strength of human will and effort. Thus, our free choices become most complete and effective through the action of a Lord who claims our obedience.

Paul's conviction resonates in a memorable phrase from St. Augustine of Hippo's commentary on First John: "Love God and do what you will." The more we love and express gratitude to God for what God has done for us, the more our own will, without effort, voluntarily conforms to God's will, and thus what we choose will reflect what God wants for our free decisions. A further pertinent statement from Augustine comes during his description of the four states of human existence in the *Enchiridion*. He describes the transition from a person guided by God to make conscious good decisions into a person whose will is in such perfect communion with God that he or she is unable to choose wrongly: "It is good to be able not to sin. It is better not to be able to sin."

The implications of these paradoxes lead to another, expressed by Martin Luther at the dawn of the Reformation in his early essay The Freedom of a Christian: "A Christian is a perfectly free lord of all, subject to none. A Christian is a perfectly dutiful servant of all, subject to all" (53). Luther owes this striking couplet to Paul, and quotes First Corinthians 9:19 and Romans 13:8 by way of explanation: "For though I am free from all… I have made myself a slave to all." And "Owe no one anything, except to love one another." Luther then continues in his own words: "Love by its very nature is ready to serve and be subject to him who is loved." To love God is to be subject to God's will. To love other people is to be subject to their needs, although of course those needs also are subject to what God wills. The source of Christian love for others, therefore, is the liberation, the deliverance, the freedom received from God.

Despite their insistence that the freedom of a Christian is actually just allegiance to God, neither Luther nor Calvin was a thoroughgoing determinist who denied even the possibility of free will. The rigid predestination emphasized by Calvin, or the severe restrictions placed on free choice in Luther's Heidelberg Disputations, might lead one to assume that they believed all sense of choice was merely an illusion. Erasmus, Luther's contemporary, certainly thought that was the stance of the Reformers. But Calvin repeatedly denied that divine providence is the same thing as inescapable fatalism. Within the overarching and mysterious plan of God, human beings do have the capacity and the responsibility of choosing rightly. Luther in turn maintained that free choice is possible, indeed common, in matters not pertaining to salvation. Choosing what to cook for dinner or how to discipline a child, for instance, remains in the hands of the doer, but believing one can by free decisions achieve one's own salvation is illusory and dangerous. (For more on these distinctions, see Timothy George's *Theology of the Reformers*, 75-76 and 204-208.) The Reformers' primary concern was resisting the works' righteousness that led to the dead end of self-justification. In that arena, the illusion that one's free choices can bring redemption is for them the road to hell.

The Christian understanding of freedom described above has the potential to transform individuals and societies. 500 years have intervened since the Reformers reiterated these biblical stances on the topic of freedom, and those doctrines still constitute the predominant official positions of modern Protestant denominations. Nevertheless, these are definitely not the prevalent public understanding of freedom in western society today. Indeed, only small pockets of dedicated believers articulate and practice them, often only in isolated areas of application. Instead, substantial reevaluation of Reformation doctrines and fine-tuning of ecclesiastical proclamations have arisen through the encounter with other views of freedom in later centuries, both within and outside of the church. It is to such alternative views and challenges that we can now turn.

Three other conceptions of freedom combine to dominate public discourse and ethical decisions. Those are the social contract theory of government articulated primarily by Thomas Hobbes and John Locke; the sense of freedom as autonomy most clearly stated by Immanuel Kant in his political/ethical writings; and the prerequisite of free choice for economic prosperity that accelerated with Adam Smith's theory of capital.

Civil Liberty and the Social Contract Theory of Government

In Chapter One, within the sketch of elements in modernity, we made an initial reference to the social contract theory of government. In a description of how the contract replaces a less secure state of nature, this statement appeared. "The new arrangement means three things: the contract could not exist unless free people chose voluntarily to develop it, every person in the contract has equal rights in the eyes of the law, and the total amount of freedom increases for all because of the order provided by the sovereign state." The social contract theory that arose in the late 17th century eventually prompted the representative democracy form of government. Locke's influence on the American Revolution and constitution may be the most obvious example, but social contract theory also accelerated the movement away from the "divine right of kings" toward rule by elected parliaments and national legislatures throughout the western world. Hobbes and Locke might have begun their advocacy of the social contract theory as a simple thought experiment, but over the last three centuries, the theory has become a prominent reality. Every such government, therefore, bears the marks of those three characteristics noted above, and that fact bears substantial implications for a modern sense of freedom.

The social contract begins with the affirmation that there is a natural freedom granted to humanity by its maker, or in the language of the Declaration of Independence, by "the Laws of Nature and Nature's God". That original freedom (and here arises a disagreement between Hobbes and Locke that influences the interpretation) is, for Hobbes, fragile and threatened, making life "solitary, poor, nasty, brutish, and short". Alternatively, for Locke life is more regulated by natural laws and thus is somewhat more sanguine. Despite that difference, in either case, the participants voluntarily choose to establish the contract (first characteristic). When one chooses to enter into a commonwealth through a social contract, civil liberty either replaces that original natural freedom (Hobbes), or supplements it (Locke). The laws of the state apply equally to every citizen who joins the contract; they have equal rights, at least in principle (the second characteristic). In the contract, people receive both greater security from the aggression of others and restrictions on their own aggression, but the gain is greater than the loss. They are, once the laws are in place, freer than they were before (third characteristic). They gain civil liberty, i.e. freedom to do whatever the law of the state does not prohibit, and protection from encroachment on that freedom by unruly neighbors. Locke insists, as noted, that the natural law also remains to restrain individuals from wrong actions.

Western democracies are fortunate that their founders initially followed Locke's sense of natural freedom rather than Hobbes', but in one key respect, that distinction has lost its original impact. The more lasting impact is that both social contract theories emphasize that free people themselves establish the contract that ensures their greater freedom. Civil liberty results from the free choice of those who decide to attain it. It is not a queen or king, nor a God who grants a divine mandate, that bestows civil liberty here. It is instead the people's own choice to gain their civil freedom. It may well be that, theoretically and originally, the free choice of the people to enter into a social contract arises from a belief that God bestows upon them their natural freedom. But practically speaking, today that concept has been forgotten in the midst of the daily exercise of civil liberties, due to multiple reasons. For one, the concept of natural law, on which Locke based his theory, no longer bears the same weight of acceptance and authority today. Although maintained in Roman Catholic thought, it has been largely set aside in most philosophic and legal circles, and talk has turned more to natural "rights". In fact, for practical purposes, citizens of a modern democracy believe their civil liberties arise solely from the social contract that they establish with their government. They, alone and in groups, are the authors of their civil freedoms. Although the state administers their liberty, they owe their freedom not to the state, nor to God, but ultimately to human choice. It comes neither by nature nor by divine gift. We create our civil liberty by contract. This is a very powerful, very influential, bottom line in the hearts and minds of modern humanity. A contract of political power used to secure opportunity and safety becomes a core understanding of human freedom.

Kant's Categorical Imperative and Freedom as Autonomy

The first dimension of freedom's modern meaning relates most to civil rights and liberties within political government. The second influences more a specific individual's freedom in making decisions. It arises as an implication of Immanuel Kant's epistemology, which we noted briefly in an earlier review of Kant's response to the skepticism of David Hume. We can now examine how his philosophical system introduces a new dimension of human freedom that challenges a more traditional Christian interpretation.

As noted earlier, Kant's *Critique of Pure Reason* distinguishes between the "phenomena" noticed by our senses, and the "noumena" or the "things in themselves" that transcend sense experience. Pure Reason, using consistent logical categories, can neither prove nor disprove the existence of such noumena, including the idea of God or freedom. However, as explained in Kant's second *Critique, Practical Reason*, operating in ethical decisions, in the realm of action, can provide other reasons for believing in God based on the force of moral obligation. If there is an obligation to act morally, then it follows that the freedom to do so must be possible. The existence of God and the idea of immortality are likewise implied. Kant calls these three – freedom, God and immortality – necessary postulates of that moral obligation. The three may be possible in the realm of speculative reason, but they are required by the inner logic of moral action.

In *The Groundwork (Grundlegung) for a Metaphysic of Morals*, a shorter, more concise document that builds on his work in the earlier Critiques, Kant gives a name to the obligatory moral law that he believes should regulate all our ethical decisions. He calls it the categorical imperative. It is categorical, in his terms, because it does not depend on contingent circumstances that might change from time to time. He states the law in many different forms. The first is this: "Act only according to that maxim whereby you can, at the same time, will that it should become a universal law" (88). A second form is this: "Act in such a way that you treat humanity, whether in your own person or in the person of any other, never merely as a means to an end, but always at the same time as an end" (101). There is great value in these statements for ethical decision-making. They protect against doing something for yourself that you would deny to other people, and they guard against using another individual merely as a tool for your own gain. Together, they evoke the tone of the Golden Rule, found in slightly different forms in many world religions. Kant's ethical precept has reinforced a sense of duty and principle into decisions otherwise decided only on utilitarian grounds.

The categorical imperative, however, establishes an alternative foundation for morality that obviates any religious connection between personal faith in a divine lawgiver and free ethical decisions (more on this later). Although in his second Critique, Kant does provide a defense of the existence of God, it is as a postulate derived from a previously discerned rule of moral obligation. God does not hold primacy of place, but appears as a consequence of a more important principle. Morality does not arise from faith in God; God arises from faith in universal morality. Furthermore, for Kant the reason you do not use other persons solely as a means to an end is that you recognize in them the freedom to make rational decisions, and to use them merely as means would violate that very freedom. The ground for treating another person with respect shifts from seeing him or her as the image of God to seeing him or her as an autonomous decision-maker. We could almost say that since Kant, what makes human life sacred is one's inviolable freedom to choose. Other comments from Kant reinforce the impression that he claims for individuals a breadth and depth of autonomous freedom hitherto unstated. A further restatement of the Categorical Imperative in the *Groundwork...* is one such comment: "Thus the third practical principle follows [from the first two] as the ultimate condition of their harmony with practical reason: the idea of the will of every rational being as a universally legislating will" (98). Each individual becomes a self-legislating body. This implies, then, in Kant's words, that "Autonomy is therefore the ground of the dignity of human nature and of every rational nature" (103).

Certainly, Kant does insist that decisions must be reasonable, universally applicable and respect the freedom of others, but such emphasis on the autonomy (literally, being a "law unto oneself") of an individual means that the only possible restraint on free choice is reason. What, though, if one chooses to ignore the restraint of reason? After all, Kant had already untethered reason from the noumenal realm, restricting its access to some dimensions of human personality. Furthermore, this "deontological" ethics, as it has been termed, removes decision-making from specific contexts, so how is one to know just what reason demands in unusual circumstances? As Kant himself insists in the *Groundwork*... "Hence everything that is empirical is, as a contribution to the principle of morality, not only wholly unsuitable for the purpose, but is even highly injurious to the purity of morals..." (93).

Kant's conception of the autonomous will of an individual has the potential to paint human beings into corners, into separate, isolated existences. Two statements from his shorter writings in *On History* demonstrate the implications of this form of freedom. The first sentences from "What Is Enlightenment?" boldly proclaim this direction: "Enlightenment is man's release from his self-incurred tutelage. Tutelage is man's inability to make use of his understanding without direction from another" (3). The third thesis in his Idea for a "Universal History from a Cosmopolitan Point of View" likewise implies a destiny of self-containment.

> Nature has willed that man should, by himself, produce everything that goes beyond the mechanical ordering of his animal existence, and that he should partake of no other happiness or perfection than that which he himself, independently of instinct, has created by his own reason. (13)

The question that haunts Kantian ethics is whether the power of universal reason, in which he places such trust, can restrain and direct the inner drive toward autonomy that he encourages, or if instead humanity will march inevitably toward "the triumph of the will".

Free Trade, Self-Interest, and Personal Identity

The civil liberty gained through social contract theory receives lofty public debate in courtrooms and the halls of legislatures. The quest for autonomy offered by Kant evokes worrisome tendencies but does connect personal independence to universal reason. Still, a third form of freedom inextricably connects our personal self-image to free choice in the marketplace. In practical terms, this last form of freedom has influenced individuals even more than the previous two, and begs a more extended examination.

The link between wealth and public prominence is assuredly nothing new. We remember Croesus, king of Lydia in the 6th century BCE and marvel at such riches. Roman senators courted rich benefactors in their quest for power. Kings and queens of colonial empires constructed lavish residences like Versailles to ensure their legacy. However, the modern era provides an extended theory for society's pursuit of wealth, the mechanism of free-market economics. Since the Industrial Revolution, the ideal of economic prosperity reaches into the hopes and homes of vastly more participants. The articulation of that process begins with Adam Smith's critique of mercantilism, connects to a view of progress arising in the early 19th century, receives stark criticism from radical Marxists and moderate capitalists alike, and prompts resentment in the many who see vast inequity in the wealth the free-market system had promised.

The year 1776 not only saw the American Declaration of Independence from England. It also, less conspicuously but with equal impact, announced a new approach to economic policy in Adam Smith's *The Wealth of Nations*. Modern economics owes much to Smith's insistence that a division of labor will enhance overall productivity, and to his definition of "stock" (the excess amount of one's possessions not needed for regular daily living) which can then become capital for investment. Indeed, the current science of economics could scarcely exist without Smith's philosophy of trade. Out of his whole contribution to the modern world, though, three aspects of Smith's theory concern us here. First is his belief that free trade is an aspect of natural liberty; second, his belief that overall consumption, rather than unlimited production, should be the final goal of economic activity; and last, his often implied though seldom stated sense of a providential invisible hand that turns individual self-interest into the greater good of all.

A group of *philosophes* of France known as the physiocrats had proposed the *laissez faire* approach to business decades before Smith used the idea to criticize English mercantilism and its protectionist practices. Mercantilism, the predominant theory of trade in England since Elizabeth's reign in the late 16th century, recommended regular intervention in economic transactions to ensure a favorable balance of trade with other countries (fewer imports, more exports, especially finished goods) and the regular accumulation of gold and silver. These, to the mercantilist mind, were the surest measures of a country's wealth, and if monopolies and multiple tariffs could enhance those measures, the monarchy should not hesitate to use them. Slowly, however, continental and English thought saw the downside of such protectionism. Too often, the wealth gained by one nation meant a concomitant loss by another, leading to wars of conquest and defense. Another practice of mercantilism was subduing the bulk of the working population. Laborers and farmers were to live at the "margins of subsistence" so that labor costs remained low. The goal was to maximize production for export, with little interest in providing goods for the native population to consume. Extra money, leisure time, and education for the working poor, it was thought, would inevitably lead to vice and laziness, resulting in harm to the economy.

The opposite belief, that government should keep its hands off the normal means of attaining wealth, was a logical extension of the more general principles of natural law. Rationalist philosophers of the early 18th century, from John Locke to the physiocrats mentioned above, believed that laws of human behavior existed, mirroring Newton's laws of physical nature. Those regularities of everyday human behavior, if unimpeded and approached rationally, would carry humanity to the height of its abilities. John Locke's insistence on natural laws protecting life, liberty, and property set the stage for Smith's theory. As Locke declared natural rights for an individual's political freedom, Smith restated that declaration for individual economic freedom. If government would restrict itself to protecting private property and helping grow wealth by providing good roads and ports, then one simple natural law of human behavior would do the rest, carrying human tendencies in the right direction. That was the law of ultimate self-interest.

The free pursuit of economic self-interest and the gain it produces helps workers spend more to improve conditions for the families they love, thereby contributing to overall expansion of the market. The marketplace thus demands growth, which new entrants into the labor force meet. Competition for those workers raises wages; competition for new products accelerates innovation; innovation creates ever-newer fields of endeavor, needing yet more workers who will earn better wages. Hence, the more one person seeks to gain a greater share of wealth, the more others will also benefit from the expanding economy. All of this progress is almost automatic (remembering of course that the process requires much human time, sweat, and toil, and an unending supply of laborers and raw natural resources). Eventually, though, each participant in the market economy contributes unknowingly to the material betterment of all. The ingrown desire for personal gain provides more commodities for more people to enjoy.

Furthermore, because free trade, compared to mercantilism, emphasizes the production of consumable commodities rather than the national accumulation of gold and silver as the most significant marker of wealth, the primary focus of trade shifts toward the consumer. Even the poor are better able to join the trend upward toward wealth because the law of supply and demand requires more workers who in turn become new consumers. This is the theory Smith championed, joining the chorus of rationalist philosophers who saw such an economic dynamic as one more law of human nature.

In *The Wealth of Nations* and even earlier in his book *The Theory of Moral Sentiments*, Smith occasionally refers to this seemingly inevitable progress as the work of "an invisible hand". Two quotations from *The Wealth of Nations* connect to portray this view: "It is not from the benevolence of the butcher, the brewer, or the baker, that we expect our dinner, but from their regard to their own interest." "The individual intends only his own gain, but is led by an invisible hand to promote the general good." (Bk.4, ch.2)

Debates have ebbed and flowed about whether Smith intended to portray a providential God behind the marvelous process that turns individual selfish desire into communal good. That debate can remain for others to decide, but it is important to recall that in his earlier work Smith emphasizes the presence of an inherent sympathy in the human heart, which extends self-interest beyond the individual self and motivates the worker to provide for one's own household. Nature (or Nature's God?) displays that same sense of sympathy when turning personal self-interest into common good, Smith believes. Such inherent sympathy is also one of the factors that limit the misuse of the prosperity which some will obtain faster and more frequently. In his later work, Smith squarely criticizes extravagant spending and hoarding, which squander wealth that could be used for purposes that are more productive and are available to all people.

There is little question that the theory of free-market economy enhanced the physical well-being of millions of Europeans and Americans in the 19th and 20th centuries. The industrial revolution worked hand-in-glove with market capitalism to create marvels of engineering, communication, and wealth. Despite squalid housing conditions of factory employees, perilous occupations like coal mining, and the disruption of an earlier stable family life in rural settings, still, laborsaving conveniences, higher rates of literacy, and medical advancements engendered by expanding capitalist profits substantially improved the life span and comfort level of citizens in the modern western world.

What remains to be seen, however, is how long such expansion can, or should, continue. Questions surface here about the way Adam Smith's natural law of self-interest and emphasis on consumption of products changed public attitudes toward freedom and wealth. If it is a natural law, with accompanying human rights, freely to pursue economic self-interest, and if this is amazingly the method whereby a guiding hand translates self-interest into the best interests of the whole society, what does that say about people who, despite honest effort, always end up at the bottom of the pile? If our daily life revolves around the freedom provided by economic purchasing power, and a preoccupation with consumption of products, what does that say about the virtues of modesty and restraint? If an ever-expanding level of consumption slowly depletes natural resources and demonstrates little regard for the natural environment, how does that affect a person's view of the creation in which one lives?

Criticisms of Capitalist Consumerism

Two critics of the society launched by Adam Smith's market capitalism illuminate these issues, insisting that even a grateful public could no longer ignore the downside of capitalist growth.

The first voice comes from the economist and social critic Thorstein Veblen. He published *The Theory of the Leisure Class* in 1899. A 1973 edition contains a preface by John Kenneth Galbraith in which he describes Veblen. "No man of his time, or since, looked with such a cool and penetrating eye not so much at pecuniary gain as at the way its pursuit makes men and women behave" (vi). Veblen reveals the psychosocial dimension of economic capitalism in a group of people with the leisure and money to express their wealth in excess, laying bare their pride, their desire for recognition, and a perverted sense of honor.

Once the accumulation of wealth transcends the necessities of simple subsistence, Veblen explains, people begin to compete for an "increase in the comforts of life". This possibility is restricted for most people, but not for all. Veblen recognizes that for the wealthy, the next step is not just having comforts, but the visible accumulation and display of them. The motive for this accumulation goes far beyond the need to survive. People now pursue it because "wealth confers honor". (And how could people know to honor you unless they see your wealth?) The possession of substantial property and goods "...now becomes the most easily recognized evidence of a reputable degree of success" (37). Veblen exposes these practices as what he terms "conspicuous consumption" (63,64) which a certain segment of society displays in order to gain the respect of a culture that celebrates wealth. More and more, a person's worth is determined not just by how much money they have but by how visibly they present it to society. The public display of excess creates a built-in basis for attitudes of envy in the observer and arrogant disdain in the exhibitor, according to Veblen's observations.

The book's title emphasizes a second gulf also, between those who must do manual labor to achieve life's necessities and those who, owing to their wealth, can instead publicly display their many hours of leisure. "Abstention from labor is the conventional evidence of wealth and is therefore the conventional mark of social standing" (44). To be clear, Veblen defines leisure not as pure indolence but as the "non-productive consumption of time" (46). No doubt all people need leisure, time not oriented to productivity. Nonetheless, the point of his critique is not necessarily that wealthy people do no work, but that they strive to give the impression that they do not need to work. The extent to which they can dedicate their lives to leisure becomes for them yet another reassuring sign of their superiority to others.

Veblen concludes the analytical part of his book with two summary statements. ""The basis on which good repute in any highly organized industrial community rests is pecuniary (monetary) strength; and the means of showing pecuniary strength, and so of gaining a good name, are leisure and a conspicuous consumption of goods" (71). Even more bluntly:

> Throughout the entire evolution of conspicuous expenditure, whether of goods or of services or human life, runs the obvious implication that in order to effectually mend a consumer's good fame, it must be the expenditure of superfluities. In order to be reputable it must be wasteful. (77)

Veblen's critique is an anthropological study of human behavior that reveals conspicuous consumption and its questionable human values. A second commentator on Adam Smith's system addresses more directly the fundamental religious question about whether in such a system it is ever possible to limit the excesses of economic freedom.

In 1920, British economist R.H. Tawney published *The Sickness of an Acquisitive Society*, another critique of market capitalism from those reevaluating the impact of the 19th century industrial revolution. The substance of Tawney's complaint about Smith's natural law of self-interest is that it changes the primary reason for industry from function, or purpose, to rights. Tawney means by this that for centuries the main determinant of useful labor and industry, indeed all forms of productive activity, was whether it serves a common purpose, usually a purpose defined by a common religious or national identity. As that widespread consensus breaks down in the 17th and 18th century, Smith's new vision, grounded in Locke, replaced it.

> What remained when the keystone of the arch (i.e. religious purpose) was removed, was private rights and private interests....

> These rights and interests were the natural order...because they were the creation of Nature herself. They had been regarded in the past as relative to some public end, whether religion or national welfare. Henceforward they were thought to be absolute and indefeasible, and to stand by their own virtue. They were the ultimate political and social reality.... (9)

This perception operates in free market capitalism when individuals enter the marketplace and workforce armed with the right to use their property in any way they see fit, rather than being restricted and directed to the discharge of social obligations that had been determined by some overarching community purpose. Tawney expresses his worries about such a direction in an extended quotation:

> The exercise of the right to pursue their own self-interest offers unlimited scope for the acquisition of riches, and therefore gives free play to one of the most powerful of human instincts. To the strong it promises unfettered freedom for the exercise of their strength; to the weak the hope that they too one day may be strong. Before the eyes of both, it suspends a golden prize, which not all can attain, but for which each may strive, the enchanting vision of infinite expansion. It assures men that there are no ends other than their ends, no law other than their desires, no limit other than that which they think advisable. Thus it makes the individual the center of his own universe, and dissolves moral principles into a choice of expediencies. (17)

The inevitable result of that internal dynamic is that no one knows why or how to limit free pursuit of economic self-interest. If that progress is the natural law and natural right of human beings, especially if that progress seems to have the providential blessing of an "invisible hand", why have limits at all? Only rarely does the lingering remembrance of community purpose gain enough support to stop or even redirect the snowballing impetus of economic growth. No, in an acquisitive society, the "whole tendency and interest and preoccupation is to promote the acquisition of wealth" (17). Tawney then describes how Smith's system inevitably creates inequality through the disproportionate accumulation of wealth (20) and how it incentivizes business toward a kind of industrial warfare (27). Toward the end of his essay, Tawney expresses his conviction that a business guided by a clear purpose established by a whole community will better combine a unity of cooperation while also recognizing a diversity of talents (85). He also worries that because wealth is the primary goal of individual and corporate industry, people will neglect

> ...the necessity of discriminating between different types of economic activity and different sources of wealth, between enterprise and avarice, energy and unscrupulous greed, property which is legitimate and property which is theft, the just enjoyment of the fruits of labor and the idle parasitism of birth and fortune. (in Adler, *Great Ideas,* 922,923)

Veblen and Tawney were by no means the only prophets sounding the alarm about unrestricted freedom of economic self-interest. As the 20th century continued, philosopher Herbert Marcuse described how society moved ever further beyond a conception of adequate possessions and toward excess by the creation of "pseudo-needs". Then advertising, lambasted in books like Vance Packard's *The Hidden Persuaders,* turns static demand for a product into an elastic demand by convincing people of their inadequacies if they do not satisfy their pseudo-needs with products promoted in media.

All of these critics, early and late, emphasize that the most entrenched sense of freedom in modern civilization is likely this belief in freedom as economic purchasing power. At its best, such freedom procures longer, healthier spans of life with less crushing physical labor and wider boundaries of aspiration. At its worse, that same freedom legitimizes avarice, alienates workers from the finished product of their labor, and ignores the future impact of unrestricted use of raw materials. It also raises the persistent question of whether one can achieve genuine happiness and self-esteem from accumulation of wealth and conspicuous consumption.

What, then, has changed in society's understanding of freedom in the 400 years since Descartes, Bacon, Hobbes, and Locke laid the substratum of the Enlightenment? The first of the three developments explained above inserted free choice as the source and origin of the state and its government. The second presented a Kantian alternative framework for morality that encourages autonomous decisions limited only by reason. The third elevated economic self-interest as the key to individual and community prosperity. The public understanding of freedom becomes a mixture of government-established civil liberty, rational, autonomous moral choice, and the pursuit of happiness through economic wealth. Despite all the apparent benefits from these developments, ranging from representative democracy to impartial duty-based ethics to material prosperity, dedicated Christians will still want to testify that these changes in our understanding of freedom have not always served the God we worship or the church we love. That continues as one of the most intense theological challenges of our era.

History as Fact and Progress

As with the prior treatment of freedom, it is wise to establish a broad baseline of traditional biblical and theological understandings of history before explaining later views arising in the wake of the Enlightenment. Only then can we see the difference made by the "new definitions of reality" noted earlier by Peter Berger as the primary cause for modern disenchantment with religious faith.

History and Interpretation within Scripture

It is surprising and perplexing that the document we call the Bible, regarded as the foundational text for two historical religions, never actually uses the word *history*. One presumes that any language with a concept or an idea of something would have a specific word for that idea, but the most common exhaustive concordance of the Bible lists no references to "history" in the Old or New Testament. Some modern translations more liberally employ the word; in every case, the term in its original language would be better translated as "chronicle" or "generations" or simply "story". There seems to be no word in the Hebrew language exactly equivalent to "history". Likewise, even though the word "history" in western languages derives from the Greek *historia*, the Gentile gospel writer Luke, for example, does not employ the term to describe his enterprise stretching over two books. He tells Theophilus that he intends simply to give an "orderly account".

What do these observations portend? At the very least, they should give us pause to consider whether the practice of historical reconstruction of events, a practice embraced by the western world since Hesiod and Herodotus, is necessarily the same as the biblical understanding of the movements of events through time. It is also fair to ask about the strange disconnection between biblical theologians today who regularly talk about "salvation history" in the Bible and the assessments of philosophical commentators that scripture has little or no consistent view of history at all. (Breisach, *Historiography*... and Momigiliano, "Historiography" 383.)

Obviously, any culture that can measure time, even by distinguishing dusk from dawn and youth from old age, understands that life moves from one event to another, that some things happen before now, some happen now, and some will happen after now. Equally obviously, people everywhere learn from mistakes and try to make the future better than the past. Furthermore, it is clear that in scripture an eternal God intervenes into time, into 'historical' situations like the Exodus or the reign of Caesar Augustus. If that is what one means by history, then of course biblical figures are historical, as are all people, and God works in "history". Nevertheless, the word "history" as generally used today has assumed a much wider meaning, and it is anachronistic to imply that biblical writers meant the same thing by the word as we do today.

So how do biblical writers differ from modern exponents of the historical investigation of scripture? The difference arises primarily in the purpose behind relating events that occurred in time. The purpose of writers within the Bible is to tell the story of our relationship to God, providing testimony to the mighty acts of God and declaring the sovereignty of God over all that threatens God's people. There are five aspects comprising this purpose.

1. History as testimony to God's mighty acts reflects on the past as a guide to the future. This perhaps seems obvious and universal, but it promotes a specific orientation to time, namely that one looks backward first and forward only later. We are

more likely to discover clues to God's will in past events than in a vision of the future. It is like crossing a lake in a rowboat. You reach your goal of a particular spot on the far shore by gauging your position in terms of your starting point. You turn your back to the future, fixing your eyes on the past. The primary orientation of the biblical chronicler (we hesitate to say "historian") is toward past root experiences. A "root experience" is an event so profound that a religion could arise from it, for example, the Exodus for Jews or Jesus' crucifixion and resurrection for Christians. Scripture asks us first to remember the presence of God in those root experiences, and only then to plan for what may lie ahead. Scripture does certainly include proclamations of a future dimension; biblical figures do indeed hope, yearning for a promised land, a release from exile, a second coming of Christ, but the source of confidence in that future is revealed primarily by actions of God in the past. We remember in order to hope.

2. To know those past events, if you were not present, you must somehow have access to them. Access, though, is not through detailed empirical examination of surrounding context, but through sacred memory. Sacred memory allows participation in the past, not just review of it. In Emil Fackenheim's *God's Presence in History*, he lists the conditions necessary for a genuine root experience (11,12). The most important of those conditions is that subsequent generations must be able not merely to recall an event that once brought God's presence to the fore, but also to experience in some way the same presence of God as felt by the original viewers. The Passover ritual, for example, the Seder, is not a simple recollection of the Exodus, but a reliving of it, re-enacting its events as present reality. Exiles in Babylon at their Seder meal feel the

presence of God with much the same power as handmaidens at the Red Sea. Likewise, Christians currently persecuted in Iran or China can feel the presence of Christ in the Lord's Supper with an experience as deep as the disciples in the Upper Room did. Mere memory becomes sacred memory, which provides vivid access to the original event.

3. Biblical chroniclers, because they regard God as the primary actor, either do not recognize, or do not consider important, the secondary causes in a chain of events. Prophets become voices through which God speaks, and Moses may raise his rod to part the sea, but because biblical texts primarily are testimony, the authors rarely investigate the natural means through which God accomplishes great works. Wm. Barclay in *The Bible and History* (13,14), documents a clear example of this re: II Kings 19. The Assyrian king Sennacherib besieges Jerusalem, but his army retreats in disarray and the city survives. The Deuteronomist account merely states, "That very night an angel of the Lord set out and struck down 185,000 Assyrians." The most we learn about secondary causes is that God sends an angel. Two ancient historians from different religious cultures document the same event, however, and take pains to explain why the army retreats. An Egyptian commentator explains that the priest Sethos appeals to an Egyptian agriculture god who sends an army of field mice to gnaw and destroy the Assyrian weapons. A Chaldean observer, quoted by Josephus, says the army died from a "pestilential distemper", a plague, probably carried by the rats and mice of the prior account. The biblical passage omits these natural secondary causes because explanation is less important than testimony to the prime actor, God.

4. Biblical writers also primarily emphasize persons or events according to the role they play in setting the stage for God's intervention. Significant examples of this include the extended treatment of the Prophet Elijah's contentious battle against Jezebel and the priests of Baal, compared to the scant mention of King Ahab's massive building campaigns, military victories and unprecedented economic prosperity for Israel. The heart of the problem is one's attitude toward God. Since Ahab's accomplishments arise from idolatry, Elijah targets the underlying religious cause, not the effects. In the New Testament, compare Paul's extended analysis of the turmoil in the young Corinthian church to his lack of interest in Corinth's strategic location for trade. It is not that Paul or the Deuteronomist was unaware of political, economic, or military factors, but that they regarded them as effects, not causes, of a greater problem. The Bible regards a religious issue, an orientation toward or away from God, as the crux of the problem, and discusses the economic or political context, if at all, in that light.
5. The fifth component in the biblical view of history as testimony is rejection of what scholars have called the "analytical I". Peter Machinist, in "The Voice of the Historian in the ANE and Mediterranean" (119ff), explains that Greek writers from the start "step forward as persons". By introducing themselves as persons, each as an 'I', they distance themselves from the events and persons about which they will speak. They set themselves up apart from their topic. He calls this the "analytical I". In writings of the Ancient Near East, though, as in the Bible, he finds little or no evidence of this "analytical I". The biblical historian does not make "... a point of standing against the tradition of which he is heir." Machinist's argument is that, with few exceptions, biblical writers

reflecting on past events do not remove themselves from the tradition that gives meaning to the events, that the authors seek no external, objective stance from which to evaluate the reliability of specific pieces of evidence. They are not historians in the sense of modern historians today. They embraced a more communal, public sense of authority rather than "the authority of the human individual" which would give them an external stance for evaluation.

Combined, these five attitudes of scriptural chroniclers and storytellers provide a backdrop for later comparison to tactics and presuppositions of the historical critical approach to scripture. It is an overstatement to regard these five aspects as hard and fast rules of composition, but they do portray an overall perspective on "historical" events in the ancient world.

An additional description of the attitude of ancient biblical interpreters arises in James Kugel's honest and comprehensive book *How to Read the Bible*. Kugel restates the same debate as the one discussed in this chapter: how can one claim the theological and ethical teachings of scripture emphasized for more than three millennia without neglecting the results of modern historical-critical assessments of scripture in the last three centuries? Those recent investigations, after all, recover beneficial information about ancient cultures, allowing modern readers to identify with the figures of scripture in their original setting. However, they also often point to entirely different conclusions about the reliability and intended meaning of many passages. Kugel bears within himself the scars of battle between traditional interpretations and modern scholarship. He dedicates most of his book to showing such tension in one Old Testament passage after another, but in the first and again the final chapter, he frames his work with a conceptual explanation of the conflict between the two.

Kugel affirms that the corpus of the Hebrew Bible (the Old Testament) did not receive its settled form until after the return from Exile, perhaps as late as the 2nd or 3rd century BCE. He discerns four guidelines used by those prominent rabbinic redactors to organize, expand, interpret, and preserve in writing the earlier documents and oral traditions placed in their hands and memories. He calls these the Four Assumptions of the Ancient Interpreters. They include the following, in shortened form:

- These interpreters first assumed that the Bible was fundamentally a cryptic text: that is, when it said A, often it might really mean B.
- They believed the Bible was a book of lessons directed to readers in their own day. It might seem to talk about the past, but it is not fundamentally history; it is instruction on current issues.
- These interpreters affirmed that the Bible contained no contradictions or mistakes, that there must be some way of understanding the Bible's words to remove any such implications.
- The interpreters trusted that the entire Bible is essentially a divinely given text, a book in which God speaks directly or through directly inspired prophets (14-16).

Subsequent to this list of four guiding beliefs about scripture, Kugel traces how, in the following centuries of Jewish and Christian interpretation, many analogical, ethical, and allegorical interpretive methods sustained those early assumptions and smoothed over their bumps. For nearly two millennia, those methodologies of symbolism dominated biblical hermeneutics. In the Renaissance and the Reformation, scholars turned away from these philosophical reconstructions and turned back to the "simple" or "plain" meaning of the texts. Now scripture was not to be regarded as a door to multiple divine meanings; it talked instead about things that had actually happened in the world. Kugel next notes that it took almost two more centuries after that key shift before a systematic theory of historical criticism broke through, in works like Benedict Spinoza's 1670 *Tractatus Theologico-Politicus*. We will elaborate on Spinoza's framework below; see "Roots of Historical Critical Method".

For now, however, it is instructive to follow James Kugel's interior battle. This Harvard professor of Hebrew and practicing Orthodox Jew yearns to find some way to reconcile scripture's theological declarations of the rabbinic schools of the 3rd century BCE with observations by investigative archaeologists, linguists and biblical analysts of CE 19th and 20th. His perspective insists that the editors and authors of early rabbinic Judaism were the ones most responsible for the Bible as we know it. Those rabbis and sages added theological interpretations to the existing texts and oral traditions from 6-8 centuries before, gathering many disparate snippets into coherent stories with lasting implications for community behavior and worship of a transcendent yet immanent God. In his words: "It was truly out of the work of these interpreters that the canonized Bible emerged, and without it, one might well doubt if the Bible ever could have come to occupy the central place that it did within Judaism and Christianity" (679).

Kugel also, though, celebrates the remarkable achievements of the historical-critical method and the immense information it has added to our knowledge of the ancient world. He soberly declares that leading lights of this 19th and 20th century school of research, like Julius Wellhausen, Hermann Gunkel or William F. Albright, should rank equal to Einstein, Darwin, and Freud in intellectual achievement and intellectual courage. Indeed, this historical research ironically cemented Kugel's very opinion that the ancient interpreters in the 3rd and 4th BCE centuries were the ones who compiled and edited the earlier texts. Because of such research, we now know that Moses likely did not write the whole Pentateuch, but probably contributed oral teaching used by the different strands of editors. We see that David likely wrote fewer of the psalms than originally believed; it was instead a range of priests preparing liturgies for temple worship. And it was likely a later poet who recorded the empathetic flow of tears, not Jeremiah himself, in Lamentations. Moreover, historical and archaeological research reveals mistakes in location for multiple stories, or highly unlikely timeframes for events. We have learned that key stories in scripture are not unique, as they have parallels in the literature of neighboring cultures during biblical times, including the design for Solomon's temple that was actually patterned on earlier Mesopotamian buildings. Frequently, what the ancient interpreters turned into pivotal ethical lessons were originally just etiological explanations; i.e., justifications for why and how a particular place has a particular name. All of a sudden, the Four Assumptions of the third century rabbis are challenged or diminished at every turn. Which set of knowledge truly defines the lasting meaning of the Bible?

Even after the extensive, grateful descriptions in his book of all the information historical criticism has added to the context and message of biblical passages, Kugel nonetheless concludes that the massive achievements of the modern historical-critical method mistake sociological facts for what is foremost. He declares bluntly at one point that "... modern biblical scholarship and traditional Judaism are and must always remain completely irreconcilable" (681). Again, he says the true meaning of scripture

> ... is not the original meaning of its constituent parts, but the meaning it had for the people who first saw it as the Bible, God's great book of instruction. If it doesn't have that meaning for you anymore – if all it is etiological tales and priestly polemics and political speeches – then why are you singing it? (682)

Kugel's book and the personal intellectual tussle within it reveal poignantly the concepts that undergird the historical critical study of scripture. His considered opinion, as a highly respected scholar, is that historical criticism challenges an understanding of the Bible that has nourished Judaism and Christianity for millennia. Is he right?

Roots of Historical Critical Method

It behooves us, then, having earlier stated the views of the ancient interpreters, to investigate further the origin and meaning of the modern idea of *history* and its effect on biblical knowledge. Thus, we now must consider the second half of the question asked at the beginning of this section. If the purpose of ancient biblical writers who related a series of events in time was to testify to the mighty acts of God, what are the purposes of 19th c. historical critical interpreters as they reevaluate the meaning of biblical passages using new tools and perspectives?

Two primary philosophic themes influence the purpose of modern historical criticism. One is the particular attitude toward veracity, reliable truth, which arose with Cartesian rationalism and advanced through empiricist verification. This combination restricts reliable truth to two types, mathematical, geometrical definitions and materially measurable actions and events. The second influence is the dynamic view of historical progression previously referred to as Hegel's dialectic movement of Mind (*Geist*). To elaborate on these two influences, let us quickly reiterate some comments from an earlier chapter.

Descartes' rationalist principles include his insistence that absolute certainty of knowledge is only possible when we "… busy ourselves with no object about which we cannot attain a certainty equal to that of the demonstrations of arithmetic and geometry." Therefore, Descartes composes his highly influential philosophy so that from the start it seems to rule out the kind of stubborn, paradoxical, mythic truth that embodies religious scripture and other forms of narrative literature. These forms of intuitive and spiritual truth resist, and exist outside of, the category of the "clear and distinct ideas" that Descartes' rationalism allows. His 17th century foundational philosophy then links to a concurrent, though initially opposite, approach, the inductive observation method articulated by Francis Bacon. Reacting against Aristotle's categorization of objects based on their spiritual tendencies, Bacon insists that true knowledge of an object requires close observation of its physical properties. His model for inductive research includes breaking down a complex whole into separate parts, documenting each part, and then if possible reconnecting the parts into a whole. Inductive observation is of measurable objects, not ethereal concepts, so again, the range of subject is limited. One can be immensely grateful to Bacon's insights for the scientific method it initiated, yet also emphasize that such empiricist disposition does not admit the full range of human experience, spiritual and intuitive, into the quest for knowledge. In Bacon's system, only what we physically measure is useful and factual.

The second influence, dynamic historical progression, starts in the late 18th century with the work of Johann Herder and reaches full force with Hegel. Herder takes a turn away from the rationalism of the Enlightenment toward Romanticism, arguing for a greater awareness of how historical, environmental and psychological factors affect a person's perception of reality. Especially in his philosophy of history, Herder emphasizes the significance of context and surrounding influences on an actual event and its consequences, let alone on how one perceives such events. Hegel embraces these historical aspects of Herder's thought, and adds to it a monistic view of reality that combines human, divine, and natural beings into one entity he terms Mind or Spirit (*Geist*). Then Hegel unites both of these with a comprehensive dynamic view of history he adopted from Fichte, who insisted that reality moves forward via a dialectical process of thesis, antithesis, and synthesis. Hegel thus inaugurates a picture of history as progress toward its ultimate goal, the self-realization of Spirit.

Two practical effects upon people's understanding of scripture evolve from Hegel's composite schema. First, from what Herder contributed, Hegel would argue that the best way to understand a past event is not through a sense of sacred memory reinforced by sacramental worship practices, but instead to gather as much information as possible about the historical, economic, and cultural context surrounding an event. These variable factors may not merely influence our perception of the event or affect its outcome; they may indeed fully determine it. Secondly, from Fichte's contribution, people look to the future, not the past, for their most satisfying and useful vision of what is good. Why read a book written two millennia ago when the fuller revelation of reality awaits us as Mind unfolds itself in the future? Why consider the meaning of liberation portrayed in the Exodus from Egypt, for example, when the Spirit of Reality is methodically moving toward the fullest expression of freedom in an epoch yet to come? If history is a dialectical movement toward an ever-improving future, what are significant events in the past except grist for the mill of *Geist's* inexorable progress?

The modern age, therefore, can thank Hegel for bequeathing a seemingly unquenchable source of optimism and idealism. Nevertheless, when his legacy of dynamic historical progress combines with the restrictions on forms of knowledge in Descartes and Bacon, the level of interest in learning from the ancient scriptures diminishes profoundly.

These 17th-19th century philosophical principles, from Descartes and Bacon to Herder and Hegel, develop into a formula, a system, for investigating Jewish and Christian scriptures and other ancient texts. How, practically speaking, does that investigative system work? When modern historical critics assess a scriptural text, what steps and guidelines do they employ? Does anything in the system disprove or preclude the ancient view of history as testimony? As a start in answering those questions, let us look at two statements of the historical critical method, intriguingly similar though separated by nearly 300 years. Notice as we do so any substantial contrasts to the characteristics of 3^{rd}c. BCE methods stated previously.

In 1670, Benedict (Baruch) Spinoza, a Jewish philosopher living in Protestant Holland, published his *Tractatus* (*Treatise on Theology and Politics*), in which he outlined the first consistent modern approach to biblical hermeneutics. Spinoza had seen the devastating effects of religious rivalry in the violence of the 30 Years War. Surely, a less contentious manner of understanding the Bible could enhance peace between Protestant and Catholic forces. He, like many in the early Enlightenment, looked to the power of reason for that solution. Drawing on the rationalist belief that eventually everything can be fully explained, he says in chapter four of his Treatise that all things are constrained by universal laws of nature to exist and act in a determinate way. We can thus deduce even the meaning of mysterious scriptural texts by seeing them in terms of a few principles or general axioms. To do that, though, we need to approach scripture quite differently than in past generations.

James Kugel lists the basic premises of Spinoza's method:

1. Scripture is understood by Scripture alone. Rabbinic midrash and allegory are misleading and useless. Only Scripture's own words are to be considered.
2. To understand Scripture, we must know all the details of its language, its world of ideas and context, rather than imposing on it our own later views.
3. Begin by assuming that Scripture means what it says even when it disagrees with our own conceptions. Accept a statement as literally true unless it contradicts a similar statement somewhere else in scripture.
4. To understand the Bible, we must investigate how the books were compiled and combined, including how later editors might have altered its original form.
5. There actually are many contradictions in the Bible. Therefore, it is best to concentrate only on the things on which its writers agree. (31-32)

Spinoza offers a very early version of the combined tactics that would slowly achieve pre-eminence over the next 300 years. Many slight alterations gradually tightened and clarified his initial insights, but the same general themes persist, as evidenced in another statement of the historical critical method from the mid-20th century. An

Ecumenical Study Conference held at Waldham College of Oxford University in 1949 produced this listing of the investigative steps: 1. the determination of the text's beginning and end (the scope of the single pericope); 2. the literary form of the passage; 3. the historical situation, often termed the *sitz im leben*; 4. the meaning that the words had for the original author and hearer or reader; and 5. the understanding of the passage in the light of its total context and background out of which it emerged. (Krentz, 2)

Comparing the Two Views

It is possible now to summarize the tenets of both the ancient and the more modern approach and observe their differences.

Ancient: Scripture as Testimony	Modern: Historical Criticism
The Bible is divinely inspired and has no ultimate contradictions. Apparent contradictions can be resolved.	The Bible does have many historical inaccuracies and contradictory passages. It is best to concentrate on what all contributors agree is accurate.
The past is a guide to the future. We read these past stories to see what they say about God's action in our life now.	The most important meaning of a text is what it intended at the time of its composition, not the meaning for interpreters in chronologically later eras

Ancient: Scripture as Testimony	Modern: Historical Criticism
Knowledge of past events is through sacred memory, sacramental re-enactment, and retelling the story.	Knowledge of past events is through systematically discovering the *sitz im leben*, the original surrounding historical and cultural factors affecting those events.
The Bible is a cryptic text. Hidden meanings can elicit symbolic interpretations.	Interpretation should look for meaning in the plain, literal sense of scriptural texts, reducing symbolism, allegory, and ecclesiastical maneuvering.
The biblical interpreters see things within the original tradition they inherit; they do not assume an external objective standpoint for analysis.	Objective observers will discover that the Bible is a collection of stories from various human sources; it describes origins of names and places, specific historical events and cultural practices.

Given these contrasting lists of tactics in method, it is instructive to see how their differing orientations affect the interpretation of a particular passage. No single set of verses can completely capture the opposing tendencies, but using insights from Kugel's *How to Read the Bible*, let us examine the results of the two approaches to an exemplary story, Noah and the great flood. (70-80)

Kugel states that ancient readers of the story would recognize it as a portrayal of a righteous God who has the ability to take life but also to save it. That much seems evident. Other questions linger, though, even for those ancient readers prepared to accept it at face value. For instance, what had Humanity done that was so bad that God chose to destroy them? Was it Cain slaying Abel? Was it the lustful appetite of the "sons of God" for the daughters of earth? And what is meant by God's threat that "their days shall be 120 years" because of the wickedness of humankind, "whose hearts are continually evil"? These conundrums faced the earliest compilers of scripture, but their response was to work through the contrasts by staying within scripture and finding key phrases of explanation. Reading the phrase about 120 years not as a prediction of how long the average human would live, but as the amount of time God would allow humanity a chance to repent, the ancient compilers found hidden meaning in a cryptic text. If Noah preached repentance to a sinful humanity for that long, yet humanity ignored the plea from God's messenger, God used that "righteous man, who was blameless in his generation" for a divine purpose that all others rejected. The flood, therefore, becomes a story of divine justice finally exercised after plentiful patience, a warning for future ages not to repeat the stubborn negligence of their predecessors. Yet even though God could justly have ended all earthly life, God spared some, a remnant of all animals and a righteous human family, to preserve creation. This is a story to tell repeatedly, a lesson that travels through the millennia to our time. Its final crafters stay within their received tradition, thus demonstrating the ancient assumptions listed above.

Toward the end of the 19th century, new research opened up a different way of regarding the flood story. Professor George Smith of the British Museum reported the discovery of cuneiform tablets telling *The Epic of Gilgamesh*, a Chaldean story of the flood. Though some important differences existed, the Mesopotamian epic was mostly similar to the Genesis flood narrative, showing that other cultures also had accounts of this massive infusion of water that nearly destroyed all life. There must have been a literary connection between the two cultures. Either one text is dependent on the other, or both are derived from an earlier common source. Given the archaeologically established dates of the two documents, the Babylonian epic surely preceded the Genesis account, so doubts arose about the divine inspiration of the Genesis story if it depended on the writers of an enemy culture. It appears instead to take its core narrative from the Gilgamesh epic and introduce later some more specifically Hebrew ideas about sin, immortality, and covenant. The more scholars investigated the text, the more evidence emerged that the story had been pieced together from different editorial strands at different times. For these modern commentators, the flood story provides a glimpse into how the Bible was written, including the influence of other ancient cultures and the specific shaping of someone else's original story toward theological themes that developed in later Judaism. The story in Genesis also showed numerous duplications and contradictions, like how many pairs of animals entered the ark, providing further evidence of the all-too-human character of this seminal story of Hebrew culture. These are the issues, the focus of attention, for the skilled modern scholars who opened up a different approach to the story of Noah and the flood.

Kugel's treatment of these two approaches to the flood story culminates in the dilemma at the center of this current section on history. How, if at all, can both approaches to a biblical passage, two different views of history, unite into one comprehensive statement of the meaning and lasting significance of that passage? Kugel acknowledges a central contention by defenders of the historical critical method. Why, they say, should their focused research into the origin of a text, and their negation of a text's supernatural inspiration, necessarily imply that they are uninterested in the lasting moral and spiritual messages of the scripture passage? Is that not still a possible addition to investigation of origins, etc.? Kugel wonders, though, whether they are honest about their loyalty to that other dimension of meaning. He explains it this way: "...the very idea that one should approach the Bible as a great book of divine instruction... is a creation of the ancient interpreters." Historical critics may perhaps borrow this premise out of faithfulness to an earlier worldview, but nothing in the historical critical method itself could come to that conclusion. Hence,

> The quandary in which modern scholars... find themselves derives precisely from their straddling two positions at once. On the one hand, they feel they have to do away with all the ancient biblical interpretation, including its Four Assumptions.... On the other hand, they still wish to preserve the *idea* of the Bible and the traditional role it has played in their religion. The result is always an elaborate, and often quite eloquent, apologetic – but an apologetic nonetheless. (79-80)

A second highly respected Old Testament theologian, Walter Brueggemann, expands the objection that Kugel sounds. The following extended quotation is from his *Theology of the Old Testament*. It reminds us of the philosophic presuppositions that undergird historical criticism.

> By the end of the eighteenth century and into the nineteenth century, history had acquired a very different dimension and significance from all previous understandings. First, history had taken on a positivistic character, so that events came to be

regarded as completely decipherable, to the exclusion of any inscrutable destiny. This change entailed that events have a simple, discernible, unambiguous meaning from which all mystery can be squeezed out. Second, in the nineteenth century the idea of history as development came to be crucial, so that events came to be seen as progressively arranged in sequence. Events without inscrutable density but with progressive sequencing leave nothing for theology to do. Thus, history could and did become an autonomous enterprise, without reference to any larger or coded significance. (11)

To be clear, Brueggemann sympathetically appreciates why nineteenth century biblical scholarship moved toward this form of biblical interpretation. These two means of establishing and defining truth met with laudable success in other fields; theologians could not simply ignore them. Furthermore, applying them to historical research of the Bible produced many benefits, such as furthering the liberation of the text from authoritarian ecclesiastical dogma, a step crucial in the sola scriptura orientation of the Reformation. Brueggemann elaborates on his earlier comments:

> The practical effect of this scholarship was that it did indeed leave biblical interpretation free of church authority. In an odd way, critical scholarship continued the effort of Luther and the Reformers in providing space for the text as distinct from church interpretation. (14)

Nonetheless, he continues "The unrecognized outcome, however, is that the Old Testament was largely appropriated in the metahistory of the Enlightenment – a metahistory that eschewed the hiddenness, density, and inscrutability of the text" (2). And yet, Brueggemann insists, these forbidden characteristics are precisely what make the Bible the Bible.

> The Bible is a voice of revelation not to be confused with, encumbered by, or contained in any human categories of interpretation that make the voice more coherent, domesticated, or palatable....This 'voice of the Bible' speaks its truth and makes its claims in its own categories, categories that are recurringly odd and unaccommodating. (3)

The question that has shaped our discussion is not yet entirely resolved. Which orientation to history provides the best access to God's living Word imbedded in this gift of scripture? Are the precious books of the Bible that nourish the faith of diligent readers primarily testimonies to previous mighty acts of God, or ancient historical documents best explored through factual research by an objective observer?

Preachers in typical pulpits today will attempt a combination of the two approaches for sermons. She or he, if diligent, will research historical context surrounding the passage, perhaps using form criticism, literary criticism, and redaction criticism. From those investigations, the preacher hopes to glean insights into the original intentions of the Old Testament scribe or New Testament gospel writer. For instance, who does not now better identify with the guests at the marriage in Cana since researchers have detailed ancient Jewish wedding customs? Who cannot better picture the dispute over the agape meal in Corinth now that we have seen diagrams of Greek domestic architecture?

And yet, having gathered this information using historical critical sourcebooks, the preachers then leap to the conclusion that they can transfer that information into ethical and spiritual recommendations on how to live a faithful life thousands of years after the text's final editing. This is despite the fact that those historical-critical sourcebooks based their research on presuppositions that the primary meaning of a passage concerns only the original writer in the original context and that the passages in which we place so much trust contain factual inaccuracies and multiple contradictions. How much do those presuppositions and underlying philosophies of modern analysis allow any exegesis of a passage to escape their implication that the relevance of a passage must be restricted to measurable empirical facts or universal rational laws? Consider the blunt assessment of Ernst Renan, who in his *Life of Jesus* says in effect that all truth is scientific, and that since the supernatural is unverifiable, therefore the supernatural is not. (In Owen Chadwick, 217)

The church today, in its approach to scripture, dwells within this tension. Because God acts within time, in what we now call historical moments, we will always want to know more about those first moments and how God's presence affected people. To neglect the historical context promotes either a vague overuse of symbolism or a naïve literalism, a fundamentalism that ties itself in knots over clearly conflicting messages from one book to another. But while employing historical critical studies to gain such knowledge, we unwittingly swallow a whole set of presuppositions that question the very possibility of supernatural truth, a truth that transcends its original context and can be seen as revelation rather than as historically conditioned incidental facts largely irrelevant to contemporary issues of faith. This, its reinterpretation of history, is the second challenge modernity poses to traditional understanding of Christian beliefs.

The Good Life

The central issue of this third challenge posed by modernity surfaces abruptly in the following statement from the respected ethicist Paul Ramsey in *Basic Christian Ethics*:

> The ethics of idealism constitutes the chief rival of Christianity because so often the ethics of self-realization and Christian ethics have been identified as one and the same; and idealism is the chief rival of Christian ethics because what idealism calls "the good" Christian ethics calls sin or idolatry, namely, the intentional pursuit of self-realization. (Ramsey, 301)

Unraveling the implications of both parts of Ramsey's declaration constitutes the majority of what follows. We will try to offer balanced summaries of what Ramsey and others call philosophical idealism and ethics of self-realization, noting strengths that make these attractive to Christians in modernity, as well as the dangers posed to an explicitly God-centered ethics so key to the church.

If we wish to state bluntly the difficulty in untangling these two ways of seeking the good life, let us reflect on two more contrasting statements. One comes from a little-known but representative voice in the biblical tradition; one is a classic declaration from modernity's most authoritative voice.

> The tragedy of humanity in our time is the certainty that what we see is what alone exists, that what we create is alone worthy, that by virtue of an existence whose origins we do not understand and whose beauty we did nothing to merit, we are all that is worthwhile. We suffer the peculiar blindness of those who only

see the visible. (Wolpe, *The Raleigh News and Observer*, January 19, 2012)

> Nature has willed that man should, by himself, produce everything that goes beyond the mechanical ordering of his animal existence, and that he should partake of no other happiness or perfection than that which he himself, independently of instinct, has created by his own reason. (Kant, Third Thesis, ...*Universal History*, 13)

Those two viewpoints portray starkly different visions. Yet, if we hope to affirm the possibility of cooperation between the two options, we can quote a further statement from Ramsey himself that opens a path for mutual benefit.

It is

> ...the author's conviction that, especially in formulating social policy, contemporary Christian ethics must make common cause with the ethics of philosophical idealism. We must become debtors to the best insight available at the present stage of thought, instead of trying to overleap the centuries in order to embrace too closely Plato, Aristotle or the Reformers.... (xiii)

As with most investigations, it makes sense to begin with a definition of terms, specifically what philosophical idealism means. Clarifying that general category provides context for a description of what citizens of the 18th - 20th centuries would likely include in their definition of the good life. Only through considering these can we examine and contrast what the good life might mean to a disciple of Jesus Christ.

Philosophical Idealism

This volume's previous forays into many philosophical concepts underlying modern thought provide background for this summary of *idealism* in its philosophical sense. People casually use the word in everyday speech to refer to someone whose "head is in the clouds", who lives in "an ivory tower" divorced from the harsh realism of daily existence. That is not what the term means in its explicit philosophical use (though we have permission to wonder about an informal connection).

The modern interpretations of idealism (there are many variations) have their roots in Descartes' and Locke's revision of what Plato earlier meant by an "idea". Stated simply, Plato defined the word as what one "sees" through an intellectual vision, rather than through the physical senses as they assess objects. To Plato, there is an idea of justice, an idea of balance, etc., and, importantly, these ideas exist prior to perception by a human mind. They are objective, pre-existing standards of meaning that shape their corresponding material reality. Modernity, though, tends to believe that an idea only exists when the mind perceives it, and there is no sure evidence that what one sees in the mind connects reliably to an external reality. What we "experience" is a mental event. We certainly can have the idea of a tree, and thus see a tree in our mind, but we may be dreaming, or we may mistake a telephone pole with moss on it for a tree. Ideas, to Descartes and Locke, are immediate objects of the mind, but that idea may not derive from or relate to any particular physical thing. Posterity regards Descartes as a rationalist, not explicitly an idealist, but his work hints at an inherent connection between the two.

As the centuries move on, Idealism becomes the collective name for the perception that what we think we know about the external world depends upon the ideas in our minds but not necessarily on a solid reality outside the mind. Indeed, later variations of idealism came to regard the ideas in our minds as creating the only reality we can actually know. That subsequent line of reinterpretation began in England with Bishop Berkeley, who emphasizes that what we think is the external world could actually be nothing more than ideas. The development later crosses to the continent, to the German thinkers Johann Fichte and Friedrich Schelling. They extended implications of Immanuel Kant's *First Critique* to say that all we know of external reality is what we ourselves have made it. In Kant's epistemology, remember, there may be actual objects of our experience, i.e. things existing in space and time, but they are without meaning to us until they have been shaped by the categories of the mind. They have no recognizable existence outside our thoughts. Fichte pushes Kant's restrained view to its logical conclusion that the mind constructs reality. What Kant called "critical idealism", Fichte maintains, stops before it should. He and Schelling are the founders of German Idealism, one developmental step beyond Kant. Hegel extends this concept further still, with a significant redirection, when he maintains that everything that exists is actually part of one single mind, or Geist. In Hegel, Idealism receives its most influential and lasting form. Hegelian Idealism, so influential over the last two centuries, implies that Geist moves toward its eventual full realization of itself. This development, combined with other modern emphases on achieving autonomy, prompts individuals to seek their own self-realization by pushing back the limits on their freedom.

It is not necessary here to delve again into the details of these developments, but what they mean for the present topic is that, at least philosophically, such idealism helps humanity approach the world with the confidence that what they envision in their mind's eye can shape reality. Admittedly, not even a small percentage of inventors, organizers, authors, and other molders of culture would consciously embrace, or even imagine, such an abstract philosophical concept as they built the machinery or wrote the books that fueled industrialization and spread the optimism of the last three centuries. Nevertheless, philosophical idealism provided the atmosphere, the spirit of the age, which spurred such growth and encouraged the dreamers and planners of modernity to envision, and then create, their manifold pictures of a splendid future.

To illustrate this development in attitude, consider the following assessment of why and how the industrial revolution gained momentum. Patrick Allitt is Professor of History at Emory University and the author of *The Industrial Revolution* lectures for The Great Courses series. He traces a group of early English inventors and investors in the pottery, coal mining, iron making, and transport industries who united in the belief that traditional methods of labor in those fields could be improved and accelerated. They initiated a reevaluation of tradition and a new era of critical thinking based on

> ...the idea that tradition should not always constrain us and that careful thought can enable us to do what our ancestors never even attempted. In this sense, industrialization has immense anti-traditional implications.... The overall effect of industrialization has been liberating; in fact, democracy correlates closely with industrialization....(Allitt, 4-5)

Coinciding with the rise of philosophical idealism and its originating insights, therefore, is a practical attitude that the past does not have to determine the future, that one can envision a new and better way and then apply engineering to accomplish that vision.

This example of practical, technical thinking by Allitt suggests how philosophical idealism provides the underlying motivation of modernity as it transitions from isolated philosophers to popular culture, viz. *that we can improve the quality of life by advocating three movements: from custom and tradition to education and innovation, from superstition to science, and from hierarchical authority to liberty and equality.* From John Locke, Voltaire, Kant, and J.S. Mill to the industrialist in a factory and the homemaker at the market, some variation of that threefold goal captures the soul and substance of the modern vision of the good life. Although all three of these goals are interrelated and cumulative, we will nonetheless attempt to demonstrate in separate sections their progress, as evidenced in specific cultural and economic events and trends.

As we examine the development of these three goals of modernity, a significant progression will reveal itself. The original ideas behind each movement spring at least partly from religious roots in late medieval and Reformation thought. This helps to explain the affinity between Christian ethics and the idealist ethics of modernity. However, as decades pass, the source of authority for and the means of accomplishing these ideas shift toward more secular principles and motivations. Owen Chadwick admirably documented this transition in *The Secularization of the European Mind in the Nineteenth Century*, which we will utilize at times to highlight the ambivalent attitude of the church then and now toward modernity's conception of the good life.

From Custom and Tradition to Education and Innovation

Widespread education of the masses without regard to social class did not begin until late in the 19th century. In England, for instance, prior to that time, wealthy families could hire tutors and send their youth to exclusive "public" boarding schools and colleges. Small charitable schools for the poor offered a modicum of education, but the gap between aristocratic families and working families was profound. The Sunday School movement that Robert Raikes began in 1780 provided five hours of education a week, mostly reading the Bible and repeating the catechism. By 1830, Sunday School assisted nearly ¼ of elementary age children, who worked in mills and mines during the week. Nonetheless, out of 4.3 million children age 5-10, only half attended school at all in 1870 when the Elementary Education Act passed. (cf. Robert Raikes, Wikipedia) The Enlightenment goal of prosperity through universal education had to overcome severe class distinctions, economic shortfalls, and political intransigence throughout Europe.

In considering education and innovation in the face of custom and tradition, though, it is crucial to remember that impetus for education came from multiple sources, including developments in the church. Long before the achievement of full public education, the 15th century invention of the printing press and the investigative research of late Renaissance literary figures had already initiated a movement toward wider literacy. Early 16th century scholars in the humanist tradition, like Thomas More in England and Erasmus of Rotterdam, devoted their lives to spreading a love of learning, and in Erasmus' case, soundly criticized reactionary Catholic clergy and their restrictions on access to scripture. His careful edition of the Greek New Testament proved a boon to the reformers who followed. Luther's subsequent translation of the Bible into German showed an inner conviction that more people should learn to read, for the Word of God in scripture illuminated the path to salvation. Calvin's insistence in Geneva that schools be expanded and include girls is further evidence that the idea of widespread literacy was already advancing when the first hints of the Enlightenment were still a century away.

Likewise, it is hard to imagine a series of political and religious events more influential than the Protestant Reformation in shaking the foundations of customs and traditions that had held the allegiance of commoner and nobility alike since Constantine. What greater innovation in the Christian religion of the time could there be than to shift the interpretation of salvation from justification by merit to justification by grace through faith! What more massive political upheaval could one imagine than driving a wedge into the monolithic western church, further unleashing the idea of nationalism!

It is important to post these familiar facts to buttress our belief that the ideas of widespread education and challenge to tradition are not modern inventions; they have roots in the 15th and 16th centuries, including in the founders of Protestantism. (One might quip, in advance of this and the following sections, that a picture emerges of grateful but independent older children who yearn to be free of their parents to establish their own authority and choose newer routes to success.) In religion and education, as in life itself, core beliefs from the parental home may linger, but enough changes can render those beliefs unrecognizable and carry children far from their roots. These changes will assume greater importance in later centuries, so to those two differences, radical doubt and historicism, we turn next.

Radical Doubt: The asking of questions and expressing doubts about answers has been part of the educational process since Socrates, but a marked intensification of the role of doubt in learning occurs with Descartes' *Meditations*. His search for absolute certainty, for that which cannot be doubted, begins, paradoxically, with doubt about everything. He questions his sense impressions; he wonders whether the divine being is actually evil enough to mislead us; he questions his prior beliefs and presuppositions. Finally, he is fully convinced that there is only one indubitable thing, *viz.* he is a thinking being who exists: "I think, therefore I am." From that solitary standpoint, he reconstructs the existence of God and a reliable universe. His quest to eliminate doubt, to vanquish skeptics, is complete. He can now believe with certainty. Descartes' legacy to the scientific method is immense, for it utilizes the same path to certainty, regularly questioning previous results and experiments until all doubt dissipates. The more this type of reasoning is taught in schools and universities, the more Descartes' use of radical doubt to achieve certainty etches its way into the hungry minds of students, mostly for good, but also for ill.

The difficulty of Descartes' method is that from the start it separates faith from knowledge. We cannot, in his procedure, start with a presupposition, a faith, that God is good. We can only arrive at that, or any conviction, through the process of logical reasoning proceeding from his, i.e. Descartes', own existence. More recent thinkers, from Thomas Kuhn in *The Structure of Scientific Revolutions* to Michael Polanyi in *The Tacit Dimension*, argue that there are not two widely separated paths to understanding something, one named knowledge and the other named faith. As stated in Lesslie Newbigin's *The Gospel in a Pluralistic Society*:

> There is no knowing without believing, and believing is the way to knowing. The quest for certainty through universal doubt is a blind alley. The program of universal doubt, the proposal that every belief should be doubted until it could be validated by

evidence and arguments not open to doubt, can in the end only lead – as it has led – to universal skepticism and nihilism.... (33)

No educational specialist, no researcher in a lab, no astronomer in an observatory, can be entirely free of certain presuppositions, or faiths, which guide their path to knowledge. They always have some implicit purpose they are seeking to verify, some basic trust in a universe reliable enough for repeated experiments. The application of radical doubt as the key to reliable knowledge is one change in modern thought that may carry the goal of expanded education into territories unacceptable to its initial advocates. We can and should reject many customs and traditions in the name of education and innovation, but others will thankfully remain with us. It would be lamentable to live without traditions big and small, whether manners at the dinner table or belief that wisdom can be conveyed from generation to generation in story and song.

History and Historicism: The previous paragraphs focused on the role of radical doubt in the scientific method, because the teaching of science in schools has so significantly increased over the last two centuries. Attention to both "hard" science and the social sciences occupies a much larger place in grade school and university curricula. To a slightly lesser degree, this advance also pertains to the teaching of history.

Earlier, we discussed the effect of newer interpretations of history on the approach to Holy Scripture, but here we concentrate on a wider impact. It is still important to reiterate reservations that anachronistic assumptions affect biblical historical research. However, we cannot deny, nor should we wish to, that God enters into specific moments of time and that in this respect Christianity is an historical religion compared to many other world religions both ancient and current. That fact leads to another dispute about how much newer views of history may not mesh well with earlier ones. As Owen Chadwick states it, "… modern historical consciousness arose within Christendom. The question therefore meets us whether history was one of the children which Christendom begot and which slowly began to change its father" (189). In particular, Chadwick targets one dynamic. In Christian theology, which emphasizes incarnate acts of God,

> To be religious events they must be of meaning in eternity. To be events of history they must be moments in time. In one sense, the great question of the nineteenth century was the question whether historians, by probing the moments of time associated with religion, could affect its meaning. (191)

This debate comes to a head in mid-19th century theories about historical determinism, or historicism. At its broadest, this theory argues that human events and inclinations are defined by their history and context. Historicism divides into different schools according to the level of strictness applied. Some advocates insist that historical and contextual factors are so determinate of action that no possibility of choosing otherwise exists. Strict historicists use extensive empirical investigation to explain how cultural, economic and political contexts predetermine behavior. Other, less strict advocates, do not attempt intricate assessment of causes but do affirm that the movement of history overall has an irrevocable direction, so personal freedom is profoundly limited by history's set movements. While relatively few public historians today would subscribe to a deterministic viewpoint, typical high school history texts regularly interpret economic, cultural and political contexts preceding significant historical events as their sole causes. Unconsciously, this form of writing history gradually influences society's approach to understanding the motives and personality of an historical figure, eliminating, or simply discounting, invisible emotional/spiritual motivations. It may also obscure a more ancient way of discerning the meaning of a past event through repetition of the story about it or re-presenting the event in the context of a sacramental liturgy.

Arguments about historical necessity permeate philosophy and religion in any century, but the specific threat of historicism in our current inquiry is to Christian views of revelation. Can we know anything with assurance except by inductive investigation of cultural environment? Does the eternal dimension of religious truth diminish to nothing as the historical facts about origin and context increase? If the meaning of the life of Moses or Jeremiah or Jesus derives primarily from their particular historical context, and we direct abundant attention to those cultural and material details, is our ability to see beyond them and into a theological interpretation reduced? Critics of these historical methods, from Kierkegaard on, point instead to the gap between historical knowledge about Jesus and the greater meaning of that person's life. H. Richard Niebuhr states this forcefully:

> There is no continuous movement from an objective inquiry into the life of Jesus to a knowledge of him as the Christ who is our Lord. Only a decision of the self, a leap of faith, a metanoia or revolution of the mind can lead from observation to participation and from observed to lived history. And this is true of all other events in sacred history. (*The Meaning of Revelation*, 83)

All who, rightly, advocate investigation of the historical context of biblical events (or even 'secular' events) nevertheless must not confuse such investigation with an encounter with the living God who emerges both from and beyond those contexts.

By focusing on the radical doubt and the inclination toward historicism that imbue our approach to the world, this section has displayed two aspects of modern education that can either enhance or mislead our understanding of the world and its creator. Combined with the right motives, critical doubt can test old conclusions to produce better new ones, and historical investigation of context can help us avoid misunderstanding events in the past. However, when doubt pretends to absolute rejection of all presuppositions and beliefs, or when history tends toward historical determinism, these otherwise valuable gifts of modernity will at best mask, and at worst injure, our ability to apprehend the living Word of God. In that case, education and innovation become misleading alternatives to the customs and traditions they renounced. This part of modernity's quest for the good life, through education and innovation, offers many positive developments, but also some that prove counterproductive when overextended and disconnected from their pre-enlightenment roots.

From Superstition to Science

In recent centuries, many critics have contended that religion and science are visceral opponents, specifically Christianity and modern science. First published in 1896, Andrew White's two-volume *A History of the Warfare of Science with Theology in Christendom* summarizes what he sees as a long battle for the soul of humanity. White's intention is slightly less combative than the title suggests. He wishes to free science from outmoded medieval categories of Christian thought, hoping to unleash greater scientific progress and allow a purified religion to provide a more contemporary moral foundation. It is hard to disagree too much with that, except how it reduces religion to morality. Nevertheless, his reasons for and method of accomplishing his goal are clearly suspect. Subsequent scholars have thoroughly debunked White's "research" in the book as conjectural and misleading. He utilizes quotes out of context, invents statistics, and convicts by generalized association. His work also reveals a distinct anti-Roman Catholic bias prompted by a late 19th century fear of too many immigrants diluting American society. Today, his book garners little respect. White had, however, captured a dominant sentiment in 18th and 19th century academic circles in America and Europe, *viz.* that greater freedom from religion would aid science. In the minds of French Enlightenment philosophes like Voltaire or Diderot, religion equals superstition. The less of it there is, the better for humanity. Diderot's massive Encyclopedia contained dozens of articles on aspects of emerging science, but no article on Jesus Christ.

One question thus before us is whether the *philosophes* are right that superstition permeates religion, and to gain the good life modern thought must remove religion from any connection to science. In reality, the issue is far more complicated than such blunt pronouncements suppose. A complementary relationship between Christian thought and the advancement of science existed throughout Christian history, though with plenty of bumps and bruises along the way. The following pages seek to reveal that relationship, showing how faith encourages and guides scientific inquiry, but also the chastisement that science can provide the church when religion clings to outmoded conceptions of nature's ways.

In *Spiritual Theology*, former Princeton Seminary professor of philosophy Diogenes Allen devotes a chapter to *The Book of Nature*. He evokes the enduring theme in Christian thought that God communicates with us through two books, nature and scripture, and ultimately (often a very long time indeed) there are no lasting contradictions between the two, for God's truth is originally, and finally, one. Allen's chapter traces early and medieval church thinkers who celebrate the way scientific inquiry and even technological development reveal new dimensions of divine presence. From Basil of Caesarea and Augustine of Hippo in the 4th and 5th centuries, through Bonaventure and Julian of Norwich in the 13th and 14th centuries, a continuous strand of saints of the church believe that the proper contemplation of nature, aided by scriptural guidance, can lead to greater appreciation of God's handiwork. More importantly for the current topic, some view the productive work of craftspeople and artisans as one means of sanctification, for as the material world improves through their labor, they fulfill our calling to restore the image of God lost to humanity in the fall of Adam. One, Hugh of St. Victor, wrote in 1120 that labor and technology could improve life on earth, as our service to God. Allen summarizes the teaching in Hugh's *Didascalicon*: "Technology and commerce help restore us to our proper relationship to nature, which is one of stewardship, and which improves our earthly life so we may approximate more fully our original condition in paradise." (119) Technology is an acceptable part of the human quest for knowledge. This and all other true knowledge leads to God. Technology, in other words, "has the potential to be spiritual". Even as theoretical knowledge is a remedy for ignorance, and practical knowledge combats vice, technological knowledge overcomes our human weakness as we attempt to mend the broken image of God.

Early pioneers of modern science retained the view that investigation and contemplation of nature can reveal the divine presence and elevate the soul toward God. Johannes Kepler, one of the first to embrace Copernicus' heliocentric theories and show that orbits are elliptical, was a devout Lutheran who felt he could glorify God through his mathematical and astronomical studies. His scientific notes often mingled with prayers and exclamations of divine praise. Robert Boyle advanced the study of chemistry and helped establish the Royal Society in England. He also financially supported early missions to Asia and America, wrote essays on Christian ethics and insisted that science could illuminate God's workings in nature. History often forgets that Isaac Newton combined world-shaping discoveries of gravitational force and basic laws of motion with extensive writings on biblical interpretation. He insisted that gravity was an active principle God used to impose order on the world. Nearly two centuries later, Michael Faraday developed field theory in physics and was the first to convert mechanical energy into electrical energy. He also served as elder and deacon in a small Christian group called the Sandemanians, regularly visiting the sick as an emissary of his church. (Christian History Institute, #67-72.)

These short historical reminders solidify the reality that from the 4th century to the 19th, distinguished natural philosophers (as scientists were first called) saw no conflict between their Christian faith and their research. These pioneers demonstrated their belief that religion was not mere superstition and that a better life through scientific research meshed with Christian faith. Nonetheless, ecclesiastical reactions to two revolutionary discoveries, including an instance of overreliance on a questionable concept, reveal why public opinion still sometimes entertains a "warfare" model.

The "Galileo Affair" of the early 17th century centered on the heliocentric/geokinetic theory of Copernicus (that earth revolves around the sun) and Galileo's recent proof of it through newly acquired telescopic evidence. The theory appears to conflict with certain scriptures, including verses in Joshua when the prophet stopped the Sun's setting to lengthen the day. Galileo argued that scripture had to be interpreted in light of ongoing discoveries, that ancient texts often accommodated their message to the original audience's ability to understand. The Inquisition panel called in to investigate the dispute ruled that Copernicanism was absurd and heretical, but it also took no punitive action against Galileo.

However, the newly called Council of Trent, in an attempt to combat Protestantism, banned the kind of biblical interpretation Galileo advocated, so later the church brought him to trial for violating a previous order to be silent about heliocentrism. Galileo was forced to recant and received a light sentence of home confinement. Throughout the 20-year ordeal, theologians and scientists on both sides debated the value of Galileo's conclusions, which were sometimes borne out (telescopic evidence) and sometimes later refuted (earth's movement as the cause of tides). Although a Roman Catholic commission in 1979 later admitted its errors in the matter, the 17th century church's intransigence and resistance to a challenging theory buttress the argument of those who would wall off religion from interacting with science. (An extensive and balanced account of the affair is available in Lawrence Principe's lectures *Science and Religion*.)

The theory of evolution provided a second opportunity for division two centuries after Galileo. Our examination of this larger and more recent challenge will reveal how the church's doctrinal dependence on one scientific discovery can lead to difficulties when a later discovery upends the first.

It is in some ways surprising that Charles Darwin's *The Origin of Species* in 1859 would raise a controversy stark enough to bedevil certain church groups even to this day. Nearly two centuries earlier, when the Danish geologist Nicholas Steno catalogued striations in exposed rock among the hills of Tuscany, most natural philosophers began to conclude that the earth was far older than a literal reading of the biblical account implied. Agronomists since antiquity had enhanced crop production by selectively choosing the best plants as progenitors for others and eliminating the weaker strains, utilizing a type of "survival of the fittest". In addition, cross breeding of animals spurred the English Agricultural Revolution of the 18th century, so the public understood that one form of life could transition to another. Furthermore, from an ideological perspective, Hegel's progressive view of history had launched a forward-looking vision of dynamic improvement. Why could not that vision apply to nature itself?

Still, two specific elements of Darwin's findings troubled the waters of Christian faith, especially in England and later in Germany. One was the implication by Herbert Spencer and others that natural selection eliminated weaker beings, favoring only the strong, emphasizing survival as the only good, leaving little room for an ethics that relied on a merciful God present in the workings of nature. The other was the insistence that the variations that led to new species originated randomly, removing a divine designer from the process and introducing a chaotic uncertainty to life. It would be hard to overestimate the impact of these two aspects of evolution or the challenge they posed to the settled worldview about nature. Let us examine the context and implications of each.

Regarding the ethical issues, the mid-19th century found the English church primarily, and some continental denominations also, with two fears. One was the worry that the rise of historical criticism was already tarnishing the authority of scripture, introducing doubt about the veracity of the Bible. For instance, J.G. Eichhorn's 18th c. "documentary hypothesis" effectively questioned Moses' authorship of the Decalogue, undermining the literal inspiration of the Old

Testament and even its value for moral decisions. The other fear concerned how a booming industrial revolution furthered a materialistic view of life. Emphasis on growth in manufacturing and economic progress crowded spiritual concerns to the sidelines for the wider public. Explicit materialist atheism like that of German biologist Ernest Haeckel or materialist economic philosophies like Marxism worried the theological academy.

At first glance, evolution exacerbated those worries. If "man", human beings, evolved from lesser species by purely natural processes, then whence comes a human soul that could direct natural brutish inclinations toward generous social relationships? What spiritual, hence invisible, guiding force could arise from mere matter? Moreover, if the process of natural evolution takes millennia to produce even minor changes, then scripture is wrong about both the origin of life and the length of the creative activity of God in Genesis. Scriptural authority, long a prop for hierarchical enforcement of morality, loses its ability to restrain impulses or command respect. With these scary prospects, who or what would halt Spencer's application of Darwinism to a model for social relationships that sees a bitter war for supremacy? Battle lines drew up over these questions on how divine compassion fits into the natural selection process that is pivotal to Darwin's conclusions.

Darwin's other controversial tenet, that the variations arising within species arise through random incidents, met an even greater outcry from the church, especially English Protestants who had embraced the natural religion so dominant in the previous century. Remember that Newton's mechanical picture of the universe launched an almost inevitable portrayal of God as a cosmic clockmaker, whose initial activity at creation set in motion a series of physical laws governing all aspects of physical life. Although in some quarters this led to deism, which largely ignored any personal God and merely consulted the eternal laws, most churchgoers and their preachers saw in natural theology striking evidence for a designer God whose laws faithfully guided life's course. William Paley's 1802 book *Natural Theology* offered a classic argument, implying that if we see a watch lying on the ground and we open it to observe the many interlocking gears, will we not automatically assume a watchmaker? Why not then logically conclude as we look at the intricate wonders in nature that there exists a divine creator who crafted these with infinite care and foresight? Paley, by the way, was a highly respected Cambridge don, ordained to ministry yet lecturing on a variety of religious and scientific topics, also an ardent opponent of slavery. Natural theology seemed to him and the wide public to offer both a clear argument for the existence of God and the reassurance that this God's providence had designed a beautiful, functional universe.

This pervasive form of reassurance about God, however, would fall apart if indeed random, purely contingent events prompted variations within and beyond species, variations that continued merely because they suited different external circumstances in the quest for survival. Adjustments to difficulties once regarded as inspired by an attendant God of providence now can operate on their own, through purely natural means. This impasse seemed so clear and insurmountable that some theologians, like Charles Hodge of Princeton Seminary, declared in 1874 that Darwinism was tantamount to atheism.

Is it, though? In reality, the Christian response to evolution has been much more varied, and often more receptive, than Hodge's pronouncement would imply. Actually, long before the modern age, Augustine of Hippo had envisioned a divine creative process whereby God initiated an ongoing continuous unfolding of nature, with secondary causes in successive generations bringing new entities into existence, a kind of theistic evolution. This theme was repeated in an 1844 book *Vestiges of a Natural History of Creation* by one Robert Chambers. Fifteen years before Darwin's *Origin...*, Chambers insisted that physical nature obviously developed incrementally according to the natural laws of God. Notice, though, that this particular "natural law" referred to is far more dynamic and changeable than the mechanical view of laws in Newton. That signals a significant development. Instead of a heavenly transcendent God setting all things in motion before time itself began, here is an opening for a more immanent picture of God, one at work in the daily unfolding of life. There emerges the possibility of a God who intentionally intertwines with the workings of an ongoing creation, acting to redirect toward a divine purpose the contingent events that emerge unexpectedly; this, instead of God as a distant architect who developed eternal plans and then left the world to itself. Nature has a distinct freedom, as do human beings. God works with that freedom, that contingency of nature, in the same way God works with human choices.

This is the wide direction subsequently taken by most Christian responses to Darwin. Does it require a rethinking of how divine providence might work? Yes. Does it require a symbolic rather than literal interpretation of the early chapters of Genesis? Assuredly it does. But these changes in theological concepts also provide a picture of God much more in tune with the actual biblical passages that depict God. Moreover, they liberate Christian thought from a deistic view of God that bore little resemblance to the God experienced in the daily lives of believers. These are changes, perhaps overdue, that enable Christian theology to continue in dialogue with scientific developments and see divine revelation in both of the "books" God intended for our instruction.

After an initial negative reaction by most religious figures, formal scholarly pronouncements from major Christian denominations by the early 20th century had gradually accommodated to the fact of biological evolutionary development of species. Likewise, the scientific community, parts of which also regarded Darwin's system with initial skepticism, embraced this new way of regarding natural development. In both theological and scientific fields, however, resistance has lingered to the blunt instrument of natural selection. At best, some theologians interpret natural selection as a clear description of the natural world as it has fallen from God's original intention, a fallen state that God seeks to redeem. To retain God's presence within the scope of evolution's process, Christians universally hold out for some kind of spiritual force in the human being. This "soul" both transcends and imbues the physical workings of nature, guiding them toward less destructive ends. (Cf. *Whatever Happened to the Soul?*) Furthermore, within biological research, recent studies have emphasized that features like cooperation and empathy are equally as important as strength and size in what allows some species to thrive. The survival of the fittest may actually look quite different from what Herbert Spencer first posited as a dog-eat-dog existence.

Over the course of the 20th century, only Christian denominations that could not accept anything but a literal reading of scripture felt the need to create elaborate "creationist" schemes that completely reject the general outlines of Darwinian evolution. The debate continues, but with few exceptions, the intellectual grounding of the Christian faith now includes some form of biological evolutionary development instead of the ancient picture of God as initially creating each species individually.

These two instances of ecclesiastical resistance, to Galileo's defense of Copernican heliocentrism and Darwin's demonstration of evolutionary biology, do reveal occasional conservative tendencies in Christian theology. That is not a statement about political alignment, but the awareness that Christian faith cherishes its heritage. The journalist Irving Kristol once declared "Religion is both prophetic and rabbinic, on the one side a revolt against things-as-they-are; and on the other, insistent on observing the laws embedded in tradition" (E.J. Dionne, *The Washington Post*). Our religion alters its principles only when compelling truths revealed by God's Spirit through courageous opponents push it to remember that God's work is not done, that God's revelation is not complete, and that we must be ready to recognize new dimensions of God's word that may qualify the old. This openness will protect the church from accusations that religion and reactionary superstition are bedfellows. Let us hope that the attitude exhibited by early Christian pioneer scientists resurfaces in an updated version for Christ's church, one that again sees groundbreaking research as a means of discovering the wonder and wisdom of a creator God. Initial forays in that direction are present in the work of Christian professors like Ian Barbour, Nancy Murphy, John Polkinghorne, and Thomas Torrance, and through active research by Christians like former National Institutes of Health Director Francis Collins. (There is more on this toward the end of Part Two.)

The other side of the equation, however, requires modern science to recognize the need for an overarching philosophic, spiritual and moral framework within which to utilize properly its new inventions. The increased professionalization of science in the 19th century and increased specialization of research in the 20th century have channeled many scientists away from public discourse and toward a potentially myopic focus. What, after all, is society's stated purpose for the immense growth of technological inventions over the last century, other than perhaps to relieve the human body of all physical labor or create the many consumer goods that crowd our closets and garages, all so that every year the gross domestic product will grow? Are we simply caught in the cycle so clearly described in Jacques Ellul's *The Technological Society*, where every problem caused by technology requires a new technological solution, and no one thinks outside that circle? Few authors today can state theological reasons for scientific advancement the way Hugh of St. Victor did, envisioning it as a means of recovering our original relationship to God in Eden. The danger exists that research will degenerate into nearsighted scientism and eventual blind allegiance to technique and novelty. The path to the Good Life may go through, but must also go beyond, laboratory doors.

From Hierarchical Authority to Liberty and Equality

One of the most striking quotations arising from the French Enlightenment was Denis Diderot's stark denunciation of authority figures: "Man will never be free until the last king is strangled with the entrails of the last priest." As chief editor and primary contributor to the groundbreaking *Encyclopedia*, banned from publication by king and church, he had many reasons for such animosity. Personal sentiments aside, however, his quotation did capture the simmering resentment that, for too long, monarchy and clergy promoted inequity, poverty, and mindless obedience. The First Estate (clergy) and the Second Estate (nobility) controlled political and economic decisions that persistently oppressed the peasantry and to a lesser extent, the bourgeoisie. Between 1741 and 1785, the rise in the real cost of living was 62%. Due to poor harvests in 1788 and 1789, the price of bread in the year of the revolt had risen 88%, accompanied by a 25% drop in average wages (cf. Wikipedia, "Causes of the French Revolution"). That resentment boiled over with the execution of Louis XVI and Marie Antoinette in 1793. It lingers still in the insistence that France officially declares itself a secular state.

While the groundswell of bitterness may have been stronger in Bourbon, Catholic, France than in Frederick's Prussia or Anglican England, 19th century movements toward greater liberty in Italy, Austria and Russia provide examples of widespread acceptance of the trend. The earlier American Revolution, with its separation of church from state and rejection of monarchy, influenced the French soldiers who returned to find their own farms heavily in debt. The ideals of France's document The Rights of Man and Citizen and the American Declaration of Independence were highly exportable.

It will be remembered that the battle cry of the French Revolution was "Liberty, Equality, Fraternity". In the two-plus centuries since then, those stirring ideas have advanced, becoming commonplace in our western societies. One of the most succinct and effective treatises delineating those principles is John Stuart Mill's *On Liberty*. In Chapter One, we quoted Mill on five dimensions of liberty and equality. Let us summarize and reflect on those now, reviewing and celebrating their progress. After recounting the gains made in liberty and equality, however, we will also consider criticisms and warnings about where some of those principles, if unchecked, might lead, and how they relate to Christian freedom.

Individual Freedom of Choice: Mill insists that the only purpose for which a government or other authority may rightfully exercise power over a person is "to prevent harm to others. His (or her) own good, either physical or moral, is not a sufficient warrant" (9). This idea restricts the intervention of an external authority over personal choices often prohibited by church or state. All are equal before the law in personal decisions. An external authority may attempt to convince a change of behavior through multiple reasonable appeals, but it may not prohibit and punish personal behavior unless and until it clearly shows that such behavior harms others. The right of private judgement of a mature citizen in a republic is irrevocable. "Over oneself, over one's body and mind, the individual is sovereign" (10). This principle ensures privacy, protection against punishment for personal beliefs and choices, such as what one reads in the sanctuary of one's library or does in one's bedroom. Mill does not intend this freedom from punishment to apply to children, nor, as he puts it, to "backward states of society in which the race itself may be considered as in its nonage"(10).

Freedom of Speech: The liberty for private behavior is matched by the liberty for public expression. All have equal rights to speak out. Neither church nor king should have had the authority to prohibit publication of Diderot's *Encyclopedia*. No government today should have power to close down a peaceable assembly whose speaker proclaims that Black Lives Matter or that Confederate statues should remain in public squares. Mill's explicit words include, "the peculiar evil of silencing the expression of an opinion is, that it is robbing the human race..." (16) and therefore "everything must be free to be written and published without restraint" (38). He voices a straightforward endorsement of rational dialogue between opposing parties as the means of knowledge and perhaps even reconciliation. Nothing good comes of being unable to hear a dissenting opinion because it has been silenced by force. Every knowledgeable citizen of the U.S.A. recognizes this liberty enshrined in the First Amendment. Journalists treasure the protection it provides them to print accurate albeit controversial articles.

Diversity and Openness As a Means to Truth: The reason for full and open expression of opinion is to arrive at a more complete view of reality. Those who "have never thrown themselves into the mental position of people who think differently from them... do not, in any proper sense of the word, know the doctrine which they themselves profess" (36,37). Only by understanding the opponent can truly rational argument measure all the facts. This openness widens one's perspective and urges broader experience. Later, Mill quotes the German politician Wilhelm von Humboldt's view that the proper goal of humanity "...is the highest and most harmonious development of his powers to a complete and consistent whole", which Humboldt also calls "the individuality of power and development". And what is required for such development? There are two requisites: "freedom, and variety of situations", which lead to "individual vigor and manifold diversity" (57). Herein lies a central impetus behind contemporary quests for wider realms of travel and heightened extremes of experience. The freer we are to roam, it seems, the more new sensations we encounter, the better we understand ultimate reality.

Optimism about the Progress of Knowledge: The prevailing optimism of the 19th century shines out from the next principle of Mill.

> As mankind improve, the number of doctrines which are no longer disputed or doubted will be constantly on the increase; and the well-being of mankind may almost be measured by the number and gravity of the truths which have reached the point of being uncontested. (43)

The more reason is unleashed through free thought, the better off we all will be. One discovery, once confirmed, leads on to another, and the cumulative effect will be genuine progress. We can see today how a breakthrough in theoretical physics, for instance, once it is accepted as established principle, provides engineers data to develop practical applications for daily life like microwave ovens or the internet.

Self-Expression and Self-Development: With this theme, Mill most clearly echoes Immanuel Kant's quest for autonomy and Philosophical Idealism's belief in self-realization.

> ...in things which do not primarily concern others, individuality should assert itself. Where (not the person's own character) but the traditions or customs of other people are the rule of conduct, there is wanting one of the principal ingredients of human happiness, and quite the chief ingredient of individual and social progress. (56)

Merely accepting the customary traditions of culture rather than expressing and exercising one's own individual character violates the spirit of the Enlightenment: *Sapere aude*; i.e., "Dare to know." In an even blunter declaration, Mill says "He who lets the world, or his own portion of it, choose his plan of life for him, has no need of any other faculty than the ape-like one of imitation" (58). Unless and until a person furthers his or her own individual choices and faculties, that person is, in Mill's view, less than truly human and misses much of what brings personal satisfaction.

Reconsidering Mill's Conclusions

Let us draw together now these emphases from J.S. Mill's *On Liberty* and ask how the Christian church can affirm the benefits of these principles yet also warn of their excesses and unforeseen consequences.

Freedom of Personal Choice and Speech: The abiding presupposition underlying Mill's belief, and all those of the modern worldview he represents, is that freedom must steadily increase so that reason may emerge from the shadows and lead humanity toward a far brighter future. He is convinced that every person is capable of making decisions based on reason alone, decisions pertaining to profound moral and political import. Many have challenged this assumption as naïve and inapplicable to real situations. Consider, for instance, the insistence in the previous excerpts that an individual should be allowed full freedom of choice and speech unless and until such freedom negatively affects others. Is it, however, even possible to distinguish between what is purely personal and what will affect others? Is there an obvious disconnect between a person's actions in private and his or her eventual public relationship with others? Do three people meeting privately to plot the assassination of a dictator intend nothing more than to keep meeting privately to talk? Regardless of the virtue of their cause, what they do in private definitely affects what they will do in public, with consequences for vast multitudes of people. Does a man spending hours every night watching pornography on the internet in the seclusion of his apartment somehow completely divorce that preoccupation from his views about women co-workers when he returns to the office the next morning? The Christian faith has always insisted that what a person believes in the privacy of one's heart is ultimately inseparable from how one behaves in relationships. Absolute and complete purity of motive may elude even the best of us, but the idea that what we do in private has no effect on what we do in public is a misreading of the way the human mind and heart actually work.

A second critique of Mill's views on liberty and reason appeared only 14 years after publication of his book. It came from an English lawyer named Fitzjames Stephen and is explained by Owen Chadwick in his *The Secularization of the European Mind*.... Stephen contends that society exists upon a consensus of shared opinions, and those opinions are far more frequently assented to on the basis of confidence in leaders than in individual rational processing of facts. Very few people, he explains, actually make decisions based purely on reason or scrutinized evidence. "And if they were purely rational decisions, to the exclusion of other aspects of our nature besides reason, they are likely to be wrong decisions" (34). This, simply put, is not the way people think and choose. To base society on that chimera is bound to lead to trouble. It has the effect of destroying all trust in authority, even earned authority rather than merely inherited. "The result of our accepting Mill's advice to decide everything for ourselves is not decision but indecision" (35). Mill asks us to abandon accepted truths without realistically granting a means for constructing any except one's own choices, which most people are unprepared to do. That leads to "general skepticism in philosophy, general agnosticism in religion, and eventual anarchy in politics..."(35). Stephen's objections may hurt the pride of a culture that believes in an equally inherent rational nature of humanity, but they have a ring of practical truth that prompts a long pause before fully embracing this attractive call to personal liberty. The extent to which contrary desires of the will and egocentrism regularly overwhelm impartial reason is abundantly documented in human history. It also forms a central warning within Christian theology.

Diversity and Openness as a Means to Truth: It happens that I am writing this paragraph less than a week after riotous protesters stormed the Capitol building in Washington, D.C., to stop Congress from receiving Electoral College votes in the presidential election. This startling event has prompted much reflection on the role played by social media in recent politics. It caused one columnist to ask "...whether liberty and human rights can survive the digital revolution" (Von Drehle, *The Washington Post*). He hearkens back to a Supreme Court case of a century ago when Justice Oliver Wendell Holmes warned, "Freedom of expression can't coexist with reckless misuse of that freedom." Those who organized or contributed to the anarchy at the Capitol did so through the vast network of social media. Repeating fabricated anecdotes and perpetuating falsehoods often enough, they turned what would otherwise have been a reasonably debated issue into an inspired mob armed with misinformation. The openness to multiple avenues of information, the search for a diversity of news sources until finding one you like, became the enemy of genuine liberty while fueling the reckless misuse of freedom against which Holmes warned. The columnist regrettably affirms,

> Anyone who has studied the workings of religious cults or mass manias understands that the human brain, far from being an engine of searing skepticism, is highly prone to dysfunction inside sealed and self-reinforcing information loops. Digital technology makes it exponentially easier to create such loops and to lose oneself inside them. (Von Drehle, *The Washington Post*)

If Mill were alive today, in an era where misinformation seems to have no limits, would he still be as confident that Truth could be found by remaining ever open to new perspectives? By the time one finishes digesting and editing all the new perspectives that come along today, is there time and energy left for actually promoting those perspectives that have already proven most worthy over the ages?

Self-Development and Self-Expression: Finally, in defending the utmost importance of developing one's inner potential through reason, Mill occasionally makes rash statements that betray a disdain for ordinary people who do not possess his own critical faculties. It is a worrisome tendency, and it reflects the intellectual imperialism of European nations in their 19th century colonization of "backward" countries. In his advocacy of personal liberty from external authority, he recognizes that this right must be restricted for children under the care of parents and, as he puts it, for "...those backward states of society in which the race itself may be considered as in its nonage" (10, "nonage" means not yet achieving adult maturity). He bluntly continues:

> Despotism is a legitimate mode of government in dealing with barbarians.... Liberty, as a principle, has no application to any state of things anterior to the time when mankind have become capable of being improved by free and equal discussion. Until then, there is nothing for them but implicit obedience to an Akbar or a Charlemagne, if they are so fortunate as to find one. (10)

Although likely not intended as such, such statements are stark exclamations of disdain for all individuals who obediently follow the guidance of their parents into adulthood and all cultures that do not embrace the rationalist philosophy of the Enlightenment. Mill regularly elevates individualism over community. He also essentially declares that whether a person has deliberately chosen an action is more important than whether the action is good or bad. This attitude becomes visible in statements like the following, which compares someone who follows custom rather than using firmness, discrimination of facts, and self-control to decide: "It is possible that one might be guided in some good path, and kept out of harm's way, without any of these things. But what will be his comparative worth as a human being?" (58,59). In other words, to Mill you are not worth much as a person unless you employ rational faculties to enhance your freedom. This raises multiple ethical issues about treatment of mentally disabled or dying people at the mercy of a purely rationalist, utilitarian society. Will their dismissal as unworthy be an inevitable consequence of this kind of liberty?

Please do not misunderstand. The criticisms and warnings raised in the previous paragraphs do not seek to reduce appreciation for the many benefits gained by challenging hierarchical authority and establishing greater liberty and equality. The Christian church obviously celebrates the emancipation of slaves, and confesses its sin for too long clinging to mistaken notions of race and property. The Christian church celebrates the ongoing success of the civil rights struggle and movements like Black Lives Matter, and confesses its failure to lead those movements boldly. The Christian church rejoices in the success of the campaigns for women's suffrage, and the ongoing quest for gender equality, while confessing its former reluctance to shed systems of male domination. This hope for liberty and equality in modernity's vision of happiness, or the "good life", coalesces with many of the goals of basic Christian ethics and helps fulfill the church's vision of God's reconciled community.

Nevertheless, at the risk of raised eyebrows from readers, it is important to declare that ultimately, in service to our Lord, there is for Christians something more important than civil liberties and the goal of self-development. That "something" is admirably stated in this quotation:

> As Christians we do not seek to be free but rather to be of use, for it is only by serving that we discover the freedom offered by

God. We have learned that freedom cannot be had by becoming 'autonomous' – free from all claims except those we voluntarily accept – but rather freedom literally comes by having our self-absorption challenged by the needs of another. (Hauerwas, *After Christendom?* 53-54)

Because of this attitude, Christians can view other people not as unwelcome barriers to self-expression and freedom to do what one wants, but as welcome limits on our persistent self-centeredness that separates us from God.

In this current subchapter, we explained how happiness, or what we have called "the good life", appeared to the foundational thinkers of modernity as requiring three movements: from custom and tradition to education and innovation, from superstition to science, and from hierarchical authority to liberty and equality. We have tried to affirm with fairness the multiple benefits to western society from these three directions. Nevertheless, that affirmation has not been unilateral. When education overextends the role of doubt and places historicist limits on the search for truth; when scientific research forgets its Christian roots and isolates itself from larger questions of meaning and purpose; and when the quest for liberty ignores the limits that protect it from chaotic, imperialistic self-expression, a voice of protest must arise. At that point, a new band of advocates for the Christian faith must remind the world of a lasting form of happiness based on service to Jesus Christ, even when such service appears to lead one far away from what most of the world considers happiness. That perspective will always be needed to provide a vision beyond humanity's own ideas about what virtues will lead to genuine well-being for all.

| four |

Christian Faith as Counterpoint

We began the previous chapter on the challenge of Modernity to the Christian church with a quotation from Peter Berger in *The Sacred Canopy*, that "...the fundamental problem of the religious institutions is how to keep going in a milieu that no longer takes for granted their definitions of reality."

That statement expresses an ongoing dilemma to the church. In an attempt to respond to that challenge, we identified the primary newer "definitions of reality" as reinterpretations of freedom, history, and happiness or "the good life". Influencing those reinterpretations are two underlying frameworks, two ways of thinking, called rationalism and philosophical idealism. A short review of these five pervasive concepts in their modern forms will help to introduce the final chapter of Part One. Subsequently, we will emphasize how the Christian faith can serve as a necessary counterpoint that helps these concepts accomplish their best intentions without overstepping limits that threaten to undo their benefits and lead to dangerous reactions.

Rationalism, as understood in modern philosophy, is the principle that the basic nature of all reality can be known by the mind using deductive reasoning. Taken to its logical conclusion, it implies that nothing exists that cannot be understood through reason. Everything is explicable, and a single rational system incorporates all reliable knowledge. This was the premise that guided Descartes' *Meditations* and his *Discourse on Method*. His search for incontrovertible certainty led him to believe that he must move beyond traditional assumptions, intuitions, theological dogma or the observations of his senses, and seek only knowledge that possesses mathematical surety. This belief, expressed in multiple forms, has remained a dominant influence in philosophical systems of the last 4 centuries.

Philosophical Idealism is a collective name for a set of slightly differing views on reality. Generally, all variations believe that what we call the external world, or material reality, is actually the creation of the mind, either God's mind or ours. One form is termed Transcendental, or Critical Idealism, labels given to the premise that objects of our experience are appearances; we cannot prove they have existence outside our thoughts. However, the form most regularly referred to in these chapters is Hegelian Idealism, often called Objective, or Absolute, which in his system means that everything that exists is a form or projection of one Absolute Mind. We have emphasized the impact of such a view on the visionary aspirations of modern industrial and technological society, and on the interpretation of history.

As argued, these two ways of regarding the world have shaped how our modern society understands freedom, history and happiness, creating influential interpretations that sometimes coalesce with and sometimes compete with the principal doctrines of the Christian faith on these themes. Brief recapitulations of what we discussed above on these will help prepare the reader for the concluding comments about Christianity as a counterpoint.

The treatment of freedom began with an outline of biblical and theological themes that express the predominant Christian interpretation of freedom. The biblical languages use words for freedom that emphasize, first, deliverance, and, second, a state in which a person can choose without undue restraint. In both cases, God is the original deliverer and the one who ultimately removes the restraints to choice. These liberties, however, do not arise primarily through human effort; they are gracious gifts. Moreover, the deliverance does not leave one free as one's own master. It is liberation from a destructive allegiance to sin or oppression into a constructive allegiance to a merciful but holy God. This results in the frequently acknowledged paradox that a Christian is most free when in obedient service to God.

From that starting point, the chapter continued to the modern understanding of freedom. That includes, first, its roots in the social contract theory of government, which creates the understanding that political liberty is the result of a voluntary group agreement that establishes government to uphold rights and resolve disputes. Second, it includes Kant's alternative basis for morality in his categorical imperative and its presupposition that the true value of a person is his or her ability to make free rational decisions in a quest for autonomy. Thirdly, and most significantly for practical purposes, it includes the interpretation of freedom as economic purchasing power, arising from Adam Smith's sense that free trade is a natural law, that consumption is the ultimate goal of economic activity, and that the invisible hand of capitalism's dynamic will turn individual self-interest into a greater good for all. These three trends combine to define most people's understanding of freedom at the turn of the 20th century.

The second theme regarded how newer understandings of history have affected biblical interpretation and the level of respect for scriptural authority. The 19th and early 20th centuries revealed how the historical-critical method upended common conceptions on the inspiration of scripture, on how the Bible came to be, and questioned whether we could still implicitly trust its stories, laws and teachings. After delineating several factors in ancient hermeneutics (i.e., principles of interpretation) that reflect a premodern view of history as testimony to God's redemptive acts, we began to state the more modern view as well. Here we underlined two philosophical influences. Rationalism, as in Descartes' methodology, had essentially eliminated mythic stories and external revelation as legitimate sources of truth, so how to the modern mind could they merit attention? More significantly, Hegel's progressive view of history contributed to a growing public disposition that valuable insights into reality will be more likely found in the future than in the past. Hegel added to his view of history the work of Johann Herder, who had influenced public opinion by emphasizing that social and historical context greatly influence someone's interpretation of an event. This observation was not new. It had arisen nearly two centuries earlier by Spinoza, but the time was now more receptive to a historicist approach to interpreting scripture. Through the insights of two respected biblical scholars, we showed how the modern view of history imbedded in the historical-critical method can enhance, but also badly distort, how much biblical truths gain footing in the mind and heart of an eager student of the Bible.

The third topic of the previous chapter, what modern citizens regard as happiness, or "the good life", began with a preliminary note about the two-sided relationship between the ethics of philosophical idealism and the Christian faith. Sometimes the two systems fulfill and enhance one another; sometimes they oppose. Awareness of this tension prompted the definition of philosophical idealism summarized above. Once again, three components of happiness required attention. The modern quest for the good life requires these movements in society: from custom and tradition to education and innovation, from superstition to science, and from hierarchical authority to liberty and equality. Each of these was examined in turn, celebrating benefits but cautioning about potential detriments. Modern education and innovation expanded the economy, freed children to learn, enhanced public health and granted awareness of the wider world, but in the process it overemphasized radical doubt and implicitly furthered a purely historicist interpretation of how change occurs. Science successfully reduced superstition, methodically investigating frontiers from deepest mines to farthest stars, unleashing data later engineered into marvels of technology and material benefits. Yet, in the process, ever-narrowing fields of research hindered wider awareness of whether its discoveries enhanced good or evil. Finally, the French Revolution dealt a bloody blow to oppressive hierarchical authority, and "liberty, equality, fraternity" rang throughout the western world. Emancipation of slaves, suffrage for women, and a slow march toward full public equality sprang from the cry for civil and personal liberty trumpeted by Enlightenment voices. However, Mill's classic study On Liberty also revealed dangers when liberty forgets proper limits and self-realization diminishes community. Notably, in all three of these movements, recognition of early Christian roots of and support for education, science, and liberty lost ground to public alignment with more secular sources of attaining happiness.

With these brief summaries in mind, what remains for Part One of this volume is a concise statement of how the Christian faith can present a living alternative to the predominant intellectual and cultural assumptions of modernity. Throughout the previous pages, we have repeatedly affirmed the benefits of all that Enlightenment principles have accomplished over the last centuries, the progress in economic, educational, scientific and political arenas. Nonetheless, those same centuries witnessed an incessant string of highly destructive wars both small and large, oppressive colonization of peoples declared "backward" by European and American elites, nationalist regimes fueled by ideologies of hate, an avalanche of media information unable to distinguish between fact and fiction, and the burgeoning growth of consumerist materialism that threatens the planet on which we live. These are just some of the travesties that Christ-centered discipleship nurtured by local churches can lessen in the public arena. By providing a counterpoint, a radical alternative to rationalist idealism, a revitalized and conscientious Christianity can proclaim fearlessly the beliefs and "definitions of reality" that will help it reclaim lost ground and provide a check on the excesses of modernity.

This attempt to reassess the principles of modernity is obviously not the first. On the final pages of historian Gerald Cragg's *The Church and the Age of Reason*, he explains the questioning of the Enlightenment that arose in the wake of the French Revolution and the Napoleonic wars.

An intellectual war of liberation was underway. The naïve and shallow faith in the perfectibility of man, so popular in the eighteenth century, rested on the cult of reason. Rationalism, as popularly understood, affirmed that all reality can be known by the mind. Right reason could reduce society to the harmonious pattern ordained by nature and by nature's God. Once mankind accepted this liberating truth, the golden age would be at hand. This was the theory. After twenty-five years of revolutionary turmoil and warfare, Europe decided that the fruits of this philosophy were discord, violence, and disillusionment. Consequently, a resolute attempt was launched to overthrow the self-evident certitudes which had seemed so deceptively obvious to the Age of Reason (283).

Central Christian Beliefs

In what follows, we will offer central Christian beliefs that also question some of the "self-evident certitudes" in modernity that may lead to consequences more dangerous than it had imagined possible. Six themes capture the essence of what the church needs to say to the modern world.

First Theme: The ethical system based on rationalistic choice, which reached its pinnacle in Kant's Categorical Imperative, creates an increasing individualism that leads to cynical Titanism and/or isolation and loss of community. In contrast, the church creates community through the care and nurture of its members and as a training ground for public and private righteousness. In *Resident Aliens*, Stanley Hauerwas and William Willimon argue for maintaining and enhancing the traditions and practices of the church. First, they state that:

> Kant's "categorical imperative" underwrote the assumption that all people could be moral without training since they had available to them all they needed insofar as they were rational. Kant's project, therefore, was to free the moral agent from the arbitrary and contingent characters of our histories and communities. (98)

In contrast, Hauerwas and Willimon assert that Christian ethics "is not something that comes naturally. It can only be learned." They continue, "...a primary way of learning to be disciples is by being in contact with others who are disciples" (102). People's character is shaped and their deepest thoughts formed within traditions and communities. Neither God's odd choice of an insignificant Hebrew people as messenger to the world, nor the crucifixion and resurrection of Jesus Christ, is true because all thinking beings accept them as reasonable. Indeed, these acts appear quite irrational, "foolishness to the wise" as St. Paul puts it. One does not learn in a vacuum of individual deliberation. Learning Christianity's most significant truths occurs within a nurturing community that helps us to see events in our world that at times defy the logic of inherent rationality. Overt and implicit individualism in modernity forgets this.

Second Theme: The scientific method, and the philosophies which undergird it, promote a closed system of knowledge disconnected from a wider sense of purpose and meaning. Without violating the proper objectivity of research, the church can nonetheless regularly remind scientists and engineers that they cannot divorce themselves from larger teleological questions about the right application of knowledge. In *Philosophy for Understanding Theology*, Diogenes Allen and Eric Springsted explain how Galileo's theory of motion and Descartes' interpretation of it created a shift away from Aristotle's view of the Four Causes. From then on:

there are neither formal nor final causes in matter (or nature). All qualitative changes (such as color, sound and texture) are caused by *impact* in local motion of matter, whose essence is extension. He devised a view of the entire cosmos as a vast machine, with mechanical causality (impact) as the sole cause of all change. Nature as a vast clockwork mechanism became the dominant image of the universe… (122).

It is not necessary to disprove Galileo's and Descartes' schema to lament that there are negative consequences in its application. Lesslie Newbigin in *Foolishness to the Greeks* worries about this trend. If the world "… is to be understood in terms of efficient causes and not of final causes, not governed by an intelligible purpose", then it will result in "…a world in which the answer to the question of what is good has to be left to the private opinion of each individual, and cannot be included in the body of accepted facts that control public life" (79). Ongoing dialogue between church and science can help ensure that satellites in space, for instance, become effective means of communication rather than instruments of mass destruction. Although research itself should conform to objective pursuit of data, the application of research should enter into a conversation with spiritual and religious considerations.

Third Theme: Human rights, and the extension of personal liberties, must be offset both by awareness of responsibility to others and by a Christian emphasis on renouncing privileges and rights for the sake of service to others. Paul Ramsey states it this way.

> Christian ethics brings about a radical shift of emphasis with regard to 'rights'. It seeks to accomplish the shift from rights to duties, from claiming to giving one's own, from teleological

motivation for doing good to doing good to all men on account of motivation from behind. When a man stands most in the image of God... he is least concerned about his own value. (353,354)

A Christian who receives freedom through the grace of Jesus Christ does not believe it necessary to always utilize for one's own sake the rights provided by civic authority. That may seem pointless and contradictory to one who sees rights only as a self-expression of liberty.

However, the primary viewpoint of a Christian is to serve those in greater need. In scripture we find that belief in verses like Galatians 5:13: "For you were called to freedom; only do not use your freedom as an opportunity for self-indulgence, but through love become slaves to one another." If your temporary surrender of a right will work to the betterment of another, Christ asks you to make that choice.

Significantly, Ramsey sees that this attitude can redirect us toward an entirely different perspective on why rights are important. He explains, "A right is a claim on the part of the individual to use a certain ability or power he has for the public good..." Hence, "A man cannot claim a right for himself alone, just because he likes things that way; rather he claims it as a member of society contributing to the general welfare" (358,359). If the church can instill this more comprehensive view of rights into society, then persistent legal battles between people claiming their rights against one another will diminish.

Fourth Theme: While it is indubitably true that human life has improved in many areas, i.e. that recent history has been progress, it is far less certain that equal progress is present in morality, in the ethical treatment of others. The Christian doctrine of original sin provides insight into that perception. Reinhold Niebuhr addresses this dynamic in most of his writings, primarily in *Faith and History*. Chapter VI of that volume, entitled "The Identification of Freedom and Virtue in Modern Views of History", assesses modernity's proclivity to believe that rational freedom is the sufficient cure for all society's ills. He begins:

> An honest error has indeed contributed to the confusion of our culture. It did discover the fact of historical growth and it did see that specific evils, due to specific forms of human impotence, may be overcome by the growth of human power; and that particular evils due to human ignorance may be overcome by the growth of man's intelligence; and it may well have been led astray by this evidence to the false conclusion that all human problems were being solved by historical development. (98)

He draws a distinction between modernity's ability to solve problems of physical nature vs. those of human nature. While an increase in free reason may well discover a vaccine for polio or a means of channeling a raging river toward a hydroelectric dam, it will have far less success in restricting the nationalist pride that prompts wars of aggression or runaway capitalist acquisitiveness. Niebuhr unveils modernity's inability to recognize this distinction and other "inconvenient and embarrassing facts about human nature." Its optimism about human abilities

> ...was an evasion both of the dimension of responsibility in human nature and of the fact of guilt. It made man the judge of his world and of himself.... It refuted the embarrassing suspicion

that man himself is the author of the historical evils which beset him. (99)

Why are we still the authors of these historical evils? It is because we have not yet recognized that there exists within all humanity an entrenched self-centeredness, an original sin overcome only by gracious forgiveness and a life-long prayerful effort to train one's will, body and mind toward sanctification in the image of Jesus Christ. In Niebuhr's words, "That the recalcitrance of the human heart should not be simply the lag of nature but a corruption of freedom and should not be overcome by increasing freedom: this is the mystery of original sin" (101). Let the church therefore recognize that it can celebrate accomplishments that sustain the belief in progress while also insisting on the inadequacy of rational freedom to address fundamental questions of personal good and evil.

Fifth Theme: This theme furthers the implications of the previous paragraph. Because Christians believe that time and space are created, i.e. limited by something beyond them, we affirm that history itself will never be a sufficient judge of what is right and wrong. The church must remind its hearers that God stands beyond time as the final arbiter of truth. Since the rise of Hegel's sense of progressive history, it has become commonplace to use the term "history will be the judge of that". It is intriguing to observe how often such a phrase replaces a more traditional comment that God will judge our actions. Doubtless, we are not fully satisfied with the ancient formidable picture of *Christos Pantokrator* ruling over heaven and earth, sending sheep and goats to different realms. Nonetheless, to replace God as judge with history as judge implies that we only need to move further ahead to the next decade or century to recognize what was right or wrong about a previous momentous decision. Admittedly, such an idea might eventually provide some semblance of justification for particular actions. We presume, 170 years later, that the Civil War was a just cause despite its significant costs. Still, such verdicts will always be subject to revision and uncertainty. Could the government have achieved liberation of the slaves through a slower but less violent economic compensation and resettlement program, as some historians have suggested?

Niebuhr addresses the uncertainty of answers provided by future history alone through examining the biblical parable about the weeds sown among the wheat. The workers want to rip up the weeds to save the wheat, but the landowner has the greater wisdom, to wait until the harvest, when the difference will be clearer. Otherwise, you will ruin the good grain now infiltrated by weeds. Certainly,

> Insofar as increasing freedom leads to harmonies of life...a positive meaning can be assigned to growth in history.... But this truth is transmuted into error very quickly if it is assumed that increasing freedom assures the achievement of the wider task. The perils of freedom rise with its promises, and the perils and promises are inextricably interwoven.... There is, in other words, no possibility of a final judgement within history but only at the end of history.... Faith awaits a final judgement and a final resurrection. Thus mystery stands at the end, as well as at the beginning, of the whole pilgrimage of man. (232,233)

We see here his skepticism about all who feel that a well-intentioned humanity will bring an end to history by improving the world so much that it establishes God's kingdom on earth. No, God remains transcendent beyond history, eternal judge and redeemer for all creation.

Sixth Theme: Utilitarianism forms the primary ethical system of modern society, fueled by the need to win the popular vote in elections. The Christian church must continue to advocate and practice an ethic of sacrificial discipleship that transcends and limits purely utilitarian measures of what is good. In the early 19th century, Jeremy Bentham and J.S. Mill formalized a standard for beneficial legislation and private behavior. Its goal was attaining "the greatest good for the greatest number"; its method was to calculate the "utility" of any act to determine its effect on others. What enhances pleasure and diminishes pain in any action has utility. Bentham then created a "hedonic calculus" to measure utility. It considered the duration of an action's effect, its intensity, its level of certainty, its long-term vs. short-term results, and the breadth of how many it affects. Mill enhanced Bentham's work by refining a distinction between personal and social utility and by recognizing that some pursuits eventually bring more happiness although they may take more patience and temporary suffering to attain it.

However, attention to the underlying workings of utilitarianism reveals that what is supposedly a conscientious quest for widespread general happiness ultimately shipwrecks on the rock of individual self-service. Utilitarianism tries to establish what is good for others based on what is good for oneself. The "common good" really is just enlightened self-interest; in other words, you seek the good of others because in the end it will be to your benefit also. In the first place, however, it is somewhat naïve to assume that people who desire their own happiness will also desire the happiness of others just because they sense that they cannot be fully happy unless everyone is happy. Yet, even more dangerous is the subtle assumption that you can regularly do what is good for others by doing what you want for yourself.

Certainly, enlightened self-interest is better than pure impulsive hedonism. Many benefits accrue to society by extending the boundaries of awareness beyond immediate personal needs. Utilitarian legislation has its purposes. But by itself, this will never establish true, cooperative community. Real community, undiminished concern for the good of others, will only occur when we care for other persons purely for their own sakes, regardless of the effect on us. This selfless caring is what Christians call *agape*. It is love born out of the plenitude of divine grace rather than the need to receive something in return. It is forgetful of one's visible security; it gives instead of craves, sacrifices instead of acquires. It regards neighbor first and only much later how one's action affects oneself. It seeks as its model the incarnate, crucified and risen Christ, not the sophisticated idealist who believes self-interest can initiate the common good. Only when the world sees this kind of love in action will it glimpse a form of existence that transcends common reasoning and purifies the motives of those who must try to balance selfish interests into workable relationships or legislation. The greatest gift that the church can give to society is to live as much as possible in the footsteps of its Lord, unconcerned that the world may regard such obedience as unenlightened and immature.

The prior six themes present ways that the church of Jesus Christ can speak clearly to western society in the modern world, curbing its excesses and guiding its virtues toward what is finally best for humanity. As always, the overarching purpose of the church is to serve and glorify God in all relationships, in families and friendships, neighborhoods and cities, public and private. Still, in the 21st century, its greatest calling may be to serve as a vocal and active counterpoint, an alternative perspective, to governmental, educational, and economic institutions. All organizations function best when they do not regard themselves as the ultimate authority. Lord Acton spoke presciently when he declared that power corrupts and absolute power corrupts absolutely. The church, which stands both within and without contemporary society, possesses the message and the motivation to remind society's powers of this enduring truth. The church can visibly proclaim to government that an authority higher than public approval judges its decisions. The church can insist to educators that knowledge offers its best results when seen within a tradition of wisdom. The church can challenge economists to see that capital gain without moral restrictions will impoverish everyone.

No institution, no being, should assume final and absolute power except the one Being that is equipped to handle it with complete justice and mercy. The church must proclaim that belief, that principle, loudly and repeatedly in the public square, becoming prophets as well as priests. Our incarnate yet transcendent God stands both within modern culture and beyond it. One stance allows Christ to work through the beneficial human institutions created over the last 500 years. The other stance allows Christ to limit, judge, and redeem modernity, with all its promise and its perils. This is the basis on which the church reframes and restates its primary "definitions of reality" as it meets the challenges of modernity. How the church can also respond to the newly emerging challenges of Postmodernism is the topic of Part Two.

PART TWO

POSTMODERNISM

| five |

Overview and Setting; Five Central Themes of Postmodernism

Describing postmodernism is difficult. It is young, in process, and unfinished, thus precluding an observer's overarching perspective. It is both an extension and a repudiation of Modernity. It derives its meaning more from what it is not than from what it is. Its impact is multi-faceted, affecting art, science, philosophy, religion and politics. It lacks unity, and sees little reason to worry about that. Moreover, even its proponents disagree on how thoroughly to employ it. Still, worthy attempts to describe this maturing philosophic movement exist, including that of Professor Lawrence Cahoone, editor of *From Modernism to Postmodernism*, a Blackwell anthology. Cahoone also is The Great Courses lecturer in "The Modern Intellectual Tradition: From Descartes to Derrida". The majority of this chapter will rely on these works to bring order to this freewheeling subject, thereby perhaps doing a disservice to the very nature of postmodernism. Cahoone suggests five interrelated themes, which

I will utilize, explain, and summarize. Prior to expounding these themes, however, it will be helpful to elaborate the larger context in which those elements arose.

A Century of Background

One of the ironies of modern history is this: Precisely when the larger public begins to benefit from scientific and social developments whose origins are decades or centuries old, a small collection of farsighted critics senses flaws in those developments that will eventually diminish their benefits and, as the expression goes, take the shine off the apple. Most practical benefits deriving from new theories of the 17th and 18th centuries did not reach the ordinary family home until well into the 19th. By that time, a smattering of intellectual opinion had begun questioning certain fundamental assumptions of modernity. While it is a clear overstatement to claim that modernity had sown the seeds of its own destruction, it had at least sown some seeds of doubt.

Despite early Napoleonic wars in Europe and a devastating civil war in America, the 19th century became an era of optimistic progress. Hegel's Idealist march of history toward full self-consciousness, the spread of western civilization through colonial empires, the wondrous advances in medicine, transportation and education, plus the productive factories of the industrial revolution, all increased an incipient belief that the world was headed in the right direction, and gaining speed with every generation. Descartes, Bacon, and royal academies in France and England had brought clarity to the process of research. The song of freedom, sounded by Locke and the French *philosophes*, spread toward all social classes. J.S. Mill's and Jeremy Bentham's Utilitarianism systematized how to bring the greatest good to the greatest number. The Enlightenment of the few was becoming a light for the masses.

Yet, "voices in the wilderness" arose in the mid-19th century that questioned and even belittled such optimism. The brief career of Soren Kierkegaard repeatedly challenged the prevailing view of rationality exemplified in Hegel's attempt to combine faith and reason. Hegel's grand scheme domesticated both miracles and radical personal choice, whereas Kierkegaard insisted that faith and reason intrinsically oppose one another, requiring a courageous decision to believe. In the "gloomy Dane's" observations lie the roots of 20th century Existentialism and the "Theology of Crisis" of Karl Barth and others. Later in the century, the biting critiques of Friedrich Nietzsche excoriated metaphysics. Nietzsche believed that metaphysics hid a deeper reality behind artificial categories. He lambasted Christianity for undermining healthy human instincts and demeaning "this-worldly" existence for the sake of so-called heavenly reward. He even attacked the very notion of objective truth and goodness. As we will note later, many proponents of postmodernism look back to Nietzsche for seminal ideas.

A slightly different perspective arose as Karl Marx and Friedrich Engels watched industrial society bring a flood of peasants and farmers to factory floors and mineral mines. Their responses in the *Communist Manifesto* and *Das Kapital* foreshadow the ambiguity of later postmodernism. Outwardly, Marx and Engels seemed to oppose modern developments, clearly criticizing the alienation and exploitation of laborers required by the machine of capitalism. Their Feuerbach-inspired unmasking of religion as a projection of human desires starkly contrasted with the comfortable deistic natural religion fostered by Newtonian physics. On the other hand, even though they morphed Hegel's idealism into materialism, they embraced wholeheartedly his progressive notion of dialectical movement in history. Marx did not protest the technological and mechanical wonders wrought by modern science and engineering, but simply their oppressive misuse in the economic system. He did not wish to turn back the clock to a pristine era of agriculture, but rather to forge ahead through class conflict to a future classless society. Furthermore, the "meta-narrative" of Marxism was the economic equivalent of natural laws and mathematical schema that fueled modernity. Postmodern critics would later reject both.

These early intellectual protests, however, whether blunt or ambiguous in their criticism, do not explain the deep skepticism about modernity that emerged in the first decades of the 20th century. For that, we need look no further than the devastation brought by World War I, the Great Depression, and a second war more deadly than the first. Death by mustard gas, starvation, and atomic bomb speaks with a clarity no isolated philosophic debate can even imagine. Modernity's ideology had promised perpetual progress toward happiness if only the world would continue to implement the new holy trinity: increased access to education, rational application of scientific discoveries and extension of personal freedom. But the shell-shocked masses that lived between 1914 and 1945 witnessed atrocities perpetrated by highly educated, cultured classes, science rationally applied to gas chambers and carpet bombing, plus personal freedom in pursuit of wealth that led to economic collapse, a plague of suicides, and displaced, impoverished families. Europe by the end of World War II lay in ruins structurally, economically, politically, and most of all, emotionally. Is it any wonder that the western world was ready to re-examine the presuppositions of its prior beliefs, and think twice before reinstating the seductive dream of modernity? America may have seemed an exception; it emerged as the dominant world power, started an optimistic baby boom, and postponed stark skepticism for another generation. Nonetheless, a reevaluation of modernity had long hovered below the surface, and would erupt in the 1960s, first at the Sorbonne in Paris, then across the rest of the western world. Five components of postmodernism emerged to claim public attention.

Dimensions of Postmodernism

The themes named in Professor Lawrence Cahoone's summary, pp. 9-12 of his introduction:

1. Postmodernism emphasizes the complexity of meaning. Objects, people, language, history, and most everything else are interconnected with such complexity that any "metanarrative", any simple, final, comprehensive definition of them, will be misleading and inaccurate.
2. Everything we attempt to know is heavily mediated by signs, language, and interpretation. Such filters bewilder human attempts at observation. As one seminal voice of postmodernism says, "Presentation presupposes representation."
3. Postmodernism therefore also maintains that knowledge is humanly constructed. Building on Immanuel Kant's first Critique, cognition is an active, structure-imposing process. Postmodernists are "constructivists".
4. Hence, objectivity based on external standards is impossible. In both modern and pre-modern methods of knowing, the separation of observer from object distorts perception, because the norms used to judge things are themselves conditioned by the processes they are judging.
5. Finally, postmodernism claims that anything, an individual person, a word, a philosophical system or social class,

establishes its identity through exclusion, separation and repression. Analysis of any system will reveal the dark side of its identity.

The vivisection of postmodernism into these five themes obscures their epistemological connecting thread. "What, why, and how do we know?" remains, as in modernity, an enduring question for postmoderns. If the following treatment of these themes overlaps and intersects, it is because writers of this era answer the epistemological question from slightly different perspectives, with slightly different consequences for society. Epistemology can be a dark forest with twisting paths; some lead nowhere, some end back at the starting point, and some head toward the same destination but by different routes. Therefore, dear reader, since ours will at times be a laborious journey, let us begin with a little levity in the form of a well-worn parable about baseball umpires.

Three professional umpires sat in heavy dispute around their postgame beers, debating perspectives on the critical job of calling balls and strikes behind the plate. The first umpire was straightforward and traditional: "I call them as they are. If it is a ball, I call it a ball. If it is a strike, I call it a strike. What's the problem?" The second umpire was slightly more circumspect: "Well, I call them as I see them. One pitch might have actually been a ball, but from my angle, I didn't see it that way. Another might have been a strike on the corner, but I could have blinked just as it passed the plate." The third umpire, youngest of the three, was decidedly postmodern: "What are you two jabbering about? They ain't nothing 'til I call them. What I call them, that's what they are!"

This parable retells the phases of philosophic debate about epistemology. A pre-modern "realist" view of knowledge believes there is a real object witnessed, an objective, substantial fact discernable by close observation. Truth occurs when an opinion corresponds to the substantial object. A more modern view of knowledge still believes in a real, external fact, but as John Locke would note, we can only accurately know our *perception* of that object, and have no final assurance that we are right. The constructivist postmodern perspective has abandoned any faith in a real object; it believes that its perception determines the reality, or at least what passes for reality. These observations are, of course, gross generalizations, but they nonetheless grant perspective on the interconnected themes that arise and interact on the journey through the forest of postmodernism in the following pages.

Central Themes of Postmodernism

The Complexity of Meaning

The public, disappointed and disillusioned by the world wars and the Depression, sought answers for why the grand schemes of modernity had failed. Newton's mathematically precise mechanistic science had revealed its vulnerability to misuse for deadly purposes. Kant's rational ethic of the categorical imperative seemed powerless in the face of nationalist ideology. Hegel's dialectical march of history toward self-actualization self-destructed in the totalitarian nation he had predicted as the pinnacle of progress. Marx's economic materialism ended in Stalinist purges and gulags. All these scientific and political grand schemes, these "meta-narratives", had over-simplified and over-idealized what humanity could accomplish. They were tragically mistaken about the complexity of meaning, unable to account for unforeseen consequences in their flawed systems.

A *Course in General Linguistics,* published in the first decade of the 20th century by the Swiss linguist Ferdinand de Saussure, had already explored one possible explanation for the failure of the metanarratives and the resultant anxiety about modernity's philosophical presuppositions. Saussure delved into the origin and function of language. Meaning is complex, he insists, because it is a social enterprise rather than an isolated individual perception. Because meaning is conveyed through language, it requires a complicated process of relating a word to all other uses of it. The epistemological realism that guided philosophy since antiquity had presumed that language was a simple process of naming, corresponding a word to the idea or thing the word represents.

In Saussure's opinion, such realism is mistaken, because "it assumes that ready-made ideas exist before words" and because "it lets us assume that the linking of a name and a thing is a very simple operation – an assumption that is anything but true" (122). Saussure emphasizes that a word, a linguistic sign, "unites, not a thing and a name, but a concept and a sound-image." His point is that names and concepts ("signifier" and "signified" are his terms) exist within a linguistic system that affects their meaning. "Language has neither ideas nor sounds that existed before the linguistic system but only conceptual and phonic differences that have issued from the system." Language is a multi-faceted enterprise involving a combination of references to the way a word is used. "In fact, every means of expression used in society is based, in principle, on collective behavior or – what amounts to the same thing – on convention" (123). Insofar as we can understand a word at all, we must interpret it through the totality of its use. A sign, a "signifier", will always be defined and limited by the differences between it and the other signs around it. Summarizing his point, Saussure says, "language being what it is, we shall find nothing simple in it regardless of our approach; everywhere and always there is the same complex equilibrium of terms that mutually condition each other" (126).

Saussure's multi-faceted view of language, upon which conveyed meaning is dependent, diminishes one's confidence in vast systems and surefire schemes of science or history. We must postpone conclusions until the wide range of meaning in each key word is fully examined for unforeseen nuances. Otherwise, the metanarrative omits the voice of neglected partners in the conversation, with later repercussions. Certainty is farther off than confident Enlightenment thinkers presumed.

Saussure's appeal to greater linguistic patience coalesces with another tendency that undermines the certainty of modern metanarratives, and that tendency actually hides within the mechanism of one such grand scheme – *Hegelian dialectic*. Here again, postmodernists recognize that some of modernity's own inclinations undermine its optimistic confidence when they are extended beyond their original intention. To Hegel, truth will always be conditional and incomplete until it is revealed further along the path of history's moving journey. The dialectic is dynamic. An idea and its opposite arrive through their conflict at a more satisfactory synthesis, blending the best of both prior states into a resolution that seems complete. Yet, it is only complete for the moment. Inevitably, an antithesis arises to oppose the new synthesis, and the truth and meaning it conveyed is challenged, relativized, and resolved again into something hitherto unknown. Meaning therefore is also complex because it is never finished. Any description of a current state of affairs will always change in the light of future developments. One must accept the inadequacy of any attempt to discern reliable information through descriptions that correspond to objects. Only a larger view of truth, *viz*. ultimate coherence with the dynamic scheme, of which any fact is only one part, could convey the meaning of that fact. Yet, such an enterprise will always be unfinished. Certainty dwindles as conclusions constantly change according to new developments and a new audience.

One may even speculate that enduring facts are intrinsically outdated once a dynamic view of history becomes the dominant philosophy. If Darwin's observations on natural selection demonstrate that even nature's species are not fixed, that evolution alters even this physical sphere, how can we expect that language and its ability to describe anything accurately will remain reliable across time? Each new generation - perhaps each individual within each generation - will need to redefine an event or idea according to the latest developments in his or her life, and find what works for them. Facing this possibility and indeed embracing it, Jean-Francois Lyotard, one prominent postmodernist, advocates a stance (summarized by Cahoone) that:

> postmodern culture no longer needs any form of legitimation beyond expediency or "performativity". Lyotard analyzes the production of knowledge in science, as well as the discourse of everyday social life, in terms of discontinuity, plurality, and "paralogy" (logically unjustified conclusions). (259)

The metanarratives that once legitimized scientific discoveries and their social consequences lose their authority and their effectiveness. As they diminish, they take with them the certainty and confidence that marked 17th century science and 19th century culture. Meaning is too complex for easy optimism about the future. Postmodernists warn that we must be prepared to live with greater uncertainty.

Language and Mediated Knowledge

Although Professor Cahoone designates this theme as a separate category of postmodernism, it is in many respects simply a focused intensification of the ideas raised in the previous category on the complexity of meaning. The author examined in this current section, Jacques Derrida, stands out as the pre-eminent postmodernist in the field of language. The best descriptive term for Derrida's work is Poststructuralism, which begs the question of what is the "structuralism" that Derrida then extends. Let us review that background. It further explains how postmodernists turn away from some presuppositions of modernity, though it also foreshadows the complicated, often contradictory strains that constitute the wide boundaries of postmodernism.

One very broad category that characterizes modern philosophy is its focus on the human subject as the source of meaning. From Descartes' inward turn in the *Meditations*, when he considers and resolves the doubts in his own mind, to Freud's analysis of the human psyche nearly 300 years later, philosophers of modernity looked at the logic, epistemology, and emotions of human consciousness as the place to find the structure of knowledge. Despite obvious variety throughout those centuries, a common thread of the modern enterprise was to investigate how individual minds organize and define the experiences they encounter in the world around them. This *philosophy of the subject*, as it has been termed, believed that meaning comes first to the human subject and then manifests itself in the language, culture, and relationships around it.

Structuralism turned that perspective on its head, emphasizing that the culture, the language, the social structures of life, define the self rather than the other way around. Ferdinand de Saussure, featured in the previous paragraphs, foreshadowed structuralism, but the primary proponent was the wide-ranging German philosopher Ernst Cassirer. Cassirer reflected on Kant's epistemological framework, with its structures of the human mind that shape the meaning of external impressions. But he took those structures and went in a new direction. It is symbols and signs, Cassirer claims, that primarily construct reality, and those are present in cultural institutions like language, religion, science, and art. (A "sign" is simply a collective term for words, utterances, images, pictures, etc. "Semiotics" is the study of signs.) We will gain a better understanding of reality, of the way knowledge arises, if we concentrate on the signs that exist in those public realms rather than on the inner workings of the human consciousness. The structures, the systems, in which these signs operate, provide the clues to knowledge. This opens up the boundaries of the epistemological laboratory to vast new arenas of research and shifts the focus away from the human subject to the broad environment in which one lives. When anthropologist Claude Levi-Strauss applied this structuralist scheme to artifacts from varied cultures, he reinforced the idea that the meaning of signs and symbols is always part of an observable community process, rather than being dependent on some faculty within one's own consciousness.

Those who followed structuralism, however, examined it thoroughly and determined that it can be used against itself. That is precisely what Jacques Derrida, the poststructuralist, showed. Cassirer and Levi-Strauss, intentionally or otherwise, had seemed to move philosophy beyond language itself onto an observable world of culture and its measurable manifestations. However, any possible move toward scientific measurement of these phenomena is cut short when Derrida applies structuralist tactics against itself. He emphasizes that any sign or symbol, even when immersed in an observable artifact or cultural institution, is still extremely complex in meaning. It is *polysemic*. Derrida explains that any encounter with a sign requires one to read both its *synchronic* and *diachronic* meaning. It is diachronic because it has a history, and one must evaluate its meaning in the many former manifestations of itself through past generations. It is synchronic because at the very moment it is spoken, it has an extended relationship to many other signs that help define it. Derrida recalls Saussure's awareness that the differences among its many options determine the meaning of a particular sign. Therefore, the multiple differences also have to be examined and compared to the current use for a sign to become clear in its meaning. Citing how a dictionary defines a word by referring it to other words with identical or similar meaning, Derrida implies that if you look beneath and beyond any particular sign you will see that its reference to these other signs is what actually constitutes the meaning of a sign. A sign's meaning, Derrida famously states, is always non-present. Inevitably, (this will arise again in our look at postmodernism's final dimension) Derrida then shows that to use a sign and give it a specific meaning requires you to repress all other uses of that sign. All our contact with the world is through signs, and all of our signs represent one choice of the many options of meaning for that sign. Here is the origin of Derrida's famous dictum: "presentation presupposes representation" (Cahoone, intro. *From Modernism...* 10).

Derrida next turns toward examining philosophical statements and "deconstructing" them. He creates a novel French word *differance* that is not spelled like but is pronounced exactly like the common French word "difference" (a, vs. e). (Cahoone, 225ff.). Derrida uses this tactic to reveal how writing down something on paper, to be read for later generations, is an irrevocable and unchangeable act, compared to speaking, which is momentary and usually more personal. Philosophical writing, which intends to reach a wide audience, must seek to control the meaning of a word, tries to fix its meaning forever. Given his observations about diachronic and synchronic meaning, Derrida says it is impossible to do this. In a wide-ranging series of articles, he examines different philosophical statements and theories. By taking key words and showing their ambiguity, the way ideas cannot be understood without their opposites, he reiterates the complex, dialectical nature of any text, especially philosophical theories which try to pin down words and meanings for fixed purposes. His work in this area supported other attacks on any kind of "foundational" philosophic theories and metanarratives.

Apparently, toward the end of his life Derrida acknowledged that we cannot escape from trying to clarify ideas by using one sign instead of another and trying to fix one meaning of a sign. It is a necessary enterprise as one seeks to communicate clearly, and we must of course try to do so. However, he also re-emphasized that we will never ultimately succeed in this. His primary contribution to postmodernism is the insistence that all language and all knowledge are mediated by choices, distant influences, and implied, hidden presuppositions. He profoundly affected literary criticism.

Constructivism and Freedom

Readers of this chapter thus far have encountered three similar and interconnected terms: structuralism, post-structuralism, and deconstruction. Keeping them straight requires a good memory and intellectual discipline. At the risk of further confusion, we examine now a fourth related word: *constructivism*. Simply put, it means that primarily human consciousness constructs, rather than receives, knowledge. Derrida would "deconstruct" philosophies that have excluded the complexities of language and neglected their own presuppositions because he would wish to reveal how all knowledge is "constructed" by human consciousness rather than implanted by the external objects one perceives.

As a further illustration that postmodernism often extends themes of modernity, constructivism arises from the conclusions of Immanuel Kant's *Critique of Pure Reason*. Recall (cf. Part I, Ch. 3) how Kant had affirmed that in the human consciousness are categories of thought that order phenomena as they reach the mind and allow us to turn random impressions into useable information. This saving tactic seemed to rescue certainty in the scientific enterprise and its ability to turn isolated facts into unifying theories. In the same Critique, and as part of the same explanation, Kant stated that behind these organizing categories there is a supra-sensible reality, the noumena.

As we have seen, however, it did not take long for the slightly younger contemporary of Kant's, Johann Gottlieb Fichte, to declare a fatal flaw in Kant's arrangement. Fichte admired Kant's transcendental idealism, and went to visit him, but left their conversation not completely satisfied. The logic of Kant's system implied that the human mind actually determined what is real and what is not, since it is the filtering of perceptions through these categories that make them trustworthy and meaningful. Kant, though, had taken this direction no further; Fichte had no such hesitation. He made the radical suggestion that we should simply give up any conception of a noumenal realm and accept that human consciousness is not based on anything outside of itself. There are no "things in themselves", no supra-sensible dimension, only that which we have ourselves determined and structured according to our mind's categories. Self-consciousness defines reality; let us be honest about it, he would say. Once we admit that we can know nothing except our perceptions of objects, and that it requires our own mind to decide what the meaning of those perceptions will be, there is no other option than constructivism, Fichte argued. Certainly, he did emphasize the social nature of consciousness, for an individual encounters others, and thereby accepts limits on one's own freedom to assert one's interpretation. But that dialogue reinforced rather than diminished an individual's awareness of constructivist freedom, since the only reason to limit freedom is out of respect for someone else's freedom.

Not every commentator on Kant in the early 19th century agreed with Fichte's conclusion that the logic of Kant's system necessarily leads to constructivism. His argument that human consciousness has no grounding in anything outside itself was an overextension, claimed Fichte's student Arthur Schopenhauer. Nonetheless, Fichte's insight seemed to carry the day, with significant impact on Hegel, Nietzsche, structuralism, and eventually the postmodernists.

A connection also exists between Fichte's constructivist perspective and existentialism, especially the definitive phrase of Jean Paul Sartre: "existence precedes essence", stated in the seminal essay called "Existentialism is a Humanism" (vii). The phrase means that one's personal existence and choice precede any inherent nature or identity. It is the opposite of metaphysics, which implies that a divine plan or an eternal nature precedes one's existence, as a *given*, to which one conforms. In a similar lecture, "Existentialism" Sartre declares: "Man is nothing else but what he makes of himself.... We mean that man first exists, that is, that man first of all is the being who hurls himself toward a future and who is conscious of imagining himself as being in the future."

Therefore, using an explicit definition of "subjectivism", Sartre explains, "...it is impossible for man to transcend human subjectivity." (169)

Like Fichte before him, however, this radical freedom to choose is a social act, not isolated individualism. In the act of choosing, one becomes completely responsible for that choice, aware of the effects it will have on other people. The choice defines not just oneself, but what one expects all people to be. "Our responsibility is much greater than we might have supposed, because it involves all mankind." This can create anxiety, anguish, once one realizes the weight of that responsibility. Sartre summarizes his philosophy in a paragraph from the same lecture:

> If existence really does precede essence, there is no explaining things away by reference to a fixed and given human nature. In other words, there is no determinism, man is free, man is freedom. On the other hand, if God does not exist, we find no values or commands to turn to which legitimize our conduct. So, in the bright realm of values, we have no excuse behind us, nor justification before us. We are alone, with no excuses. ("Existentialism", 171)

Explicit postmodernists distance themselves from Sartre for what they term his glamorizing of a "heroic subjectivism", his occasional support for the metanarrative of Marxism, and because his philosophy neglects the complexity of communication in language. Still, as will be seen in the following section, the constructivism of postmodernism shares with Sartre at least the general sense that existence precedes essence, even if a Derrida or Lyotard would step back from utilizing that idea as an explanatory scheme.

The Immanence of Norms

From this book's earlier chapters, you can discern that postmodern thinkers reject any attempt to justify knowledge by basing it on direct correspondence of a description to an object. The philosophical realism associated with this method requires an external reference point that purports to provide a foundation, a basic starting point on which perceptions depend. We might think of this external foundation as eternal forms that provide archetypes (Plato), stable universal laws of Nature (Newton), or the God whom we can trust not to deceive us (Descartes). No matter: any philosophy ancient or modern will now come under the microscope of postmodernism's deconstructionist critique. Writers like Derrida, Foucault, and Lyotard are clearly anti-foundational. The external-internal split implied in the dualism of another realm parallel to or preceding this one, plus a second dualism when an objective observer stands apart from and looks at an object, create an untenable situation in the eyes of postmodern thinkers. In the words of Professor Cahoone:

> ...dualism often functions in a philosophical system to put the means by which we know and judge things *outside* the things judged, e.g., by making the validity of the rules of reason or morality *independent* of nature or human convention. Normative immanence in contrast asserts that the norms we use to judge processes are *themselves products of the processes they judge.* (p.11)

If a philosophy, whether epistemological or ethical, begins its argument with an appeal to an "outside other" as a fundamental starting point, deconstructionists will challenge the ambiguity of its language, reveal its self-serving rationalizations and expose the social relations that led to its supposedly irreproachable foundation.

Where did this opposition to an external authority originate? Enlightenment principles from Kant, Fichte, and Hegel might have set the stage for a next step, but the revolutionary philosophy of Friedrich Nietzsche actually took it. Postmodernists like Michel Foucault explicitly use him as a springboard for their thought. In the late 19th century, Nietzsche provided a persistent, biting critique of epistemology, morality, and truth. Commentators on Nietzsche identify two themes in his thought that combine to make him the progenitor of postmodernism: his critique of metaphysics and his insistence that language necessarily falsifies reality.

From the early "Truth and Lies in an Nonmoral Sense", through ...*Zarathustra*, and then *The Genealogy of Morals*, Nietzsche insisted that there is nothing "meta" about metaphysics. Such attempts to found meaning on a being or essence outside the sheer physical facts are illusory. Morality is not based on unchangeable laws handed down from God on Mt. Sinai, but is self-created for the sake of "pleasant, life-preserving consequences". Morality arises from a slave mentality that postpones gratification to an afterlife because one is too powerless to improve things now and too cowardly to try. Moreover, the very concept of a permanent truth is a false projection,

> [a] moveable host of metaphors, metonymies, and anthropomorphisms: in short, a sum of human relations which have been poetically and rhetorically intensified, transferred and embellished, and which, after long usage, seem to a people to be fixed, canonical, and binding. Truths are illusions which we have forgotten are illusions.... (*"Truth and Lies..."* 112)

What one party in an argument sees as careful use of critical reason appealing to a lasting standard, the wiser party knows to be a mere rationalization of one's will trying to create a self-serving power. The standards by which we judge right and wrong or good and evil are not transcendent. They are within the human will. What matters more than the apparent "truth" of a claim, i.e. its apparent correlation to a state of affairs, is whether the belief is life affirming and allows the actor to feel strong, free and fulfilled.

Secondly, Nietzsche's academic training in classics and philology convinced him that evaluation of languages should be at the center of philosophical thinking. This alone will reveal the "immanence of norms". With a slight variation in emphasis, Nietzsche foreshadowed postmodern linguists, contending that by using language we artificially order and simplify experiences, distorting them, robbing them of their original power. He criticized the use of "concepts" to categorize groups of individual experiences. Again from *"Truth and Lies..."*: "We obtain the concept, as we do the form, by overlooking what is individual and actual, whereas nature is acquainted with no forms and no concepts, and likewise with no species, but only with an X which remains inaccessible and undefinable for us" (112).

Nietzsche seems to acknowledge that humans face an inevitable dilemma, similar to that admitted by Derrida noted above. The concepts and forms that are so convenient in measuring and identifying objects are part of a "fundamental human drive which one cannot for a single instant dispense with in thought, for one would thereby dispense with man himself." But alas, through this drive, "a regular and rigid new world is constructed as its prison from its own ephemeral products, the concepts" (114,115). Required by the need to communicate beyond isolated exclamations, human language nonetheless distorts, over-simplifies and traps the fullness of a singular event within misleading abstractions. Language falsifies the urgent, primitive experience into which Nietzsche so much wants to be drawn. Knowing that this falsification occurs unmasks all attempts to ground our beliefs in standards outside of ourselves. All norms are immanent, part of the internal process of human perception.

One might wonder why these stinging criticisms from Nietzsche took 75 years before postmodern authors adopted, adapted, and popularized them. The delay likely occurred because his fierce assault threatened the strongest institutions of society. Aside from his stark challenge to the entrenched church and its religious morality, Nietzsche also undercut the irreproachable scientific objectivity that had guided research since Newton. Newton's universal laws of gravitation in science matched religion's external authority of a heavenly God. One does not give up such "transcendent" norms lightly.

Developments in both fields in the 19th and early 20th centuries, however, indicate a budding awareness that, since the Enlightenment, metaphysics can no longer legitimately undergird faith, whether that be faith in an external authoritative God or in unchangeable mechanistic laws of physics. Protestant liberalism turned toward the study of history and internal feelings of dependence to buttress convictions. Indeed, decades before Nietzsche, Friedrich Schleiermacher announced that new direction. Likewise in science, theories of relativity demonstrated that (at least in extreme situations) Newton's laws did not apply. Quantum physics similarly overturned certainty about atomic structure, especially when Heisenberg's Uncertainty Principle demonstrated how changes in observation affect changes in perception. Recognition that the "immanence of norms" challenges even sacred fields of science and religion played its part in slowing the march of Nietzsche's insights forward into explicit postmodernism.

Analysis of Privileged Power

Postmodernism, since its explicit emergence in Paris of the 1960s, has influenced fields of philosophy, art and architecture, and linguistics. It contributed to philosophy's growing suspicion of *foundationalism*, opened up new fields of unrestrained expression to artists and new visions for architects, and furthered critical examination of language forms in literature and conversation. But by far the most public, political impact of postmodernism lies in its analysis of power, specifically how words, concepts, conventions, and public institutions unconsciously establish and maintain entrenched power for dominant, privileged groups. This truly revolutionary new direction draws upon insights from four sources. From Nietzsche comes the idea that language falsifies reality and projects power. From de Saussure comes the awareness that the key to the meaning of something is all the differences that distinguish it. From structuralism comes the emphasis that the semiotic frameworks of culture and language more reliably reflect meaning than does an examination of human consciousness. And especially, from Derrida comes the conclusion that to emphasize one meaning of a sign you must repress others. The predominant representative of this new direction is Michel Foucault, who draws these various insights together. The predominant expression of this analysis is its critique of the systematic and entrenched oppression of racial/ethnic, sexual, and social minorities.

Foucault seeks to define a new basis for establishing truth in a world where, he believes, realist correspondence of idea to external object has been thoroughly discredited. Plainly, he contends, truth is a humanly devised and accepted framework. In his essay "Truth and Power", he offers this alternative structure: "Truth is to be understood as a system of ordered procedures for the production, regulation, distribution, circulation and operation of statements" (253). A collaborative effort will establish the ground rules. That collaboration should, though often does not, include all those social groups affected by the eventual outcome of the mutual decision. As this collaborative effort seeks to establish ground rules for determining truth, it must be consistently aware of what he calls the "three-fold specificity" that has inevitably influenced truth constructions in the past: class position, the conditions of current life and work, and the politics of truth in society. This warning reflects Foucault's underlying conviction: "Truth is a thing of this world; it is produced only by virtue of mutual forms of constraint. And it induces regular effects of power." Again, in the same essay: "Truth is also linked in a circular relation with systems of power which produce and sustain it..." (252).

The extent to which common conceptions of truth in the past have been linked to power has had devastating effects on repressed groups with minimal political and economic power. In a second essay, "Nietzsche, Genealogy, History", Foucault claims that the supposedly sacred and objective laws of a democracy are too often "...a calculated and relentless pleasure, delight in the promised blood, which permits the perpetual instigation of new dominations and the staging of meticulously repeated scenes of violence" (246). In the same piece, he claims that even society's quest for knowledge suffers from the same vicious motives of preservation of power for the dominant classes. "The historical analysis of this rancorous will to knowledge reveals that all knowledge rests upon injustice (that there is no right, not even in the act of knowing, to truth or a foundation for truth) and that the instinct for knowledge is malicious..." (250). These are bold and startling statements, yet to many representatives of disenfranchised minorities, they declare a reality hidden from the eyes of those comfortably in power. Let us examine the reaction from some of those representatives.

"A Genealogy of Modern Racism", quoted below, is a chapter from Princeton Professor Cornel West's earliest book, *Prophecy Deliverance! An Afro-American Revolutionary Christianity*. West embraced his combined heritage of African-American Baptist Christians, the nonviolence of Martin Luther King, Jr., and the fiery political challenge articulated by the Black Panthers and Malcolm X. He combines that heritage with expert training in the history of philosophy, which provides his thought with insights missed by purely political commentators. West states the theme of his analysis in this way:

> I shall argue that the initial structure of modern discourse in the West 'secretes' the idea of white supremacy. I call this 'secretion' – the underside of modern discourse – a particular logical consequence of the quest for truth and knowledge in the modern West. (299)

By combining classical Greek stereotypes of facial beauty and emerging scientific insistence on detailed observation, the western intellectual tradition first devalued African facial structure and then reinforced its racist attitude by supposedly scientific disciplines like phrenology (the reading of skulls) and physiognomy (the reading of faces). West cites numerous racist remarks from Enlightenment philosophers, most of which depend for their opinion on the authority of "naturalists, anthropologists, physiognomists, and phrenologists." One such comment from a supposedly enlightened figure, Voltaire, will suffice:

> The Negro race is a species of men as different from ours as the breed of spaniels is from that of greyhounds.... If their

understanding is not of a different nature from ours, it is at least greatly inferior. They are not capable of any great application or association of ideas.... (306)

Cornel West exposes the racism of many Enlightenment thinkers and demonstrates that such attitudes were rooted in the very traditions so valued by modernity. He concludes: "This inquiry accents the fact that the everyday life of black people is shaped not simply by the exploitative (oligopolistic) capitalist system of production but also by cultural attitudes and sensibilities, including alienating ideals of beauty" (308).

Feminist epistemologists Sandra Harding and Susan Bordo, in further excerpts from Cahoone's anthology, employ investigatory tactics similar to West's but turn the spotlight toward the issue of gender. Reiterating West's claim that 17th century science and the 18th century Enlightenment established an epistemological framework that intensified and perpetuated oppression of minorities, they then analyze how that has sidelined the contributions of women. In an article "From Feminist Empiricism to Feminist Standpoint Epistemologies", Harding summarizes their effort: "...inquiry from a feminist perspective can provide understanding of nature and social life that are not possible from the perspective of men's distinctive activity and experience" (342). Harding then discusses five dimensions of that different perspective:

1. Craft labor, as distinct from market capitalism, had united hand, brain, and heart
2. Women's emphasis on sensuous, concrete, and relational dimensions of knowing were subjugated

3. The dualisms of subject/object, mind/body, reason/sense and inner/outer could be reduced by the consideration of women's perspectives
4. The changes required to recover a more unified view
5. Certain important historical cultural changes have set the stage for a more feminist epistemology

Susan Bordo focuses Harding's five dimensions into a penetrating assessment of Cartesian method. Her article's title presages her conclusions: "The Cartesian Masculinization of Thought and the Seventeenth Century Flight from the Feminine". Her analysis radically challenges the whole epistemology of scientific observation in Descartes and Francis Bacon. One extended quote from her article illuminates what she sees as Descartes' grievous mistake.

> The Cartesian reconstruction has two inter-related dimensions. On the one hand, a new model of knowledge is conceived, in which the purity of intellect is guaranteed by its ability to transcend the body. On the other hand, the ontological blueprint of the order of things is refashioned. The spiritual and the corporeal are now two distinct substances.... For the model of the universe which results, neither bodily response (the sensual or the emotional) nor associational thinking, exploring the various personal or spiritual meanings the object has for us, can tell us anything about the object 'itself'." It can only be grasped "...by measurement rather than sympathy." (355)

Obviously, she would hope, like Harding, that this ontological blueprint can be reversed or at least moderated and that postmodern epistemology will incorporate these feminist insights.

Bordo extends her assessment of Descartes into an historical review of that whole era in which modern scientific method was developed. Drawing upon the research of feminist historians, she concludes that the century of 1550-1650, in which Descartes' objectification of nature arose, was a "particularly gynophobic century." That research has exposed "... a virtual obsession with the untamed natural power of female generativity, and a dedication to bringing it under cultural control." Hence, "The project that fell to both empirical science and 'rationalism' was to tame the female universe" (356-358). Only when this gynophobia is exposed and eliminated can a more comprehensive and less restrictive method of exploring nature arise.

The insights of West, Harding, Bordo, and similar deconstructionists can also apply to other oppressed cultural minorities. Iris Marion Young, for instance, investigates the idea of "respectability" in western society, which dictates unwritten rules of public behavior. "Respectability consists in conforming to norms that repress sexuality, bodily functions, and emotional expression" (372). Oppression of some social groups occurs when dominant groups set standards according to that unseen, unacknowledged sense of what is (to them) respectable behavior. Indeed, the strongest characteristic of respectability is its invisibility to those who have constructed it and live unconsciously within it. A case in point is exclusion of and even violence toward homosexuals. Young (in "The Scaling of Bodies and the Politics of Identity") insists that "confronting homophobia involves confronting the very desire to have a uniform, orderly identity, and the dependence of such a unified identity on the construction of a border that excludes aspects of subjectivity one refuses to face" (381). All who seek to live a publicly respectable life are now challenged to examine whether that desire for orderly lines of social conduct may hide prejudices and hateful attitudes toward those who are different. Uncomfortable as that may seem, it is an act of "consciousness raising", which Young sees as a necessary prelude to genuine social justice.

Conclusion

The authors just examined in the last section unite in appreciating the deconstructive tools of postmodernism. They see the unseen, the presuppositions, the structured language and oppressive institutions that dominant groups take for granted as simply "the way things are". But most of these authors, seeking greater political and personal liberty for oppressed groups, would stop short of turning the tools of deconstruction upon themselves. If we employed Derrida's tactics with unrelenting thoroughness, as he did against Structuralism, the quest for justice in modern liberation movements would reveal its own presuppositions and its unconscious use of restrictive definitions. As this chapter ends, are we not left wondering how one defines the useful limits of deconstructionism, and where it leads to hopeless, self-defeating criticism of all things?

To repeat, the five dimensions of postmodernism delineated by Professor Cahoone are the complexity of meaning, language and its mediation of knowledge, constructivist freedom, the immanence of norms, and the analysis of privileged power. I trust this initial treatment of these five has granted readers an impartial and useful general perspective. One goal has been to show that some roots of these five themes arose in the modern era, either in its advocates or in its critics. Primarily, however, we have trusted the words of the postmodern commentators themselves through extended use of quotations from their writings, in the hope that their original explanations will best represent this complex philosophy of postmodernism. The next direction for this Part Two will carry us more directly into the world of the 21st century Christian church, into how its theology and its daily acts of faith have been affected by Postmodernism and have responded to it.

| six |

Christian Faith and the Postmodern World

The previous chapter introduced central components of postmodern tendencies, conveying both background to their origins and potential uses. Given a preliminary acquaintance with this new era, it is now possible to reflect on the possibilities, challenges, and accommodations that today affect Christian faith, its doctrines and its practice.

For nearly a century, Christian writers of varied backgrounds have attempted to assess the pluralism, reevaluation of language, and rejection of Enlightenment presuppositions in postmodernism. Tracing those assessments, we begin with a hopeful prognosis about how the crumbling of Enlightenment pillars opens space for Christian doctrine to re-emerge as a legitimate intellectual possibility. The next section of the chapter counters that optimism by re-emphasizing certain themes that, taken at face value, would rule out any explicit cooperation between postmodernism and Christianity. The ensuing section discusses some of the movements within recent Christian theology that recognize the new situation and try to develop appropriate responses. Chapter Seven concludes Part Two with a cautious encouragement of three proposals that take insights of postmodernism and employ them effectively within boundaries of a recognizable Christian framework.

Before we begin that effort, however, note an important clarification. The word *postmodern* can refer to either the general era since the early 20th century or to the explicit school of poststructuralist philosophers embodied in the French writers of the mid-1960s and beyond, thinkers such as those noted in the previous chapter: Michel Foucault, Jacques Derrida, or Jean Lyotard. Some of the theological responses in the following pages address specific issues raised by these postmodern writers, more accurately called "poststructuralists"; other authors address the larger era and its wider causes.

New Space for Faith

One voice who saw promise in the postmodern challenge to modernity was Diogenes Allen, former Stuart professor of philosophy at Princeton Theological Seminary. In two places, an essay in *Postmodern Theology* and his own *Christian Belief in a Postmodern World*, Allen expresses his optimism that the pillars of the Enlightenment, which had relegated Christian doctrine to the sidelines, are themselves exposed as unworkable by the discoveries and insights of recent decades. He sees four new gaps in the Enlightenment armor against faith-related knowledge.

First, Allen states, "It can no longer be claimed as a commonly accepted philosophical and scientific tenet that we live in a self-contained universe." (*Postmodern...*, 21). A self-contained universe is one in which there is no need, and indeed it is practically impossible, to consult anything outside the physical universe for meaning. Such epistemological systems, like those of Hume and Kant, however sophisticated, are incomplete and misleading. This is recognized both by religious and non-religious commentators in recent debates. (Allen specifically cites the work of William Rowe, an analytical philosopher.)

Although it is accurate to say, with Hume and Kant, that an examination of the contingencies of nature does not establish or prove the existence of God, such examination can nonetheless prompt the question of the possibility of God's existence. Although physical examination of phenomena can detail how and why individual events occurred, it cannot speak to why there is a universe in the first place, about why, as is often asked, there is something instead of nothing. Likewise, it is legitimate to ask, and try to answer, why there is this particular universe instead of something different. What is more, the stance that there is a God who exists outside the physical universe is not just a whim of personal opinion. The existence of orderly laws in physical phenomena might point to a dependable external agent with just as much likelihood as the existence of chaotic, destructive events points to none. The existence of awe-inspiring beauty within nature might point to a benevolent outside agent with just as much likelihood as cruel human and animal behavior might point to the absence of such benevolence. At this point, Allen affirms that we do not have to prove one or another view, just allow that both views can be reasonably possible.

In addition, new developments in the physical sciences have challenged the picture of reality developed in the 17th and 18th centuries. Quantum theory and relativity present a substantially different picture of how the universe works, restoring contingency, denying the prior Enlightenment assumptions that a positivist, mathematical reading of physical reality is the single key needed to understand the world. Allen contends that Einstein's general relativity theory lends credence to picturing the universe as a whole, thus legitimating the question of where did the whole come from (*Christian Belief...*,70). Other cosmological theories, like the Big Bang and the accompanying "Anthropic Principle" lend credence to the idea of a designing power at work in creation. Again, though, neither of these new interpretations of creative power should overreach into an attempted proof of a divine cause. As Allen says succinctly in *Postmodern Theology:* "These developments in philosophy and science only show us the possibility of God. But the possibility is raised by developments in the very domains which earlier had been used to close off the possibility. We have had quite a *volte face*" (22).

The second pillar of the Enlightenment that is faltering under new scrutiny is its inability to develop an adequate foundation for morality, one that transcends simple enlightened self-interest. We noted some of what Allen means in the introduction to a previous chapter and in a discussion of happiness in Part One (page 64), so the treatment here will be brief. People simply lost confidence in a moral system, whether for individuals or society, based purely on rational analysis. Kant's categorical imperative, for example, insisted that all one needed to become a moral person and create a moral society was rational ability and the will to only act in such a way that your actions could become a universal law. All ethical decisions could be objective; specific historical and personal circumstances would be largely irrelevant.

As we have seen, however, one of the key themes of postmodernism disputes the very idea of objectivity, insisting that adopting an attitude of rational objectivity distorts your view of what you observe. It is dualistic, presuming a superior condescension outside and above another. We earlier recognized one of those condescending attitudes in J.S. Mill's assessment of primitive cultures that did not seem to possess the critical abilities of a 19th century English gentleman. Inevitable hidden presuppositions, the "immanence of norms", completely compromise any attempt to decide complex moral questions by universal rational laws. The attitude of postmodernism is suspicious of any such "foundational" proposal that bases all knowledge on one vehicle like rational evaluation. Too many "irrational" things happened in the first half of the 20th century to prolong the idea that objective rational analysis provides an adequate basis for morality. A public disillusioned with reason as the source of social ethics may instead choose to anchor respect for others in sensing the image of God reflected in all created beings.

If objective reason ultimately fails in its ability to conquer evil intentions, then a third pillar of modernity, inevitable progress, will also crumble. As explained in Part One above, people had come to believe that a combination of widespread education, scientific advancement, and the freedom to make their own choices would lead them into a snowballing movement toward the perfect society. Feeding this sentiment were abstract philosophical ideas like Hegel's movement of Spirit toward full self-realization. Progress would not only be possible, but essentially inevitable, because that is the direction to which the world-spirit moved. For common citizens living in the late 19th and early 20th century, with Bessemer furnaces and aspirin and cures for childhood diseases, progress did indeed seem to gallop toward a time when all that troubled them would be resolved.

Yet, inevitable progress is one more of those "metanarratives" which postmodern writers excoriate as simplistic and dangerous. The complexity of meaning that these authors recognize affects not just language, but people, history, and science. The doctrine of inevitable progress over-simplified and over-idealized the benefits of progress. Accordingly, it underestimated the potential that what seemed to work well in the short run could bring disastrous consequences in later unexpected arenas. The iron that hardened into steel in Bessemer furnaces produced smoky pollutants that caused untold cancerous deaths. That is just one obvious example of the need to recognize the multiple factors that should cause proponents of progress to reconsider their ideological and technological optimism.

At the heart of the previous two crumbling pillars described above is what Allen labels the fourth Enlightenment belief that postmodern thinkers criticize. It is the assumption that knowledge is inherently good. He explains the force of that belief, and its vulnerability, in *Christian Belief...*:

> For centuries science has been regarded as unquestionably a force for good. We are indeed immeasurably better off because of it. But our conviction that science is intrinsically good and scientists inherently benefactors of humanity arose largely because the morality that was part of the Greek and Christian heritage guided and restrained to some extent the uses to which scientific knowledge was put. Today we are becoming increasingly aware that there is no inherent connection between knowledge and its beneficial use...." (5)

An ingrained societal Christian ethic, even in many who no longer claimed personal belief in God, helped direct the use of technological and scientific knowledge, but as that ethic gradually loses influence and familiarity, discredited and sidelined by Enlightenment alternatives, that key resource for directing new inventions toward beneficial results is diminishing.

One particular individual in the early 20th century presents a keen example of how the same scientific discovery can lead to either great benefit or great destruction. Fritz Haber (1868-1934), was a German chemist who won the Nobel Prize for Chemistry in 1918 for developing a method to synthesize ammonia from nitrogen and hydrogen. The result was anhydrous ammonia, which has become the main ingredient in crop fertilizers throughout the developed world. Wikipedia notes an estimate that nearly two-thirds of annual global food production uses this fertilizing method, thus supporting nearly half the world population over the last century. However, the same synthesizing process can be used to weaponize chlorine into a poisonous gas, one that caused such suffering and death in World War I. Therefore, history also considers Haber the "father of chemical warfare". He personally supervised the use of the gas at the Second Battle of Ypres.

Fritz Haber would provide a clear example for Allen to show how nationalistic patriotism, for instance, employed potentially good discoveries to destructive ends. Raw technological power, untethered and disconnected, contains within its own process no restrictions on use. It is susceptible to multiple larger ideological frameworks that manipulate its power for what Christian ethics might declare sinful ends. The postmodern awareness that knowledge is not inherently good helps reclaim the idea that sin, even original sin, is not an outmoded concept, and that there are dimensions of human decision-making much stronger than objective intellect. Society still needs to implement the technology based on public standards regarding good or evil.

Considering the combined effect of the postmodern challenge to these four key characteristics of modernity, Allen contends that Christian belief should be seen once again as both intellectually coherent and relevant, that a new respect can and should be afforded to Christian doctrines about creation, ethics, and social practice. His hope prevails in statements such as this:

> The recognition that Christianity is relevant to our entire society, and relevant not only to the heart but to the mind as well, is a major change in our cultural situation. The transition is hardly complete, but this is the vista which a postmodern world reveals. (*Postmodern...*, 25)

Obstacles to Cooperation

This premise from Diogenes Allen about four crumbling pillars of the Enlightenment focuses the question whether a particular writer welcomes wide themes from the chronological era of postmodernism or embraces the ideas of the specific French poststructuralist school. Allen utilizes 20th century developments in astronomy, mathematics, and philosophy that re-open the door to Christian ethics and theology, but he mentions Derrida or Foucault et al. only obliquely. This next section will attend more to key components of postmodern poststructuralism as listed in the prior chapter. It will unsurprisingly point out that poststructuralism also presents substantial obstacles to Christian faith, obstacles that blunt some of the promise of larger trends within postmodernism. In that regard, many other authors, like Allen, utilize certain postmodern insights yet remain wary of more stringent poststructuralist proposals. (cf. Lawrence Cahoone's list of "Critical Appropriations", *From Modernism...* 222). Some are willing, for example, to employ the deconstruction tactics of Foucault or Derrida if those tactics help denude their particular adversary, but stop short of embracing fully the poststructuralist platform. It is clear, if these writers represent one viewpoint and poststructuralists the other, that two stances can look at the same postmodern themes and, by employing them to vastly different lengths, will arrive at vastly different conclusions.

Three themes from the previous chapter figure prominently in the following assessment of how some postmodern thought may stymie Allen's sense of hope. The themes are clearly interrelated, but we distinguish them here to emphasize different aspects of their challenge.

Epistemological Relativism: Clarity is Elusive

Ferdinand de Saussure's groundbreaking study of linguistics emphasized an increasing awareness of the complexity of language. He believes that the meaning conveyed by language is a social enterprise, not a simple correspondence of a word to the idea or object that it represents. Saussure insists that the word, the sign, exists before the idea, which it "creates" through a social conversation. Jacques Derrida then expanded Saussure's insight into a wider awareness of how words have both diachronic meaning (a word has a history) and synchronic meaning (a word has current wide relationships). All the multiple differences that distinguish one word from another must be examined to glimpse even a hint of the word or sign's full meaning. Furthermore, there is a multiplying effect at work. Every time the sign tries to signify something, it starts a new chain of meaning in a new context.

Derrida celebrates this increasing complexity of meaning as a way to instill humility into those metaphysicians who would create vast ideological frameworks. As noted briefly in the previous chapter, in his 1968 lecture "Differance", Derrida draws on Nietzsche and Heidegger to explain why humanity needs this hesitancy arising from complexity. "Differance is the "active (in movement) discord of the different forces and of the differences between forces which Nietzsche opposes to the entire system of metaphysical grammar, wherever that system controls culture, philosophy, and science." In a subsequent paragraph, Derrida intensifies both the necessity for and the inevitable threat of differance:

> ...differance is not. It is not a being-present, however excellent, unique, principal, or transcendent one makes it. It commands nothing, rules over nothing, and nowhere does it exercise any authority. It is not marked by a capital letter. Not only is there no realm of differance, but differance is the subversion of every realm. This is obviously what makes it threatening and necessarily dreaded by everything in us that desires a realm, the past or future presence of a realm. (234, 236)

Because poststructuralists wish to dismantle metaphysical and other metanarratives, they promote interpretations of language and discourse that disrupt ordinary communication and carry dialogue into a spiral of complexity.

Most of us can recognize that there are warnings here with at least a slight ring of familiarity. Religious thinkers have always known they must pause and reflect before they attribute particular qualities to God. The *via negativa* of classical theology recognizes that God is best described through subtraction (what God is not) rather than addition (what God is). Christians influenced by what is sometimes called "the Protestant Principle" insist on divine transcendent sovereignty above all attempts to limit God. Obviously, significant gains to theology also arise from a postmodern insistence on complexity of meaning. Contemporary theologians rightly affirm that metaphysical frameworks, whether Cartesian rationalism or Baconian empiricism, have compromised and misinterpreted our experience of God. By refusing to defend a metaphysical scheme, like Newton's "watchmaker universe" that once seemed to support religious faith, we can avoid tragic mistakes like upholding passionately the literal reading of the creation story, or callously explaining an infant's tragic death as if it were a part of God's desired plan.

Yet, from a practical perspective, postmodern insistence on the complexity of meaning makes the task of theology in the church almost impossible. When abstract thoughts must be deconstructed interminably, when discourse is pressed toward a spiral of hidden influences, then the attempt to speak clearly to inquiring minds in sanctuaries and classrooms is doomed. The search for clarity of expression is futile, unless clarity is defined as a massive clearing-away of all that is familiar so that we will stand speechless before a vast multitude of differences. Deconstruction certainly can initiate a purifying cleansing, but it tightens a straitjacket around any attempt at reconstruction of meaning. It is a positive outcome if we can shed the restrictions of positivism or rationalism and come to recognize that texts can contain and convey multiple meanings. However, loss of a unifying core of belief will send Christians scurrying into individual corners of identity and turn the body of Christ into scattered appendages.

Proclamation from Christian leaders requires affirmation of certain personal and social values and denunciation of others. Whether quietly and persuasively or abruptly and publicly, Christian proclamation seeks conversion from one thing to another, and for that, clarity of belief and courage to declare a particular position is necessary. Rowan Williams, recently the Archbishop of Canterbury, addresses this in his contribution to the essays in *Postmodern Theology*.

> Here we come up against the most central issue in the whole of this discussion. How are we to speak of judgment in a fragmented culture? The language of judgment presupposes recognition and communication, the possibility of shared points of reference. To pass judgment is to propose and in certain circumstances...to effect a definite 'placing' of what it is that is being judged.... (98)

He then describes the contrast between a real community of active persons that makes and implements key decisions and a society guided more by what some have called epistemological relativism.

> Hence, in a radically pluralist society, the society as such increasingly withdraws from judgment. It will contain groups who continue to believe that judgment is possible or imperative, but the social system overall sees its job as securing a pragmatic minimum of peaceful coexistence between groups, by a variety of managerial skills and economic adjustments. (99)

It is admittedly unfair to attribute all the ills of the society just described to postmodern authors whose works had only recently emerged publicly when Williams' critical description appeared. A wide variety of social influences contributes to isolation and disengagement. (cf. Jameson, "The Cultural Logic of Late Capitalism"). However, if Derrida pushes his view toward a consistent conclusion, scrutinizing theological language inexorably, the church's voice will be lost amidst that "pragmatic minimum of peaceful coexistence". Some may rejoice in that prospect. I trust there are also many who believe it provides only a dull shadow of genuine community.

Suspicion of the Past: History Is Misleading

Previous chapters of this volume dedicated numerous pages to the topic of history and its alternate interpretations, both in the context of Hegel's progressive realization of Mind and in critical biblical research. Within postmodernism, debate about history takes on yet another dimension. One influential composition by the poststructuralist Michel Foucault, "Nietzsche, Genealogy, History", reopens the discussion on the reliability of historical accounts and their ideological presuppositions. The essay employs themes and quotations from the full range of Friedrich Nietzsche's works, especially re-presenting Nietzsche's explicit definition of "genealogy" as the key to an "effective history" that should replace more conventional, traditional views of history. Foucault's essay is precise and difficult, but rewards examination here as a prelude to comments on how such a view challenges even chastened biblical interpretation and confidence in a providential God. We intend to restrict our focus to Foucault's use of Nietzsche's term "genealogy" and avoid the more far-reaching statements and implications in Nietzsche's larger work, *The Genealogy of Morals*.

On the first page of the essay, Foucault promotes the necessity of "genealogy" as it debunks utilitarian moral schemes of interpreting history. Genealogy

> ... must record the singularity of events outside of any monotonous finality; it must seek them in the most unpromising places, in what we tend to feel is without history – in sentiments, love,

conscience, instincts; it must be sensitive to their recurrence, not in order to trace the gradual curve of their evolution, but to isolate the different scenes where they engaged in different roles. (241)

This search for sentiments and instincts in multiple isolated events Foucault calls "descent", a translation of Nietzsche's word *Herkunft*. In accordance with both Nietzsche's and Heidegger's quest to find a form of meaning antecedent to metaphysical frameworks like Plato's theory of forms, Foucault believes that this journey of descent, this "genealogical" search, will undercut the generalizations about history that end up in systems like the doctrine of inevitable progress or Marxist interpretations of materialist stages. Employing the descent will help us

> ... discover that truth or being do not lie at the root of what we know and what we are, but the exteriority of accidents." Again, "The search for descent is not the erecting of foundations: on the contrary, it disturbs what was previously considered immobile; it fragments what was once thought unified.... (244)

The disorienting effect in the search for descent is desirable, Foucault believes. He would argue, again following Nietzsche, that traditional ways of writing history always assumed some sort of suprahistorical perspective, whether that be of a divine planner or a rational mind unencumbered by pesky details. It attempts to study history from outside of history, rather than within its messiness, thus distorting what history conveys. Accurate knowledge is impossible in such an enterprise, he contends. History written from a suprahistorical perspective regards its work as allowing a person to rediscover and recognize oneself at the end of the long investigative process that leads up to the present moment. But this framework must be dismantled, and a better form of knowledge will emerge. He explains:

> Knowledge, even under the banner of history, does not depend on "rediscovery", and it emphatically excludes the "rediscovery of ourselves". History becomes "effective" to the degree that it introduces discontinuity into our very being.... "Effective" history deprives the self of the reassuring stability of life and nature....
>
> It will uproot its traditional foundations and relentlessly disrupt its pretended continuity. This is because knowledge is not made for understanding; it is made for cutting. (p. 247)

If and when Foucault's "effective" history then considers events in the past and seeks to interpret them without the presuppositions and "suprahistorical perspectives" he so resists, what is its strategy? He attributes the misuse of history to its Platonic metaphysical foundation, and thus fashions a three-part method that frees the past from what he sees as the Platonic modalities of history. To wit:

> The first is parodic, [as, to parody; the Greek *paroidia* is a burlesque song, d.h.] directed against reality, and opposes the theme of history as reminiscence or recognition; the second is dissociative, directed against identity, and opposes history given as continuity or representative of a tradition; the third is sacrificial, directed against truth, and opposes history as knowledge. (249)

If indeed we can understand Foucault's cryptic words here, the first tactic seems to allow the false suprahistorical scheme to parade in public, indeed, to encourage its showmanship, and then to expose its shallowness through farcical parody, ala "the emperor's new clothes" or the court jester who belittles the king and gets away with it. The second tactic points out all the factors that contradict and complicate the simple metanarrative foisted upon reality in an attempt to create a unified identity. This effort reveals that such an identity is weak, a façade that needs to be dismantled so that history "...will not discover a forgotten identity, eager to be reborn, but a complex system of distinct and multiple elements, unable to be mastered by the powers of synthesis..." (250).

The third tactic is particularly difficult to apprehend. Foucault argues that the idea that history brings knowledge must be sacrificed, removed. All who claim that they are studying history, and who hope to arrive thereby at beneficial, constructive knowledge of themselves and the world, do not understand the malice of their own activity. In his words: "The historical analysis of this rancorous will to knowledge reveals that all knowledge rests upon injustice (that there is no right, not even in the act of knowing, to truth or a foundation for truth) and that the instinct for knowledge is malicious..." (250). Therefore, Foucault believes the only honest thing to do is to jettison the great 19th century frameworks of knowledge like those of Fichte and Hegel. Through these three tactics, Foucault proposes a more "effective history", a "genealogy" of separated information, which cuts through all the intellectual pretense of past centuries and reminds us repeatedly of how attempts at comprehensive schemes of historical investigation are worse than futile.

Let us attribute to Foucault a genuine attempt to discover a level of truth (a word he uses with reticence) that is antecedent to Platonic metaphysics. With Nietzsche and Heidegger, he tries to find meaning – in this case, within history – that is accurate and untainted by ideology, more raw, more original, and closer to real human emotion. If that means surrendering the illusion that history can convey knowledge, he accepts the prospect. It is certainly not an illusion, however, to recognize how strenuously Foucault's premise would challenge, indeed demolish, many cherished central tenets of the Christian faith. Both in the interpretation of scripture and the development of relevant doctrine, the church has always tried to keep one eye on historical events in scripture and the other eye on the history of civilization. It does so to find signs of a providential God at work in the events of figures from Abraham of Haran to Abraham Lincoln and beyond. It is not an exaggeration to say that despite other differences, Christians, Jews, and Muslims all regard their God as the Lord of history, intervening in the daily affairs of earthly life. To surrender any attempt to find knowledge about God and knowledge about humanity through the study of history would leave religious believers in a morass of directionless apathy.

This declaration of peril is not to imply that there is no merit in Foucault's warning about mistaken sweeping schemes of historical meaning. Long before poststructuralism arrived on the scene, it was common in academic and theological circles to warn that, to the historian, there is no such thing as bare facts untainted by ideological perspective. "Lessons from history" too often have been summoned to buttress patriarchal domination, racial segregation, and a bevy of other oppressive practices. We have seen earlier in this volume how historical-criticism, utilizing empiricist investigation, favors one particular view of biblical knowledge and neglects others.

Still, for example, does not an awareness of the historical situation of the exiles to Babylon prompt closer identification with their raw emotions of guilt, loss, and fear? Is it not knowledge of Roman methods of execution that permits deeper sympathy for the passionate suffering of a particular criminal hung on Golgotha hill? Does not useful information as in these examples enhance rather than hide the deep human feelings that Foucault and Nietzsche seek to uncover? Why then is it necessary to subject such lessons of history to the three-fold debunking strategy Foucault proposes?

It is not my intention, and it is well beyond my ability, to disprove Foucault's theory that he can develop a more effective history based on Nietzschean "genealogy". Nonetheless, it is crucial to state clearly what will be lost if in the postmodern era the church withdraws from all attempts to trace the hand of an active God in historical circumstances. Foucault's suspicion about the unreliability of history stands firmly as a second obstacle to greater public respectability for Christian faith in the future. History obviously can be misleading, but that only increases the responsibility of the church and its members to hold one another mutually accountable for the best possible interpretation of divine activity throughout the ages.

Humanly Constructed Knowledge: No External Standards

Readers of previous chapters have heard more than enough about Immanuel Kant's interpretation of the human mind's categories that clarify, or even create, meaning from sense data. That principle contributed to the epistemological concept called constructivism, the belief that all knowledge is humanly constructed. Poststructuralists subscribe to this belief at least in part because of their objection to how metaphysical and other metanarratives create a dualistic foundation for knowledge and morality. Every dualistic scenario distinguishes an exterior source of reference, an outside from an inside, a preceding standard or a universal standard that judges its subject matter. Postmodernists, however, drawing on Nietzsche's critique, disavow any supposed use of critical reason that appeals to a lasting standard, and instead emphasize that such reason is merely a rationalization of the human will trying to create self-serving power.

All norms used "to judge processes are themselves products of the processes they judge", as Professor Cahoone explained in the previous chapter. Poststructuralists call this the immanence of norms. Nothing is truly transcendent or outside of what it considers. All norms are constructed within situations; neither objective scientific measurement nor eternal religious laws are what they seem.

If, however, the postmodern world accepts completely the human construction of knowledge, if it affirms without exception the principle of the immanence of norms, and rejects implicitly any external standard in epistemology, then it would revolutionize and overturn any clear concept of a transcendent, eternal God. Whether the Christian faith could survive that assault is questionable indeed. Following are three crucial areas among many in which Christianity presupposes at least some form of external standard, a God who stands outside human activity and intervenes to establish an authoritative claim.

The Transcendence of God: All primary western religions include the idea of a God who creates from a stance that begins outside time and space. Debates do exist whether the phrase "in the beginning" necessarily implies a *creatio ad nihilo,* but in Genesis the creation of light and dark, sequence, definable space and time, exist because a compelling word came from outside the stormy waters of chaos to bring meaning. The very contingency of physical nature arises because it is separate from, though interacting with, an external source. The freedom and effectiveness of scientific investigation would falter if nature were a full pantheistic infusion of the divine, or if it had no presumption of regularity, as the historian of science Stanley Jaki has shown in his essay "The Biblical Basis of Western Science". Because of the belief that God's initial act of creation stands outside of physical nature, science maintains an independent sphere of research. Concomitantly, the investigation of nature can neither prove nor disprove the existence of that creator God.

This is relevant for ecological issues today. Interpreting the whole creation – from planetary systems to microscopic enzymes – as a gift granted by a benevolent God engenders an attitude of grateful stewardship. Nature is a bequest placed in human hands to maintain, enhance, and protect such a treasured gift. Douglas John Hall conveys how this idea of stewardship, in which humanity exists in relationship with the God above us and the earth around us, does not create an oppressive, rapacious attitude toward raw material, but a cautious and respectful approach to nature aptly fitted to 21st century environmental perils. He conveys this persuasively in *The Steward: A Biblical Symbol Come of Age*. Surely it is not necessary to maintain an antiquated picture of God, sitting upon the heavenly clouds waving a majestic hand, to insist nonetheless that there is an external dimension to the God of creation. This God could still work intimately in and with the evolutionary contingency of nature without surrendering all dimensions of transcendence. The very concept of creation, at the heart of Christian faith, defies the belief that humans, without reliance upon any exterior standard, construct all knowledge. On the contrary, both scientific research and religious inquiry try to discover dimensions of a real world created from outside natural or human boundaries.

The Law's External Standard: The giving of the Law, a second picture of God's transcendence or external standard, would readily elicit the scorn of poststructuralists who decry dualistic approaches to knowledge. Having carried Israel on the wings of eagles out of bondage (Ex.19), God sends Moses to the top of a mountain to receive commandments handed down from on high. Once again, an observer need not insist on literal interpretation of the images to recognize that the intention of the biblical authors includes a picture of God's transcendent authority and the law as a divine gift. The divine appearance brings with it the thunder, lightning and earthquake that accompany many pictorial epiphanies of God as a holy, unapproachable deity who can terrify as well as save. Yet, the Law itself comes as an act of mercy, intended to guide people, if obedient, into an unexpected and undeserved land of plenty. There are many dimensions to the theme of morality in scripture, but each carries an element of this picture on Sinai. The God who seeks obedience from disciples provides liberty for them and establishes a covenant with them. Throughout this covenant God stands above them to convey authority yet also exhibits empathy and guides toward a better future.

The argument is legitimate, no doubt, that versions of the commandments and legal codes are present in other Ancient Near East cultures. The Hammurabi Code, for instance, exhibits distinct similarities to parts of the covenant code of Ex.22. An alternative hypothesis therefore could contend that the commandments of Israel amount to little more than a collection of social mores and cultural restrictions that had proven effective in maintaining civil society elsewhere, humanly constructed wisdom, as it were. While such a hypothesis cannot be disproven, in some respects it misses the point. When the writers of scripture intentionally recorded and elaborated on incidents conveyed through oral tradition, it was for them a testimony. It proclaimed their belief that the force and effectiveness of moral law, however enmeshed in a culture's legal practices, comes from the inspiration of a divine authority. The God of Sinai, in Christian tradition, is not absent from mundane daily practices of courts, whether in Canaan or Connecticut, but is likewise not restricted by them. The testimony of scripture is that the ultimate source of their justice comes from an external eternal standard, the God who rules the universe. The principle of constructivism would declare that testimony invalid and deny such an external source for any law.

Christian Soteriology, the Doctrine of Salvation: This is the third central belief that, on face value, runs completely counter to a principle of humanly constructed knowledge. The classic definition of Jesus Christ in the Chalcedonian definition of 451 asserts that Christ is one person in two natures, the divine nature of the same substance as the Father and the human nature of the same substance as us. These natures unite in the one person, inseparable and without confusion. The definition is significant because it in effect unites a nature of God regarded as invisible, timeless, and transcendent to a nature of God regarded as visible, perishable and immanent. Its implication for salvation is inescapable. As expressed by Dietrich Bonhoeffer in his lectures on Christology (*Christ the Center*), Christ is the center of human existence, the center of history and the center of nature. His Christology could be summed up in the phrase: "If Christ were not human, he could not save **us**; if Christ were not divine, he could not **save** us."

Certainly, more recent interpreters of doctrine who see the world in dynamic rather than stable terms (e.g., Alfred North Whitehead) have challenged the Greek-influenced language of "substance", and here reconsiderations might be necessary. Nonetheless, Chalcedon's insistence on the union of different entities representing supposed opposites remains integral to salvation. Awkwardly stated from Whitehead's perspective, a non-temporal relatedness still unites with a temporal relatedness.

Christian theology regards the Incarnation of Christ as in some way an arrival from a pre-existent sphere into human flesh. The eternal

Logos becomes mortal. That may be better described as an "emptying" (Philippians 2) rather than through a picture of walking down a ladder from the clouds, and we may thus gain a clearer insight into the exact nature of the "humiliation". Still, the point remains that what once was external in a pre-existent sense does enter human flesh. As a derivative from that implication, the teachings of Jesus exhibit an authority greater than existent folk knowledge. The parables capture the imagination; ordinary daily events like sowing a field grant unexpected insight into a different realm of meaning, a hidden meaning that seems to come from completely outside the expected. The perplexing statements of the Sermon on the Mount shatter normal ways of thinking about the world, offering an entry into a transcendent realm. Even more significantly, the crucifixion and resurrection of Christ convey transformative impact only because the one who chooses to endure human suffering on behalf of others is one who had known no such suffering before. To the Christian believer, the love of Christ may be emulated by many, but could not have been initiated except by him. He represents the entry of an external standard, an enduring compassion that could not come via humanly constructed knowledge.

The three preceding central doctrines of Christianity, creation, divine law, and the person of Christ, despite many variations, have persistently retained the presupposition that God begins with and maintains a transcendent presence and then enters the world of humans to effect change and provide guidance. However, the poststructuralist belief that all knowledge is humanly constructed resists precisely such an external standard. This constructivism, along with the epistemological relativism and the suspicion of historical knowledge treated earlier, remain formidable obstacles to traditional interpretations of Christian beliefs.

In light of this, sprinkled within previous paragraphs I have occasionally expressed my clear skepticism about any full rapprochement between pivotal poststructuralist ideas and Christian faith. Nonetheless, I have tried objectively to present those ideas as challenges to orthodox Christian theology rather than as completely incompatible. The next section of this chapter summarizes a variety of 20th century attempts that incorporated certain insights of postmodernism with more or less long-term success. Chapter Seven will describe three arenas where this author does find possible future 21st century cooperation between traditional Christian doctrines and postmodern influences.

Recent Theological Responses to Postmodernism

Lingering influential tendencies within Enlightenment and Romanticist philosophies of the 19th century connected with newer developments among poststructuralists and called forth a stream of responses by mid-20th century theologians trying to make sense of the rapidly changing religious landscape. Following are five such attempts. Our intention is not to present exhaustive information about any of these "schools" of thinkers, but to describe a few central ideas within these schools as they relate changes in culture, science, politics and epistemology to poststructuralism and to traditional theological doctrines.

Death of God Theology

In 1966, the editors of *Time* magazine caused a public controversy by placing the question "Is God Dead?" in bold letters across the cover of their April 8 issue. The feature article mostly documented decreased church attendance and reduced public interest in traditional religion, but it also introduced to the world a small group of writers lumped into the category "Death of God Theology". Gabriel Vahanian, Paul van Buren, William Hamilton, and Thomas J.J. Altizer occupied the limelight for a decade before the media moved on to cover the Moral Majority and other eye-catching religious controversies. Less public attention, however, did not diminish the importance of the questions raised by these theologians.

Greater variety existed among the members of this school than was initially evident, but they all shared an observation: traditional theism held less authority over mid-20th century American culture than it had before World War II. Vahanian emphasized the loss of a sense of the sacred; van Buren declared that the word "God" had no empirically measurable definition; Hamilton insisted that there was no longer any recognizable transcendence in people's perception of the divine. To these authors, and the public they believed they represented, the God known previously had disappeared, if indeed it had ever been really present. Theism seemed untenable. Some of the school turned toward an honest atheism, some reduced the idea of God to the figure of Jesus and his moral teachings, and some created intriguing theological systems that saw the death of God as a necessary prelude to the rebirth of God. This last is the direction taken by Thomas Altizer, and it is to him that we turn, due to his continuity with themes previously addressed in these pages and his explicit reference to postmodern ideas.

Three figures from the prior century heavily influenced Altizer's theology: G.W.F. Hegel, Friedrich Nietzsche, and the English poet/artist William Blake. If one does not recognize Altizer's uncritical embrace of Hegel's *Phenomenology of Mind*, his thesis of the self-negation of God will seem unintelligible. Secondly, if one does not give any credence to Nietzsche's madman in *The Gay Science*, who declares that "God is dead and we have killed him", the impact of Altizer's claim will be minimal. And if Altizer had not glimpsed the prescient poetic and artistic vision of Blake, he would have been less likely to interpret the modern world in apocalyptic terms.

Altizer best describes how the death of God clears the way for full grace and freedom in his article "History as Apocalypse" (*Sources of Christian...*). The foundation for his thesis is the progressive view of history articulated by Hegel. The first pages of the article include this premise, "If we accept Hegel as the primary thinker of modernity, then we can see that apocalypticism and a pure or full historical consciousness go hand in hand, for the full realization of the historical consciousness brings the ancient or premodern world to an end" (579). Such a full realization of historical consciousness by the universal mind has, in fact, been reached, Altizer believes, and the first person to realize and state that publicly was Nietzsche.

> Not until Nietzsche's ecstatic discovery of Eternal Recurrence did a pure or total consciousness fully appear as its own ground and source... it continues to lie before us as perhaps the clearest and most powerful symbolic unveiling of our own interior depths. (579)

This pantheistic being, *Geist*, embodying all human and divine striving, has reached the end of its dialectical movement and issues in complete self-realization. But that achievement is also a dissolution, as its destiny is complete and its meaning, defined by its progress, is gone. With the dissolution of *Geist's* self-consciousness, the historical consciousness is gone too, and thus also all meaning defined by that process.

The next step in Altizer's progression seems to be the acknowledgement that this dissolution of self-consciousness bears consequences for the concept of God as we have known it.

> So it is that the end of history is the death of God, the death of the primal ground of individual presence and actuality, the end or dissolution of the grounding source of all integral and inherent differentiation.... For now, we are continually plunging backward, sideward, forward, and in all directions.... And that is just the reason, mythically considered, why it is no longer possible for us to name God. Nor, of course, can we name ourselves, or name anything whatsoever which is an individual and distinct identity. (580)

At this point, we know God only by what God once was but no longer is, a presence defined by absence. Altizer draws a comparison here to Jacques Derrida's idea of *differance*. Like that poststructuralist idea, even something that can be known only by its absence, "... is a full presence nonetheless, and is so if only by virtue of the fact that it is actually experienced and known" (581). Some sense of identity, whether of a unique individual or of a distinct, transcendent God, remains, but not as before. "No identity whatsoever can any longer stand forth which is only itself. But it is precisely thereby that a total and comprehensive identity is being born in our midst, and that identity is real..." (581).

Hegel's dialectic movement of history implies that what has been is now negated. Yet, that negation gives way to something more complete, more revelatory.

> Now it has always been true that history gains a new identity only as a consequence of the loss of a previous historical identity, and

> if the end of history has now occurred, that ending could make possible for the first time a total identity of history. (581)

Therefore, with the end of history and the dissolution of God, something else will replace it, a different way of knowing, a more complete, non-differentiated perception. Altizer continues: "History perishes in that dissolution, but that very perishing unveils the final and ultimate identity which is finally no less and no more than the self-embodiment of God" (583). That full self-embodiment could not happen as long as history had not ended and the previous distinct, transcendent God had not died. "For only when history comes to an end can history be known as grace, just as the only God who can be known as a totally gracious God is the God who is dead" (583).

Using more familiar theological terms, Altizer interprets the crucifixion and resurrection of God through the prism of this dissolution of history.

> Christianity has always known the death of God as the way of absolute grace, for nothing less than the death of God lies behind the symbol of the crucifixion, but not until the birth of the modern world is the death of God fully realized in consciousness and history, a realization which is consummated in an absolute or eschatological explosion of history and consciousness. Now grace is everywhere because it is nowhere.... (583)

Altizer carries his article toward its conclusion by emphasizing that he has seen this dynamic at work in Christian history, from the apostles onward.

Freedom in Christ, for either Paul or John, is freedom from the Law, a freedom which was reborn again and again in Christian mysticism and apocalypticism, and which decisively and comprehensively entered Western history in the Protestant Reformation. This is a freedom that was a primal source of what we have known as consciousness and history, and a freedom which finally released itself in the ultimate act of deicide, the murder of the creator and judge. (584)

What this process creates, to Altizer, is a kind of Christian nihilism, "...a nihilism which is the inevitable consequence of the absolute presence of the Christian God" (585). Based on his reasoning in the article above, Altizer seems able to greet this prospect with a sanguine heart.

Altizer's unique and almost incomprehensible argument at least conveys that some recent theologians can welcome the harsh Nietzschean critique of Christianity and can incorporate insights from poststructuralists into a framework that provides a certain kind of hope. It is a hope that the workings of God need not be restricted to former categories, that the mind of God can move into completely unfamiliar territory yet bear fruit. It should be clear that Altizer's schema rises and falls with a Hegelian interpretation of history, and Hegel's metanarrative has lost much of its luster recently, especially in the eyes of the very postmodern thinkers Altizer sees as potential allies. It would also be clear to careful theological critics that he either misunderstands or ignores the Trinitarian conception of the persons of God, and commits the heresy called *patripassianism* (that is, the Father also dies on the cross) in his view of the crucifixion. These criticisms would likely be of little concern to Altizer, however. If the "death of God" could indeed ever lead to a positive consequence, schemas like his would be a helpful guide to a distinctly unfamiliar future, a theology without theism.

Narrative Theology

One of the subcategories in the modern philosophical preoccupation with epistemology is hermeneutics, i.e. the way we interpret what we hear and read. The two figures most responsible for a new direction in hermeneutics, called narrative theology, are Paul Ricoeur and Hans Frei. Because Ricoeur's ideas first bridged the gap between philosophy and hermeneutics in theology, we will address his contribution first. Frei then utilized Ricoeur and others to develop more directly the perspective called narrative theology.

Paul Ricoeur was a prolific author whose published works spanned over three decades, three countries, and multiple disciplines. Raised by his grandparents in Rennes, France after his parents both died in World War I, he regarded himself as a philosopher, with emphasis on epistemology and neo-Kantian studies. He also admired the theology of Karl Barth, Gabriel Marcel, and the work of Karl Jaspers. He lived many years in a Christian community founded by Emmanuel Mounier, who developed the philosophy of personalism. After imprisonment during World War II, Ricoeur taught at Strasbourg and the Sorbonne in Paris. When he left France to teach in the U.S., the University of Chicago appointed him to the chair previously held by Paul Tillich.

Ricoeur's early philosophical work led him to evaluate forms of textual interpretation that he termed "hermeneutics of suspicion". He identified how dominant theories of Marx, Nietzsche and Freud, for instance, or Saussure's structuralism, insisted that to interpret a statement is to reveal how things do not mean what they first seem to mean. To these ideologies, "... the real significance of things lies elsewhere, beneath the surface, whether in the economic conditions of production, the will to power, or the unconscious." (For this and subsequent quotes, see David Pellauer's summary of Ricoeur's work in *A New Handbook...* 392). Ricoeur, like the poststructuralists, was not satisfied with this approach, since he believed it utilizes (despite likely protests from the authors) a presupposed metanarrative that purports to explain everything through one sweeping idea, and neglects the actual text. In effect, these hermeneutics of suspicion claim that what a speaker or author actually says is less important than what they didn't know they were saying. Ricoeur believes that is a mistaken, perhaps even arrogant, approach.

He leveled a similar critique against the tools of historical criticism when interpreters apply it to the Bible. One does not just read scripture for the imparting of historical information that illuminates the original author's intention and situation. Something more is happening in the text itself. Scripture uses metaphor, symbols and imaginative stories in such a manner that the symbols, metaphors and stories remain alive, "re-describing reality", as Ricoeur puts it. They become a kind of poetic language that involves the readers in a new world, drawing them into a relationship. Referring to the parables and eschatological sayings in the New Testament, he says these texts even "...involve the one who is presented as speaking them, thus adding a Christological aspect to their redescriptive power" (394). Ricoeur is openly uncomfortable with the entire combined enterprise of historical-criticism as it attempts to discover the original context of a scriptural passage and then make it relevant by "demythologizing" its archaic message. Biblical theology, he would argue, "...is not a question of replacing what scripture says by what it actually means, or by what, at least, makes sense to us today" (395). Instead, it is important to consider the different literary genres in the Bible, how they convey a "re-described" reality, and invite the reader into it.

From this background, Ricoeur developed an extended interest in religious narrative. One of his later works was the three-volume *Time and Narrative*, in which he claims that narratives, stories of the past and present, help us make sense of time by "...refiguring our understanding of our own temporal existence and experience" (396). Narrative does not work only with individuals, however. Even more, the hearing, learning and participating in historical narratives are keys to what Ricoeur calls our "narrative identity at both an individual and communal level. Who we are is significantly related to our stories that are meant to answer the question, 'Who'?" (396). Such narratives, in other words, help us discover and rediscover who we are and with whom we are in relationship.

Hans Frei also bore the scars of upheaval from war. He grew up in the Weimar Republic and the first years of Nazism in Germany. His parents, aware of their distant Jewish ancestry, sent Hans to a school in England, and just before the advent of World War II, the whole family managed to emigrate to the US. Through an unexpected set of circumstances at university, Frei met H. Richard Niebuhr at a guest lecture and shortly thereafter chose to study with Niebuhr at Yale. It was at Yale that Frei spent nearly his whole career. Though also ordained as an Episcopal priest, his primary vocational devotion was to his students.

In contrast to Ricoeur's prolific authorship, Frei published only two manuscripts during his lifetime. He is best known for *The Eclipse of Biblical Narrative*, which documents the substantial shift in hermeneutics regarding the Bible during the 18th and 19th centuries. He criticizes this reversal that interpreted the Bible in terms set by the culture. In his words from *The Eclipse*..., biblical interpretation "...became a matter of fitting the biblical story into another world with another story rather than incorporating that world into the biblical story" (Campbell,152). This position reflects his indebtedness to Karl Barth, doubtless through his teacher H.R. Niebuhr. Theology, therefore, has a "confessional" framework; it describes and defines the beliefs of the Christian faith as practiced in the church, beliefs based on awareness of the teachings of scripture. Its primary role is not to make Christian beliefs relevant to the world but to assist the church to know what it believes and live out its faith in active discipleship to Christ. Frei's perspective contributed to what became known as the "Yale" school of theology, contrasted to the "Chicago" school grounded in Paul Tillich's concept of correlation, which seeks to provide theological answers to existential questions.

Frei's connection to postmodernism includes how his suspicion of systematic apologetics resembles the poststructuralist suspicion of "foundationalism" and its sweeping ideological explanations. Like postmodernists, he also found a basis from which to critique the Cartesian mind-body dualism that describes human identity as a soul inhabiting the material flesh. This insight came from Frei's discovery of the philosopher Gilbert Ryle's book *The Concept of Mind*, which argues that the essence of human identity "... is not some hidden self – some 'ghost in the machine' – indirectly manifested in a person's words and deeds. Rather, personal identity is best understood through a person's public, intentional acts" (Campbell,154). From this insight, Frei could emphasize that Jesus' own identity is best discovered simply by looking at his actions and words in the narratives of scripture, rather than trying to find hidden motives and meanings through a psychological analysis, as it were, or through an examination of the original cultural context of the gospel writer.

What, then, would Frei mean by "narrative theology"? Frei himself would be hesitant to expand the term too far, acknowledging that much of the Bible is not narrative, but laws and poetry and letters. Still, he would insist that interpreters of scripture, when they encounter stories and narratives, must begin with what can be called the initial or literal meaning of that story rather than immediately looking behind and above it with historical investigation or philosophical generalities. As one of Frei's students explains:

> The initial meaning of a realistically told story is that, within the framework of the story, certain characters did certain deeds and underwent certain experiences. When a text provides a realistic narrative, as much of the Bible does, any interpretation that bypasses this literal meaning distorts the text. (Placher, 2)

When we permit the narrative to encounter and challenge us through its original presentation, we allow the actor to "re-describe reality" as Ricoeur asserted, and that can be transformative. We also know the actor better through their public actions and responses to circumstances, as in Gilbert Ryle's proposal.

One can see how the spirit of narrative theology would inspire the resurgence of a form of scripture study like *lectio divina*. One simply reads the passage repeatedly, asking different questions of it, allowing the passage to penetrate with its initial force through the blockages of prior misunderstandings. An appreciation of narrative theology also prompts such undertakings as the series of commentaries called *The Storytellers' Companion to the Bible* that employs stories from multiple sources to enhance understanding of specific passages. Finally and significantly, Hans Frei first articulated the cultural-linguistic model of the Christian faith, setting aside Schleiermacher's view of faith as an inner experience and instead seeing it as the "publicly enacted language and practices of the Christian community" (Campbell, 154.) In the final chapter of this volume, we will explore that theme more extensively through the lens of Frei's colleague George Lindbeck's volume *The Nature of Doctrine*.

Process Theology

With Process Theology, a prominent question that has occupied theologians for the last century comes into full view. Can we still speak of God as a "Being", a transcendent substantial entity, when the tendency of metaphysical thought over the last two hundred years has been to emphasize a spirit of dynamic, progressive "becoming"? After all, the ground from which the emergent process philosophy of Alfred North Whitehead springs is visible in Hegel's dialectic history, the evolutionary biology of Darwin, and early 20th century developments in physics, like Einstein's theories of relativity and the quantum mechanics of Max Planck and Niels Bohr. What follows in the next few pages is a tracing of the main themes of process thought from Whitehead to his student Charles Hartshorne and in turn to Hartshorne's student John Cobb.

The relationship of process thought to postmodernism is multifaceted. Some of the themes that emerge in Whitehead's work, which predates by decades the French poststructuralist school, clearly raise postmodern questions. He criticizes the mind/body split so central to Cartesian rationalism. He acknowledges the inevitable restrictions that language places upon the ability to know and communicate, and he admits that his philosophy will always be inadequate, unable to express all the permutations of the topic.

Certainly, he also rejects the mechanistic framework of Newton and its issuance into deism. Nevertheless, Whitehead places God precisely at the center of his system, and obviously he has designed the type of metanarrative that the poststructuralists cannot abide. Hence, the enduring relationship between process thought and postmodernists has never been particularly comfortable. Still, process theology does represent one very clear attempt to respond to the inadequacies of modernity, thus paralleling the goal of more explicit postmodern writers.

As the 20th century began, Whitehead and his former student Bertrand Russell launched work on what is arguably the most important book on mathematics in recent centuries, the *Principia Mathematica*. Using axioms and inferences in symbolic logic, they sought to prove all mathematical concepts, including the most simple, e.g. 1+1=2. It was a groundbreaking work, with lasting impact, even though most philosophers and mathematicians believe that Kurt Gödel's later critique undercut its ambitious premise. But by the 1920s, Whitehead had transitioned away from mathematics and into the history of science, which in turn led to an invitation to move to the U.S. and Harvard University in that field. It was there that he wrote *Science and the Modern World* in 1925, and the even more significant *Process and Reality* in 1929.

The foundational ideas in Whitehead's new metaphysics include his insistence that reality is not primarily a collection of independent bits of physical matter with only an external connection to each other. Instead, reality consists of events that link inextricably to one another, creating an experience. As one commentator explains,

> In process thought, what is real is what happens; events are real. There is no underlying substance. The event itself is the actuality,

an 'actual occasion', a droplet of reality. Events, all of them, are also experiences; they have a subjective aspect.... Thus, subject and object are not separate types of reality but alternating aspects of experience. (Beardslee, 202)

There are not, contrary to Descartes, two different kinds of real existence, one spiritual (mind) and one physical (body) that must be linked by some external vehicle. The dualism that has beset philosophy since Descartes dissolves into one sequential movement. These experiences, in Whitehead's vocabulary, are not limited to the human mind. They can exist in even inanimate processes, from electron collisions to photosynthesis in plants. That insight will prove fertile ground for some later process philosophers and theologians.

What role might God play in this series of events, these moments of "becoming"? The series of events creates new possibilities in every moment; change is constant; every moment presents a new choice, a new opportunity for free decision. But something must provide an overarching direction to the process, an order. Again, as stated by Beardslee:

> For experience to move into coherent new forms, there must be a universally present limiting and purposive reality that offers direction to each occasion, a direction to which the occasion may or may not respond....Process thought calls this ordering reality God. (202)

However, the God who provides this ordering of reality does not do so by authoritarian fiat or by predetermined plan. Whitehead criticizes traditional Christianity for its picture of God as king, an eternal Caesar. Instead, God has a more permission-giving personality. Divine power is not the threat of punishment but the power of persuasion, encouraging each moment in the process of becoming to move in the direction of attaining the full wealth of possibility. Each moment has the option of listening and following that direction encouraged by God, but it can also refuse.

This option, the freedom of an experience to develop differently than God wishes, has substantial implications for the traditional ideas of the sovereignty and omniscience of God. God is not immutable, but changeable, indeed could not be otherwise if God offers true freedom of choice to the world's events. Every event affects God, so God also is not impassible. Rather, God stores up each event and incorporates it into the divine life, saving and cherishing each one as a factor that will influence the way God acts in the future. God's identity depends upon the world to a certain extent, since the world is in flux. In *Process and Reality*, he declares,

> In this way God is completed by the individual, fluent satisfactions of finite fact, and the temporal occasions are completed by their everlasting union with their transformed selves, purged into conformation with the eternal order which is the final absolute 'wisdom'. (347)

Even more succinctly, he says "What is done in the world is transformed into a reality in heaven, and the reality in heaven passes back into the world....In this sense, God is the great companion – the fellow-sufferer who understands" (351).

It should not be difficult to recognize the revolutionary potential of Whitehead's philosophy, not only for metaphysics and science, but also for theology. The immanent presence of God related to the ongoing processes of events replaces the image of the omniscient and transcendent God who intervenes only at certain times and places into human history. For further development of these themes, however, we will consider the work of Whitehead's student, Charles Hartshorne.

It is intriguing to think that a person who developed what some regard as a very sophisticated, abstract theology experienced two intense religious visions during his formative early years. Serving as an orderly in a medical corps during World War I, Hartshorne lay upon the deck of a ship crossing the Atlantic and viewed the vast starry skies above. What he called "close to a mystical experience" started him thinking about God as the Spirit of the whole cosmos (a view often labeled panpsychism). Scant months later in France, he looked upon a beautiful landscape and, as he put it, "saw into the life of things", solidifying his earlier experience and affirming his belief that God is the soul of the universe. These insights never left him, and launched him into a lifelong search for a metaphysical framework that would emphasize God's presence in all things. (For these observations and following comments, we are indebted to David Ray Griffin's article in *A New Handbook...*).

Years after his return from the war, Hartshorne attended Harvard, completed his doctoral work, and was fortunate indeed to be assigned as a teaching assistant to Whitehead. Though adopting many of Whitehead's ideas, Hartshorne also expanded and refined them. One of those ideas was "prehension". Each of the momentary events, which Whitehead saw as the true building blocks of reality, has the ability to "prehend", or sympathetically feel, all the prior events in the chain of experience. Hartshorne concluded that even at a metaphysical level, sympathetic love works to connect past to present to future. The "self" of anything is thus not a separate substance, but an interconnected series of experiences held together by sympathy. This new perspective, in Hartshorne's view, shows that sympathetic love is "the clue to cosmology and epistemology as well as to religion and ethics" (Griffin, 205).

He also clarified process philosophy's understanding of the relationship of God to the world, utilizing the belief called panentheism. This is not pantheism, the idea that God is entirely identified with the universe. In panentheism, God exists in all things but also has a separate identity outside those things. The universe is thus the body of God, and God the soul of the universe, but God can still influence all things in the world from outside it and can know and include it within God's own existence. Panentheism implies that God is dipolar, one pole of God being inextricably affected by the universe, and another remaining separate. This picture of God has been criticized as diminishing the perfection of God, but Hartshorne would counter that the definition of God's perfection needs to be expanded. He calls these two poles God's "concrete states" and God's "abstract essence", the model for this distinction being how a person can have both successive concrete experiences and yet maintain an abstract character that is exemplified in those experiences. In other words, contrary to traditional terminology, there is no reason why the perfection of God must be "simple" or without parts. Even as traditional Christian doctrine acknowledges both the economic and the immanent presentations of the Trinity, while maintaining their ultimate unity, so does Hartshorne claim a similar idea. God's abstract essence can be necessary, eternal, independent, impassible and unchanging, yet the concrete states of God show a God who is contingent, temporal, dependent, relative, and changeable (210-211). Hartshorne would contend, and many have agreed, that this formula presents a better understanding of the perfection of God while also accurately portraying the active, involved, changeable God of the Bible.

Charles Hartshorne's century-long lifetime of achievement included a contemporary reinterpretation and defense of Anselm's ontological argument and inroads into a new natural theology, yet his specific advancement of process theology has been our primary concern here. As Hartshorne was a student to Whitehead, so did he greatly influence the third figure we now meet. After some years as an instructor at Harvard, Hartshorne had moved to a joint appointment at the University of Chicago and the Divinity School there. It was in Chicago that he supervised the doctoral dissertation of a brilliant young student named John B. Cobb, Jr. Cobb had recently returned to the U.S. after living with his missionary parents in Japan, and from 1947 to 1952 had earned his Bachelor, Master, and Doctoral degrees. Through Hartshorne, Cobb imbibed the process philosophy of Whitehead, and Hartshorne's own turn toward process theology. Although Cobb became a renowned, multi-faceted theologian in his own right, it is his emphasis on the ethical, political and ecological implications of process thought that we now consider briefly. (For comments that follow see Suchocki in *A New Handbook...*). If in fact Whitehead's interpretation of themes like prehension is accurate, and his criticism of the mind/body dualism is justified, then reality is integrally connected and deeply relational. The Christian faith, to John Cobb, should do a much better job of presenting that reality and acting to preserve and enhance it. Also, if God's power is persuasive rather than authoritarian, then the picture of God in traditional doctrine (and in the neo-orthodoxy of Karl Barth) is misleading. It should be amended. As a committed Christian ordained to ministry in the Methodist church, Cobb dedicated a substantial portion of his writings to educating laity in churches on ethical and ecological topics.

His first book of this type was *Is It Too Late? A Theology of Ecology*. It focused on the dangers of dualistic thinking and the materialist attitude that sees nature as resource. Specifically, it documents the harm done to nature by misguided consumerist ideologies. *Is It Too Late...* was a study guide for adult education classes in churches, utilizing frank interchange and discussion to motivate members toward changing their approach to the organic world around them. Cobb offers a slightly different emphasis in later books, *Process Theology as Political Theology* and *For the Common Good*. These are direct challenges to churches to become much more involved in political decisions that affect culture, pushing legislators toward more just and participatory policies. Churches are to be self-critical about their present and past complicity in oppressive, exploitative public practices, including economic divisions. Process theology, with its insistence on relatedness, prompts professional theologians and lay leaders to recognize their connection to the social and natural environment around them and to engage in local public policy. One intriguing suggestion from *For the Common Good* is to substitute an Index of Sustainable Economic Well-Being for the index of Gross National Product, for a more conscientious and ultimately accurate assessment of the real, lasting wealth of a nation.

John Cobb, in conjunction with another of Hartshorne's students, David Ray Griffin, established the Center for Process Studies at Claremont University in California, where Cobb continued to teach until retirement in 1990. He demonstrates how an abstract intellectual system begun 70 years earlier in the mind of a renowned historian of science can become, through three generations, a driving force in ecological and ethical decisions of immense practical value for a nation seeking its way into the future.

Liberation Theology

In the decades after World War II, inspired by the social gospel and by the Second Vatican Council's calls for *aggiornamento*, theologians in Western Europe and Latin America once again raised the cry that Christian thought must dismantle the wall of separation between individual salvation and societal improvement. German thinkers like Jürgen Moltmann, J.B. Metz, and Dorothy Soelle articulated a vision ultimately named *political theology*. Soelle's 1971 book of that same name enhanced and popularized themes stated in Moltmann's *Theology of Hope* and *The Crucified God*, Metz's *Theology of the World* and Soelle's own *Christ the Representative*. Simultaneously, in Peru, Gustavo Gutierrez published his groundbreaking *A Theology of Liberation*, which forever changed the relationship of the Latin American church to culture and the organizational structure of the church itself. His work was both inspired by and prompted the writings of other liberation theologians like Juan Luis Segundo, Leonardo Boff, Rubem Alves, Jon Sobrino, and Jose Bonino. Because of specific geographical and cultural differences, in this current section we concentrate on these South American figures and their liberation theology. Later, in the penultimate pages of this volume, we will return to political theology and its intersection with other postmodern influences that undergird the cry for freedom from oppression and greater civil rights by black and feminist communities.

Two quite different cultural backdrops combined to give Gustavo Gutierrez knowledge of two worlds. Born into a working-class section of Lima, Peru, he overcame poverty and disease (osteomyelitis) in the first 20 years of his life and entered university for premedical training, switching soon to philosophy and theology. For the subsequent two decades, his life revolved around formal theological education in Belgium, France and Rome, plus a position on the faculty back at the Catholic Pontifical Institute in Lima. His dual appointment as a parish priest and professor prompted what one commentator has called his "theological realignment" (Taylor, *A New Handbook...*, 189-199). He re-entered the world of the poor, critically reoriented his academic training, and envisioned a new model for parish churches. The key components of that realignment follow, as articulated in illuminating chapters from *A Theology of Liberation*, published in Spanish in 1971, English in 1973. He elaborated on these beliefs later in a collection of essays, *The Power of the Poor in History* (1983).

As his theological development continued, Gutierrez became increasingly convinced that the saving action of Jesus Christ concerns the whole person, not just the soul. The dualism of matter and spirit so prominent in 17th century philosophy is, to him, simply unbiblical. Similarly, the earlier orthodox belief in limited atonement has given way to the belief in the universality of God's salvific will, that God extends salvation to all people (*Theology...*, 49, 50). Grace is present in all. Hence, we need not interpret salvation as if it referred only to life after death, making this world merely a test to see if we qualify. Christ's life, death, and resurrection embrace all human reality, transforming all creation, thus making it possible "...for man to reach fulfillment as a human being" (151). One implication of this means there is one history, not a divine history and a profane history that may or may not interact. He thus repudiates Augustine's separation of realms. As he puts it, "...there is only one history, a 'Christo-finalized' history" (153).

If Christ sets in motion a salvific history, eschatology (study of the "end times") becomes a central theme of that platform. Gutierrez believes that "...the Bible presents eschatology as the driving force of salvific history radically oriented toward the future" (162). He expands on that belief later in *The Power of the Poor in History*, connecting it with the idea of God's "preference for the poor":

> The God of the Bible is a God who not only governs history, but who orientates it in the direction of establishment of justice and right. He is more than a provident God. He is a God who takes sides with the poor and liberates them from slavery and oppression. (7)

Those who are oppressed may indeed find salvation in a heavenly realm after death, but they can also have confidence that history is leading to a time when they will no longer be oppressed on earth either. Nonetheless, lest his emphasis on future eschatology be misinterpreted as salvation by works or a human construction of the future kingdom, Gutierrez emphasizes that the full realization of liberation requires God's action to bring in the kingdom, which Gutierrez calls a "gift".

The previous paragraphs have recounted Gutierrez's new interpretations of standard doctrines like salvation and eschatology. As significant as his contribution on these themes may be, they are neither particularly distinctive nor revolutionary. It is three other ideas Gutierrez emphasizes that distinguish liberation theology from other progressive interpretations of Christian doctrine.

Through reflections on God's preferential option for the poor, Gutierrez senses a distinction between North American or European political theologies and those in Latin America. In *The Power of the Poor in History*, he declares that such theologies from privileged societies attempt to answer questions and criticisms from nonbelievers. What new ideas would bring such doubters back to the church? What makes Christian thought respectable in the eyes of a secular public? These are intellectual questions, he feels, arguments about the Enlightenment or science. In his home country Peru and the other colonized nations of the south, theology must speak instead to those looked upon as "nonpersons", the marginalized, whose opinions are not sought by the ruling powers because their opinions are already dismissed as worthless. Most of those to whom liberation theology directs its message are already Christian believers, but even church authorities sideline them through a hierarchical, entrenched structure beholden to the ruling classes. So he writes, "Our question is how to tell the nonperson, the nonhuman, that God is love, and that this love makes us all brothers and sisters" (193).

That observation about the primary audience of liberation theology is integral to a second groundbreaking idea, Gutierrez's vision for the church in Latin America. This in turn leads to his third breakthrough, the truly significant insistence on a new model for a theology that springs from and is secondary to involvement in local communities and their struggles. For these topics, we turn to two other liberation theologians that have developed these insights of Gutierrez, Leonardo Boff and Juan Luis Segundo.

Much in the mold of Gutierrez, Boff grew up in a poor working class family and was educated in some of Europe's leading universities. His Brazilian homeland, to which he returned, languished under a military dictatorship during the early years of his ministry at a Franciscan seminary. His superb mind and passionate concern for the oppressed drove him into a wide range of positions as researcher, author, lecturer and social activist. He was theological adviser for the Brazilian Conference of Catholic Bishops and editor of many religious journals. He was the cofounder and president of the

National Movement for the Defense of Human Rights. We examine here his book *Ecclesiogenesis*, as it is one of the foundational descriptions of the movement known as ecclesial base communities.

He begins the book with a description of the spontaneous origin of these small church fellowships. The overarching and distant hierarchy of the Roman Catholic Church fosters an authoritarian juridical understanding of relationships among Christians. That lack of local community, combined with a shortage of priests to serve smaller parishes, prompted respected lay leaders in a barrio of Rio de Janeiro to gather friends, families and neighbors into groups for catechesis and mutual support. The movement caught on fast, creating an atmosphere that, in Boff's words, "…is characterized by the absence of alienating structure, by direct relationships, by reciprocity, by a deep communion, by mutual assistance, by communality of gospel ideals, by equality among members" (4). As members see personally what gathering around the word of God can accomplish, they discover self-worth and begin to mobilize to address the oppression they deal with on a daily basis. Boff and other liberation theologians never believe these base communities can or should replace the institutional church, but they can renew and reform it. Challenged by the ecclesial hierarchy and by political leaders, Boff insisted that the base communities are fundamental and lasting, not a brief experiment. He also insists that temporal transformation of conditions and greater justice must accompany the idea of individual salvation. He served blunt notice that members of these communities will oppose the paternalism of the elite who treat the poor like ignorant children (37-40).

To the consternation of the Vatican, many base communities saw the capitalist economic system as the chief cause of their suffering. Some endorsed the use of Marxist social analysis, and most all believed that political protest and activism would arise from the grassroots. Boff's increasing alienation from the Vatican, plus his growing radical views on salvation among non-Christians, led him to renounce his ordination and to leave the Franciscan order he had served for decades. Nonetheless, the base communities that he loved and encouraged remain at the heart of the theological method that he and Gutierrez promoted. We will look at the basic features of this method through the work of Juan Luis Segundo.

Segundo, a Uruguayan Jesuit priest, actually published a groundbreaking attempt to describe theology from the perspective of the poor nearly a decade before Gutierrez's Theology of Liberation. He is the representative of Latin American writers who focuses most on the presuppositions behind liberation theology and the method it employs.

Common to all liberation theology is the underlying belief that thought must be anchored in active practice, or praxis. The word "Praxis" has Marxist roots. In his "Theses on Feuerbach" and in his notebooks, Marx insists that theoretical philosophy will never be effective unless it arises from an initial commitment to change people's circumstances, a commitment which guides the direction and sets the limits of theory (*Writings of the Young Marx*, 23, 247, et al). In turn, in Segundo's view liberation theology insists that "anthropological faith precedes religious faith", that:

> ...one cannot truly know Christ theologically, and thus 'believe' in Christ, unless one lives a Christlike life through which one comes to know Christ concretely and practically, in one's relationships with one's brothers and sisters. (Goizueta, *A New Handbook...*, 424)

The liberation theologian, therefore, begins with a spiritual commitment to the poor people of a parish and neighborhood, pledging to improve their circumstances, and then begins to reinterpret doctrine and scripture in light of that commitment. Gutierrez persistently emphasized that theology is a second act, after commitment to action, praxis.

Segundo details the way this reinterpretation works by a four-part "hermeneutical circle" that spotlights historical context and ideology's effects on reason. The implanted, committed individual begins to question ideas and doctrines that conflict with his or her specific communal situation. They then pose those questions to their overall understanding of Christian faith. The next step involves addressing the scripture previously used to defend those ideas and doctrines, resulting in a new interpretation of scripture that speaks more concretely and directly to the current situation of the oppressed poor (Goizueta, 420). This hermeneutical method does not end with a one-time conclusion. Interpretation continues as one's experiences change. Its ongoing goal is always to be able to show the incarnate word of God in contemporary context. This method bears substantial resemblance to the postmodern critique of abstract reason and unchanging, "pure" ahistorical narratives.

The fate of liberation theology in Latin America has depended partly on the theological orientation of the papacy. Neither John Paul II nor his successor Pope Benedict could accept even the distant Marxist connection advocated by Boff and others. They appointed more conservative bishops and discouraged outspoken advocates of liberation thought. The tenure of Pope Francis, however, prompted a resurgence of popular support for base ecclesial communities. Furthermore, the international impact of liberation theology and the idea of small, supportive "cell groups" continues to reach far beyond the original movement in the neglected communities of Latin America, especially into places where people treated as "nonpersons" yearn for recognition and a remedy for the grinding oppression they have suffered.

Dietrich Bonhoeffer's "Nonreligious Christianity"

Both Liberation theologians like Gutierrez and Death of God thinkers like Thomas Altizer trace some of their insights back to Dietrich Bonhoeffer, the young German pastor/professor whom the Nazis executed just weeks before the end of World War II. Only 39 when he died, Bonhoeffer's writings enjoyed a rapid rise to prominence in the 1950s and 60s, when Protestant pastors in Europe and the U.S. read *The Cost of Discipleship*, *Life Together*, the *Ethics*, and especially his *Letters and Papers from Prison*. As research by his friend and biographer Eberhard Bethge and others progressed, other works like his lectures on Christology, two essays called "Creation and Fall" and "Temptation", and a brief monograph on the Psalms appeared on the bookshelves of those who admired his theology and his final act of sacrificial discipleship.

Bonhoeffer's writings, like the thinkers already noted in earlier pages of this section, reflect the tension between postmodernism and traditional Protestant theology, but his particular Christocentric resolution of that tension proposes a truly challenging option for the church's future. His earlier works, rooted in patristics, Luther and Karl Barth, undergird and foreshadow his more radical later statements about Christian faith in the modern and postmodern eras. Our treatment of his work, regrettably oversimplified, will divide into four related categories. The first is his theology of the cross and its resultant focus on Christ as the Crucified One. Second is his emphasis on God as the Lord of history, with Christ present differently in different historical moments. Next is his critique of "religion", leading to his advocacy of a "religionless Christianity"; and finally, his positive view of "worldliness" that led him to welcome "the world come of age."

Theology of the Cross: In prior chapters we have noted how, in the Heidelberg Disputation of 1518, Martin Luther listed 28 theological theses that define how Jesus Christ is and is not revealed to the world. Among those, #19 says, "That person does not deserve to be called a theologian who looks upon the invisible things of God as though they were clearly perceptible in those things which have actually happened." #20 continues, "He deserves to be called a theologian, however, who comprehends the visible and manifest things of God seen through suffering and the cross." #21 concludes the theme, "A theology of glory calls evil good and good evil. A theology of the cross calls the thing what it actually is" (Tappert, 66). Luther's sole intention in these tenets is to assert that philosophical thought, whether based on abstract concepts or empirical investigation, cannot truly discern the hand of God at work in the world. Because all human thought begins with the nearsightedness of its own perspective, it will always see only what it allows itself to see, and cannot penetrate to the "invisible things of God". To look upon the world from the perspective of the cross, however, which turns common presuppositions on their head, is to grow closer to seeing things as they actually are in the domain of God's rule.

Bonhoeffer embraces Luther's description wholeheartedly. In one of his very earliest writings, "Concerning the Christian Idea of God", Bonhoeffer asserts:

> The last 'reality' for all consistent philosophical reflection must be an ego….Thinking does violence to reality, pulling it into the

circle of the ego, taking away from it its original 'objectivity'. Thinking always means system and system excludes reality. (*Gessamelte Schriften*...101)

God is often a hidden God who reveals Godself in the opposite of what is expected. In St. Paul's language, God "destroys the wisdom of the wise" because for Christ wisdom is foolishness and weakness is strength. Bonhoeffer will continue to insist throughout his career that only those who have experienced the suffering that comes with the cross will be able to understand and properly demonstrate what God is doing in the world. From his early writings to his last, Bonhoeffer speaks about Christians learning to take "the view from below", standing by those who suffer, acting on behalf of them, becoming like their Lord, who Bonhoeffer in his letters from prison later calls "the man for others". This is not just a call to discipleship, therefore. It is also the equivalent of a hermeneutical principle, for only those who undergo sacrifice on behalf of others will understand how God reveals Godself to people of faith. All truth, to be known as such, must run not through the filter of abstract principles or empirical verification, but through the person of Jesus Christ.

History and the Forms of Christ: In Christian theology, God's actions within history, in specific identifiable contexts, demonstrate that God is not an abstract idea but a living being. Furthermore, the God who acts in history directs time from a beginning to an end, intervening from without and acting from within the processes of history to redeem and providentially guide God's people. To Bonhoeffer, this means that we encounter God in daily events, repeatedly asking, "Who are you?" Bonhoeffer begins his lectures on Christology with that precise question to Christ (*Christ the Center*, 28-31). This is the only question that draws us into dialogue with

Christ. Questions beginning with "what" or "how" already imply that Christ is an object, a thing to observe rather than a person who in turn questions us. In his *Ethics*, Bonhoeffer develops this theme with an emphasis on the particular form Christ takes to address us in different situations. He comes to us always as a person, but sometimes as the Incarnate One, sometimes as the Crucified One, and at others as the Risen One. As we encounter Christ, he calls us to conform to his image "… formation comes only by being drawn into the form of Jesus Christ. It comes only as formation in his likeness, as *conformation* with the unique form of Him who was made man, was crucified, and rose again" (80).

This dynamic, rooted in the awareness that only when Christ confronts us as a person will we avoid the egocentric circle of interpretation, now becomes for Bonhoeffer an interpretive framework for viewing the work of Christ in history. Not only does Christ speak to an individual; he speaks also to an age, an era. As the *Incarnate One*, Christ reveals concretely the reality of his humanness, and shows to those seeking conformation to him that they must be fully human. To the kind of religion that sees salvation only as an escape from harsh earthly reality, or denies the good things of life out of fear of entrapment, Christ the Incarnate One emphasizes how the fullness of good human existence is a redeemed gift of God.

Christ forms himself as the *Crucified One*, and draws others to this form, when those who live as fully human, responsible beings realize that nonetheless they are people sentenced by God. They are found wanting because of the sin that remains within them, a sin that despite their best intentions has harmed many people because of the entrenched institutions and destructive practices in which they participate. Only as they realize the depth of that sin, and are conformed to the Crucified One, do they know the real God. "It is only as one who is sentenced by God that man can live before God. Only the crucified man is at peace with God" (*Ethics*, 75).

Yet at times Christ also comes to the world and to individuals as the *Risen One*. In the midst of our enjoyment of a full human life, conformed to the Incarnate One, followed by the acceptance of our sin when conformed to the Crucified One, we also, then and only then, realize the coming hope and redemption that results when Christ the Risen One reveals the truth of his resurrection. Now the individual, and the age, becomes a new creation. "...wherever it is recognized that the power of death has been broken, wherever the world of death is illumined by the miracle of the new life..." that is where the Risen One has taken form in a person or an age (79).

These manifestations of Christ in the forms of his existence are Bonhoeffer's way of seeing the living God at work in the world. He does not attempt a classification of historical periods through this threefold framework, but we will see that he does use the forms of Christ to speak to individuals, to the church and to society in what he calls "the world come of age".

Religion and Religionless Christianity: Partly under the influence of Karl Barth's critical interpretation of religion, and more keenly because of the failure of the official German church to resist the rise of Nazism, Bonhoeffer in his later writings staunchly criticizes the way well-intentioned faith in Christ deteriorates into self-serving religiosity. By the time he was writing his letters from prison to his family and to Bethge, Bonhoeffer had concluded that only a "religionless" Christianity should survive in the modern world.

The religiousness, or religiosity, of western Christianity consists in his opinion of two misguided motivations that manifest in three ways. One of those prime motivations he describes in a letter of July 18, 1944. "To be a Christian does not mean to be religious in a particular way, to make something of oneself (a sinner, a penitent, or a saint) on the basis of some method or other..." Later he laments that too many religious people take this route because they are "...in the first place thinking about one's own needs, problems, sins and fears..." rather than simply "...allowing oneself to be caught up into the way of Jesus Christ" (*Letters...*, 361). Concerned primarily about their own welfare, religious people attempt to justify their actions and even their very existence by creating their own self-fulfilling identity based on themselves rather than on Christ.

The other motivation connects to the first. Because of the focus on one's own needs and problems, the religious person tends to picture God as a god of power, in a triumphalist manner, someone whose power can alleviate those needs and problems. Yet, Bonhoeffer warns that really the main difference between genuine Christianity and all other religions, including misinterpretations within Christianity, is that true faith can see the hidden and suffering God, whereas "Man's religiosity makes him look in his distress to the power of God in the world..." (361).

These two motivations, self-justification and seeing God only in terms of power, work their way into three expressions of religiousness. They are two-sphere thinking and its resultant individualism, interpreting God through metaphysical categories, and the misuse of religion for personal privilege.

Thinking in two spheres is Bonhoeffer's pejorative label for the tendency to contrast two different realms of life, "...the one divine, holy, supernatural and Christian, the other worldly, profane, natural and un-Christian" (*Ethics*, 196). Far too much of our Christian heritage promoted this bifurcation of reality. That has led to the inability of modern believers to act in such a way that they "... never experience the reality of God without the reality of the world or the reality of the world without the reality of God" (195). (Note here a similarity to the postmodern protest against dualism). The negative result of two-sphere thinking is that the whole person also becomes separated within oneself, and dwells mostly in the individualistic tendencies of self-satisfaction, insulated from the corrective disciplines that a diverse community would provide. Individuals focus so much on salvation from one's own sins that they become inward looking and neglect larger surrounding issues.

The second negative characteristic of religious Christianity is its insistence on defining God through metaphysical categories, and using those metaphysical constructions of God as an explanation for the mysterious universe. Bonhoeffer wants to dissociate Christian faith from all metaphysical presuppositions. Too many of the metaphysical schemas throughout the history of theology cast the idea of God's transcendence in spatial terms, as if divine transcendence means God is up in heaven waiting to swoop down when needed, a kind of *deus ex machina*. We regard God as transcendent because God provides answers to the questions we cannot yet answer. Yet, when those answers do come, through further scientific research, God becomes less needed. In a letter to Bethge on June 8, 1944, Bonhoeffer expresses his grave concerns that the modern world does not need God anymore. "Man has learnt to deal with himself in all questions of importance without recourse to the 'working hypothesis' called God....It is becoming evident that everything gets along without 'God' – and in fact, just as well as before" (325).

The third mistake made in religious Christianity Bonhoeffer calls "privilege". By this word, he means two things, one personal and one institutional. The individual Christian is too prone to seek an estimable, advantaged social position afforded to church members in some societies. This may be less a problem today than in the middle of the 20th century, but the practice of adding membership in a church to one's dossier in order to cement one's reputation as responsible and kind is not entirely passé. The country-club church still exists in many places, where church connections create convenient business connections, and the inner pride that some Christians feel for belonging to the "right" church in town is quite pervasive even now. More worrisome to Bonhoeffer, though, is the institutional privilege that the church has embraced because of the separation of realms that Luther had promoted. The blind acceptance of Nazism by the official *Reichskirche* stemmed from the belief that the church could remain separate from politics and leave that realm to God's appointed representatives of the state. Such a belief creates the attitude that the church is guardian of religious truths, and that it should stick to that realm. This affords the church the mistaken impression that it has the privilege of not getting its hands dirty in political affairs. However, such isolation allows the perpetuation of unjust governments simply because they currently hold power. Whatever the realm of privilege, personal or institutional, it once again makes religion oblivious to the Christ who suffers on behalf of others.

These two motivations, and the three ways they become manifest, prompt Bonhoeffer to lament what the church has become, and to promote a "religionless" Christianity as the only possible alternative to proclaim to a world that has come of age.

The World Come of Age: In the significant June 8 letter quoted above, Bonhoeffer also shares with Bethge his assessment that western society has reached an entirely new status in relation to God and to earlier ages.

> The movement that began about the thirteenth century... towards the autonomy of man (in which I should include the discovery of the laws by which the world lives and deals with itself in science, social and political matters, art, ethics, and religion) has in our time reached an undoubted completion. (325)

As noted by other thinkers in the mid-20th century (including most of those noted earlier in this section) changes in philosophy and science have arrived at a watershed of ideas, including the irreversible launch of political freedom, the irrevocable trust in human reason, and the end of static metaphysics in favor of progressive dynamism. Detractors of this so-called revolution, reflecting on the myriad failures to execute these ideals, would dispute the certainty with which Bonhoeffer speaks. Actually, Bonhoeffer nowhere insists that this progress is complete or that it is ethically or spiritually superior to previous eras. He simply insists that the "autonomy" of free human reason is here to stay, cannot be reversed. The world and its leaders have come to maturity; have "come of age"; they have arrived at the right kind of worldliness. This fact makes the religiosity and preservative, privileged posture of traditional Christianity all the more outmoded or repugnant to the "worldly" leaders who influence the future.

Bonhoeffer's next belief is even more unsettling to the ears of comfortable religion. It is Jesus Christ himself, in his form of the Incarnate One, who urges people to shed the former trappings of Christian security and become truly "worldly" in the best sense of that word. Bonhoeffer commends the maturity and worldliness of modern leaders that prompt them to live right in the midst of earthly, human concerns, rather than retreating from the world as if it were profane. His peripheral involvement in a plot to overthrow Hitler placed him in the company of responsible, successful "worldly" leaders, very few of whom came from the church. By immersing oneself in daily human struggles and victories, the Christian could come to know the incarnate and earthly Christ, the Incarnate One. Furthermore, to those who have already come of age, who thrive in the midst of a full daily life, Bonhoeffer urges them to take the next step in discipleship, to connect personally with people outside their successful circles, to risk their success for a greater cause, to aid the broken. In so doing, they suffer alongside those oppressed by disease, political repression or ignorance. Then, in that identification with those who suffer, the truly worldly, mature people discover the presence of the Crucified One, the Christ, "the man for others".

Bonhoeffer thus shows (as he puts it) how we can understand the world "...better than it understands itself..." "Thus the world's coming of age is no longer an occasion for polemics and apologetics, but is now really better understood than it understands itself, namely on the basis of the gospel and in the light of Christ" (329). The God revealed in Christ the Incarnate One speaks clearly to the still religious church that it must leave its defensive walls and its misguided picture of divine transcendence and live right in the middle of earth's difficulties and joys. Beyond that, Christ the Crucified One urges the worldly man and woman to find their deepest longing and calling in the company of the man for others. In such a world, where religious, defensive Christianity has proven useless, a nonreligious, effective Christianity may look very different. As he writes to his infant nephew:

Our earlier words are therefore bound to lose their force and cease, and our being Christians today will be limited to two things: prayer and righteous action among men. All Christian thinking, speaking, and organizing must be born anew out of this prayer and action. (300)

We can see in these themes of Bonhoeffer's "nonreligious Christianity" many ideas that have resurfaced in the last half century, as theologians have tried to relate the person of Jesus Christ and the Christian scriptures to the current world of postmodern society. Three such promising trends form the substance of the following, final chapter.

| seven |

Prospects for Cooperation

Deconstructing Cultural "Isms"

At the end of an earlier chapter that had presented an overview of postmodern characteristics, we stated a lingering question, "… are we not left wondering how one defines the useful limits of deconstructionism, and where it leads to hopeless, self-defeating criticism of all things?" That question arose when considering the stark comments of Michel Foucault, such as "Truth is a thing of this world; it is produced only by virtue of mutual forms of constraint. And it induces regular effects of power." Also, "Truth is also linked in a circular relation with systems of power which produce and sustain it.…" Foucault contends, in short, that basic beliefs of a culture, and the language that culture employs, are artificially constructed to sustain prevailing positions of power.

A reply to that earlier question about useful limits may now gain clarity as we consider the first prospect for cooperation between postmodern themes and the practices of Christian faith. The scourge of cultural "isms" – racism, sexism, and classism – provides a timely, significant arena for employing deconstructionist tactics in the quest for full equal opportunity in society. In that earlier chapter, examples of these "isms" appeared in comments from Cornel West, Susan Bordo, Sandra Harding, and Iris Young. With those examples in mind, we now can turn the discussion toward the role of the church in addressing these problems.

Throughout its history, the Christian church has tried to establish justice in society by treating all human beings with the respect and dignity owed them as people created in God's image. It is freely admitted here that the church has not been consistently successful in such efforts, and has indeed perpetrated instances of oppression. Nonetheless, many Christian churches over the last decades have demonstrated that they can be significant allies for groups seeking to expose entrenched, repressive, discriminatory cultural practices. In that effort, churches have been guided by the best of the Christian gospel and the best of modernity's insistence on human rights and personal freedoms. Moreover, the postmodern awareness that racism, sexism and classism are systemic, rooted in longstanding, self-serving power structures, has most likely given some current churches a renewed impetus to address these persistent inequalities.

A current case in point is the national debate about teaching critical race theory in schools. It is controversial precisely because the theory seeks to illuminate the systemic, ongoing nature of racism. A second glaring issue concerns the persistent social and economic factors that entrench women, especially women of color, in recurring poverty. Issues of this nature reveal the need to "deconstruct" the institutions that perpetuate these injustices, to reveal and confront the atmosphere of entrenched power that overrides well-intentioned personal efforts to make things better. What role can the church play in that deconstructionist effort? This will be addressed in two parts. First, what can the Christian faith contribute to the deconstruction? Second, how must the Christian church itself change in response to postmodern criticism of its doctrines and practices?

The Christian faith maintains four enduring beliefs that it can offer to the current dialogues about systemic racism, sexism and classism: an insistence on the corporate nature of sin; the necessity of complete repentance to overcome the effects of sin; its affirmation that personal worth is a gracious gift that empowers the recipient; and an eschatological vision, which sustains hope.

The belief that an individual's sin carries substantial consequences for the surrounding community, and that the sin of a community substantially influences an individual's action, resounds throughout the Bible, especially in the Old Testament. Phrases like "The iniquities of the fathers are visited upon the children for many generations" (Ex.34:7) embody the awareness that sin transcends time. Purity codes, intended to protect the community from threats to health and virtue, reflect the interrelatedness of life. The repeated apostasy of kings ends in massive destruction of cities and exile centuries later. In the mythic story of humanity's fall in Genesis, even the ground will be punished, yielding thorns and thistles. Christian theology has understood from its very start that sin is entrenched in public institutions and that it embodies an invisible misuse of power. In his autobiographical critique of small town racism, *Blood Done Sign My Name*, Timothy Tyson recounts how even well intentioned children breathe in an atmosphere of racist presuppositions and discover only later, or perhaps never, who they have become.

Definitions of sin arising in recent decades within the Christian community have accentuated this corporate nature. In *Political Theology*, Dorothy Soelle argues:

> ...the sinner is the collaborator (seemingly harmless from the point of view of the natural consciousness) of a structurally founded, usually anonymous injustice. Accordingly, for political theology sin would be collaboration and apathy. (89)

Delores Williams interprets sin as participation in the social structures that lead to the defilement and devaluation of black women (Williams, 557-561). Rosemary Radford Ruether insists that a modern definition of sin must resist its "victim-blaming" tendencies (e.g. Eve) and instead recognize the patriarchal misuse of such stories (Ruether, 539). To recognize that sin is entrenched in institutions that perpetuate power, not merely individual instances of injustice, is a significant contribution of the deconstruction of unjust "isms".

The second important theme in Christian theology that supports what would now be called a "deconstruction" of embedded injustice is the complete doctrine of penitence. To emphasize the complete doctrine is to affirm that true repentance requires more than just a temporary feeling of regret about one's sin. Understood in its fullness, the traditional doctrine of penitence includes four parts: personal sorrow and remorse for what one has done; a public confession of guilt, perhaps to a priest, confessor, or in the midst of a congregation; an acceptance of forgiveness, sometimes expressed as absolution of sin or assurance of pardon; and, significantly, an act of satisfaction, which means reparation for the injury caused by the sin. One has not fully satisfied the ritual of penitence unless the final act tries to repair the relationship that was broken or change the circumstances that caused the sin in the first place. In monumental social issues like racism, violence against women, or exaggerated economic disparity, some form of repair, whether that be Affirmative Action, strengthening of domestic abuse protective orders, a modern equivalent of the biblical "jubilee year", or explicit monetary reparation, is required before society can begin to free itself from lasting injustice.

It is striking to recognize that certain postmodern writers confronting systemic injustices of society utilize a framework that bears a certain similarity to this traditional doctrine of penance. Both Rosemary Radford Ruether ("Feminist Theology..."), and Anne E. Carr, *Transforming Grace*, describe the three tasks of the women's movement in churches. Carr notes (7-10), "Both logically and chronologically, its first task is critique of the past", by which she means awareness of the problem, confronting the misleading images that have created the problem, naming the sin, as it were. Following this naming of the problem comes a step toward reclaiming confidence, which might be compared to the feeling of freedom that arises with forgiveness. In the feminist framework it means "...the recovery of the lost history of women in the Christian tradition." Every medieval saint, every unrecognized abbess of an influential convent, every Anne Hutchinson who challenged male Puritan authority, helps women recover hope that they can overcome the past and believe in the possibility of a redeemed future. The third aspect of this framework for progress Carr names "revisioning Christian categories in ways that take seriously the equality and the experience of women" (7-10). This is the "reconstructionist" element, the movement to make the changes needed to prevent the continuation of the injustice. It is a set of actions reminiscent of the final step of satisfaction in genuine repentance. Hence, whether it is consciously recognized or not, the doctrine of penance reveals its relevance to frameworks for change in some postmodern efforts.

The third contribution of Christian faith to elimination of systemic injustices concerns the lack of self-worth felt by many who endure discrimination or seemingly inescapable poverty. In one of his earlier writings, *Race Matters*, Cornel West devotes one chapter to "Nihilism in Black America". To address the fundamental issues of racism, he says, we must delve into the depths of "...the murky waters of despair and dread that now flood the streets of black America" and "face up to the monumental eclipse of hope, the unprecedented collapse of meaning, the incredible disregard for human (especially black) life and property in much of black America...." West bemoans "...the profound sense of psychological depression, personal worthlessness, and social despair so widespread in black America" (12-13).

The immense task ahead in removing such despair and chaotic meaninglessness will encompass multiple more visible political and economic tactics. Nonetheless, one key spiritual truth can ameliorate self-recrimination and helplessness, *viz.* the foundational belief that one's greatest sense of worth comes not from personal wealth or publicly recognized accomplishments, but from the realization that one is loved by a gracious God. This gift of gracious favor simultaneously provides two assurances, that God has gone to extreme limits of sacrifice to show us that we are worth saving, and that God has redeemed us to carry on the divinely appointed ministry set before us. That is the full meaning of the doctrine of salvation, which combines both justification by grace and sanctification by inspired action. Exclusive emphasis on either half of this dynamic leads to cheap, meaningless grace or self-defeating works righteousness.

If Cornel West is right that nihilism, the inability to believe in anything, devastates the inner lives of people mired in senseless violence and grinding poverty, then verbal and visible assurances of being loved by a gracious God and being called to a worthy effort will grant them self-respect, lifting their eyes from the ground and toward the horizon. As West reminds us, "...people, especially degraded and oppressed people, are also hungry for identity, meaning, and self-worth" (13) The church must not stop proclaiming this central doctrine of the Christian religion, even as it also rolls up its sleeves in more visible signs of support.

Even as hope arises out of gracious acceptance by God, hope also springs from the fourth belief that sustains those combatting systemic racism, sexism, and classism. Undertaking a generations-long dismantling of power structures requires clinging to the belief that ultimately justice is possible, despite current frustrations. The church offers such a promise in its eschatological vision of the new creation established by God at the end of history. The most visible emphasis on this vision within recent Protestant thought has come from the German theologian Jürgen Moltmann.

In two of his earliest books, *Theology of Hope* and *The Crucified God*, Moltmann offers a framework for theology that moves through the present to the future, through the crucified God to the resurrected God, and from the resurrected God, through time, toward the eschaton when the new creation will be revealed. The church cannot act effectively in the present unless it interprets the present in light of the future of the crucified and resurrected Christ. In Moltmann's words: "The theologian is not concerned merely to supply a different interpretation of the world, of history and of human nature, but to transform them in expectation of a divine transformation" (*Theology of Hope*, 84). All our actions, including the way we use reason to think about things, is influenced by faith that the crucified God becomes the resurrected God, the same God who then will bring ultimate justice at the end of time.

That is God's promise, and it motivates us to follow Jesus here and now. Faithful discipleship foreshadows, prefigures the final just acts of God. Again, from *Theology of Hope:*

> The promissio of the universal future leads of necessity to the universal missio of the church to all nations. The promise of divine righteousness in the event of the justification of the godless leads immediately to the hunger for divine right in the godless world, and thus to the struggle for public, bodily obedience. (225)

The promise undergirds the mission, and when we act with faith in the promise, we are able to demonstrate on earth examples of the ultimate, final justice that God will bring about at the end. These occasional victories grant hope of a final victory, whether we live to see it or not. Moreover, the promise of God for a final judgment prompts followers of Jesus to become impatient with the status quo, and inspires them to work harder to follow Christ in all things. (The summary of Moltmann's framework comes from Lorenzen, *A New Handbook...*, 304-315). An event, an act of God in the unknowable future, grants hope and persistence to advocates for justice today.

The four contributions explained in the pages above are ideas, theological doctrines that articulate ways the Christian religion can inspire and assist the dismantling of the unjust isms of past and present society. To explain and promote such theological ideas is appropriate to a volume like this. However, let us be clear that the effort to deconstruct entrenched systems of power will not succeed through ideas alone, but requires the church actively to invest time, money, and energy, and frequently to sacrifice its comfortable existence.

Part of that sacrifice of comfort will come as postmodern thinkers turn their criticism toward the church itself, calling it to review and amend some of the same cherished doctrines listed above to better suit an era of full equality for previously oppressed minorities. Whether welcome or not, this critical self-examination is one other way the Christian church can contribute to deconstructing today's "isms".

Black, Feminist, and Womanist theologians specifically criticize the traditional interpretations of words like sin, pointing out that the historical emphasis on sin as pride has reinforced a servant mentality that runs counter to the sense of self-worth and accomplishment needed by oppressed people. Delores Williams, in her article "A Womanist Notion of Sin" reminds that society must take more seriously Black women's "depleted self-esteem" (560). The sole focus on pride distorts sin's multivalent meaning, forgetting that apathy, violence, and the dehumanization of another are equally sinful, and usually more destructive to women and people of color. This misreading of sin then leads also, in Williams view, to a perverted view of the cross. She opposes seeing Christ's death as a substitutionary atonement. As one commentator on Williams' work explains, it is a mistake to equate Jesus' death with the act of redemption. "Limiting redemption to crucifixion creates serious problems for oppressed persons because it sets the precedent that the sacrifice of one's life for the gratification of others is a virtuous act" (Sheilah Jones, *A New Handbook...*, 517). Instead, the cross should be regarded as a symbol of human evil attempting to foil the plan of God, an attempt that was defeated by the resurrection.

Reevaluating and deconstructing the Bible and its authority is also a tenet of the feminist critique. Even if parts of the Old Testament signal liberation, other parts of it restrict and demean women's roles. St. Paul in the New Testament is guilty of stark phrases commanding women to be silent in church. Commenting on both biblical authority and ecclesiastical authority, Rosemary Radford Ruether proposes a second source of authority when discerning the will of God, "The patriarchal distortion of all tradition throws feminist theology back upon the primary intuitions of religious experience itself…" (Ruether, 542). The Reformation's exclusive allegiance to the Bible as sole interpretive authority, and Roman Catholic allegiance to church tradition, both lose credence in the eyes of feminists. Seeing entrenched patriarchy and centuries of injustice, they begin to add their own experience of God's presence in the midst of oppression as an equal source of wisdom.

The exclusive maleness of God that predominates in scripture also comes under attack. Ruether states that we must begin to see "…the legitimacy of encountering the divine as goddess" (535). Not all feminists follow Ruether to that point, but even the more moderate realize the need to deemphasize masculine language for God in the Bible and instead find the rich diversity of scripture's way of naming the Lord. Anne Carr, in *Transforming Grace*, offers a trove of more neutral images in scripture and theology, emphasizing the way God is relational, liberating, incarnational, empathetic. Carr evokes Whitehead's phrase that God is "the great companion", "…the fellow sufferer who understands" (152). Phrases like "the ground and dynamic power of Being", or "the incomprehensible horizon of Holy Mystery", though initially awkward, actually convey neglected ways of speaking about God, enriching and broadening our sense of who God really is.

These challenges by feminist theologians represent a form of deconstruction of the church's own traditional language. Nothing short of a whole reevaluation, they contend, will lead to greater inclusivity and justice. This critique of the church itself is necessary to dismantle the isms that currently mock the Christian contention that a resurrected, compassionate Christ is alive and active in the world. The church should welcome this dimension of the postmodern challenge to traditional institutions, even if there are also legitimate reasons why it can reject the most radical implications of poststructuralist deconstructionism.

Cultural-Linguistic Interpretation

Throughout this volume, one of the persistent underlying themes has been how the Christian faith can articulate eternal truths amidst widely varying cultural and historical contexts. The second topic chosen to show a connection between postmodern critiques and traditional formulations of beliefs presents a late 20th century attempt to address that enduring question. The primary guide for these next pages will be Yale Professor George Lindbeck and his groundbreaking book *The Nature of Doctrine: Religion and Theology in a Postliberal Age.*

Both a cultural context and a theological context help explain the problem Lindbeck wants to address. A few years after completing *The Nature of Doctrine...*, he contributed an essay to *Postmodern Theology: Christian Faith in a Pluralist World* in which he laments the loss of a central cultural language, a shared heritage of thought like what the Bible once provided for western societies. Whether employed by earnest believers or agnostic critics of the faith, the rich images and poignant stories of the Bible granted a common reference point allowing for communication, plus standard presuppositions about how the world works. Biblical literacy was prevalent in home, marketplace, and laboratory, even if scripture's commandments were often conveniently neglected. Yet over the last century, increasingly culture has been "de-Christianized" and "de-biblicized", with the result that disparate ideologies no longer have common ground for beginning a lasting conversation. In his words:

> With the loss of knowledge of the Bible, public discourse is impoverished. We no longer have a language in which, for example, national goals...can be articulated. We try to deal with apocalyptic threats of atomic and ecological disaster in the thin and feeble idioms of utilitarianism or therapeutic welfare. (47)

Lindbeck does not offer this assessment in bitter resentment, but as a summons to discover a timely format for reimagining how scriptural and theological literacy could first reinvigorate the church, and then – possibly and distantly – recreate an effective platform for conversation even in an increasingly pluralist culture.

Moving from the cultural to the theological context, Lindbeck couches his description in the dilemma of how to unite the often-divided Christian Church, i.e. to achieve doctrinal reconciliation amongst branches of Christianity without loss of key, indispensable beliefs. Surveying the contemporary theological scene, he remarks on multiple reports from ecumenical conferences declaring that participants no longer see substantial differences in their beliefs about once contentious doctrines like the means of grace, justification, or sacraments, even though denominations have not substantially changed their historic formal declarations of belief (*The Nature of Doctrine*, 15). Can these groups be theologically reconciled without admitting their original beliefs were mistaken and abandoning them? Does the changed historical situation, which has reduced tension and necessitated cooperation, allow for a fresh look by all?

Could ferocious debates of the past be seen now from a completely different, inclusive perspective?

In sum, Lindbeck wants to be able to identify "... the criteria we implicitly employ when we say that some changes are faithful to a doctrinal tradition and others unfaithful, or some doctrinal differences are church-dividing and others not" (7). He contends that neither the premodern view of doctrine, and of the Bible, nor the modern view of these, is adequate. The more ancient view, usually found in Roman Catholic and Protestant fundamentalist groups, believes that biblically based doctrines "function as informative propositions or truth claims about objective realities." The modern, liberal view of doctrine he calls an "experiential-expressive" view of religion. It emphasizes the way doctrines are "...symbols of inner feelings, attitudes, or existential orientations" (16). To Lindbeck, neither the ancient nor the modern liberal approach provides adequate foundation for what is needed in the postmodern era. He seeks to craft a better alternative in what he will call a "cultural-linguistic" approach.

The initial explanation of what this new phrase means starts with Lindbeck's awareness that increasingly in the last century (possibly referring to the work of Wittgenstein and Gadamer)

> ... emphasis is placed on those respects in which religions resemble languages together with their correlative forms of life and are thus similar to cultures.... The function of church doctrines that becomes most prominent in this perspective is their use, not as expressive symbols or as truth claims, but as communally authoritative rules of discourse, attitude, and action. (17,18)

Doctrines, then, as the public expression of that communal authority, are regulative guidelines, or simply rules. Rules, he argues, "retain an invariant meaning under changing conditions" (18). He offers the example of how it is necessary to drive in the left lane in Britain but the right lane in America. There are always exceptions, as when the attendant with the stop/slow reversible sign instructs you otherwise, but the rule holds, and we recognize the difference between a temporary exception and the enforceable rule. Likewise, we recognize the extent to which cultural differences can influence the rule.

In an example from a specifically theological context, the debate at the 1529 Colloquy of Marburg, when Lutheran and Reformed Protestants could not agree on the exact meaning of "this is my body", doomed any hope of union or cooperation. Yet, centuries later, that debate diminishes in importance, while ecumenical cooperation flourishes. If we regard doctrine more as a regulative guideline, a rule, rather than an expression of ontological difference, the details of disagreement can be regarded as just that, details. Of equal importance but in the other direction, the rule maintains full allegiance to the presence of Christ in the Eucharist, granting it a greater sense of authority than if the doctrine is regarded simply as a symbolic expression of human emotion.

The next step for Lindbeck is to expound a wider descriptive definition of religion, since both doctrine and the scriptures operate within a religious framework. A cultural-linguistic view sees religions "… as comprehensive interpretive schemes, usually embodied in myths or narratives and heavily ritualized, which structure human experience and understanding of self and world." Further, a religion sets about identifying and describing what is "…'more important than everything else in the universe,' and to organizing all of life, including both behavior and beliefs, in relation to this" (32,33). He then expands on this:

> It is not primarily an array of beliefs about the true and the good (though it may involve these), or a symbolism expressive of basic attitudes, feelings, or sentiment (though these will be generated). Rather, it is similar to an idiom that makes possible the description of realities, the formulation of beliefs, and the experiencing of inner attitudes (33).

Therefore, "Like a culture or language, it is a communal phenomenon that shapes the subjectivities of individuals rather than being primarily a manifestation of those subjectivities" (33). Obviously, this last sentence is the reason Lindbeck calls his a "cultural-linguistic" approach to religion.

To proceed, let us try to answer two questions: How have postmodern themes contributed to this cultural-linguistic framework for religion, doctrine, and scripture, and what benefits does this new framework provide to Christians trying to understand their place in a postmodern world?

Certainly, two interrelated postmodern influences on a cultural-linguistic approach to religion are the awareness that language is central to any system of meaning and how complex that meaning can be. The previous chapters emphasized that these are two of the five central postmodern themes. From Ferdinand de Saussure's insistence that language is a social enterprise to Jacque Derrida's insight that any sign has both synchronic and diachronic reference points, it is clear that any attempt to convey meaning must recognize the cultural and historic contexts of what it is trying to say. This need not imply that nothing exists outside of language. There are external influences affecting the social enterprise when it assigns meaning to words and images. And it need not imply, as Derrida himself acknowledges, that the fact of language's complexity must stop us from even attempting to make clear statements about what we want to communicate. Still, before making those statements, we pause and admit our awareness of a vast reservoir of unknown influences. Hence, a sense of modesty and caution arises about truth claims that pretend to universal applicability.

That modest pause connects to one major debate on the contemporary religious scene in an increasingly international, pluralistic world. Lindbeck includes a chapter in *The Nature of Doctrine* on "Many Religions and the One True Faith". He addresses therein the thorny issue of how to promote interreligious dialogue that is neither completely relativistic nor dogmatically proselytizing. How can one speak with clarity of conviction about the rightness of one's faith yet acknowledge the potential of being wrong on a very multifaceted topic? His discussion of this is extended and complex, but he believes that a cultural-linguistic outlook provides the best option for a middle ground. He sets up the two poles of the debate by again comparing the traditional model of orthodox affirmation of propositional truth and the liberal model of experiential-expressivist symbolic representation of inner feelings. At the risk of generalization, we could legitimately say that the first would tend more to dogmatic insistence on a single truth, the second toward assuming the similarity of all religions. The cultural-linguistic approach, though, has an advantage over the others because it can clarify the categories of the debate. Because, he writes, in this approach:

> ...religions are thought of primarily as different idioms for construing reality, expressing experience, and ordering life", it "...focuses on the categories (or 'grammar' or 'rules of the game') in

terms of which truth claims are made and expressive symbolisms employed. (47,48)

Such clarification is the key to less accusatory contentious dialogue, which would otherwise stop the discussion as participants retreat to their respective corners to lick their wounds and prepare their next verbal assault. It also, nonetheless, allows free statements of convictions as part of an attempt to provide a vision of what may be better not only for oneself, but for all. This can apply to discussion between world religions and to dialogue within a single religion divided into once-combative denominations.

We will not attempt to follow Lindbeck's full treatment of his path toward modest and productive interreligious or intrareligious dialogue, but in a later chapter, he does offer one very useful tool, which he calls "A Taxonomy of Doctrines". Again in this system Lindbeck regards doctrines as rules, regulatory standards, rather than necessarily ontological truths, and those rules can be different varieties. Some rules, he states, are unconditionally necessary, "part of the indispensable grammar logic of the faith" (85). He cites the "law of love" in Christianity as one such essential. Other rules, though, can be conditionally essential; e.g., the role of pacifism in that law of love. Pacifism may not always be the best way to love. Of these conditional types, some may be permanent and others temporary if conditions change. He takes one further step, dividing temporary conditional doctrines into reversible and irreversible. An irreversible doctrine, for example, might be the condemnation of slavery. For centuries, the church accepted the consensus of classical cultures that slavery was an inescapable necessity, but condemnation of slavery has now become standard across the wide spectrum of Christians, and is to all intents and purposes irreversible.

Disagreement about details of Lindbeck's taxonomy of doctrines is certainly legitimate, but he has articulated a way for the church to address historical changes without abandoning beliefs and doctrines central to its existence. This has granted modern Christians an indispensable tool for reducing the barriers that separate us and divide the body of Christ. The greater possibility of church unity without uniformity is one gift of the cultural-linguistic model as it incorporated postmodern criticisms.

A second gift embedded in the cultural-linguistic model is its ability to incorporate postmodern objections to the restrictions that historical criticism placed on biblical interpretation. Two new ways of considering a scripture passage began to emerge as the 20th century closed. Sandra Schneiders, Professor of New Testament and Spirituality, clarifies one of those as her contribution to the *Postmodern Theology* volume. "Does the Bible Have a Postmodern Message?" she asks. Lamenting that exegesis of scripture has become an increasingly specialized discipline, open only to experts in ancient history and linguists, she sees an opening to a new path in the postmodern view of literature. The "locus of revelation" in a text "…is not the events behind the texts, nor the theology of the biblical authors, nor even the preaching of the texts in the community, but the texts themselves as language that involves the reader" (61). Thus, she argues:

> …the positivistic objectification of the text which resulted inexorably in the dilemma of the subject-object paradigm of understanding by analysis has begun to give way to a hermeneutical paradigm of understanding by participative dialogue. (62)

We don't stand outside the text to comprehend it, we enter into "…genuine dialogue with it as it stands. Through this dialogue reader and text are mutually transformed" (62). This insight about participation as a repudiation of the subject/object split is also clearly stated by John Donahue in a very useful appendix to *The New Interpreter's Study Bible*.

> In place of a split between the object (what can be known) and the subject (the one who knows), postmodernism questions pure objectivity in both science and literature, and it stresses participatory knowledge, with emphasis on the reader and the reading process.... (2264)

Lindbeck himself expounds the second advantage of this new way of looking at scripture. We honestly should thank the critical method for its illumination of historical context, but we can equally point out its deficiencies, one of which is its insistence that there is only one right answer when interpreting a text. "Modernity has been deeply prejudiced against treating a classic as a language or lens with many meanings or uses with which to construe reality and view the world." Texts were viewed primarily "as objects of study", implying that they possessed only "...a single meaning ascertainable only by specialists..." ("The Church's Mission"... 50). But now "...the intellectual climate is changing, and the one we are now entering is congenial to the close reading of texts in order to see what the world looks like in and through them" (51). This implies that a text can be multivalent, multivocal, as it were, with a new voice and a new meaning to each different age that reads it. Lindbeck's cultural linguistic model incorporates this insight, thereby providing a clearer path by which the Sunday sermon, this exchange between pulpit and pew, is not regarded as a lecture from an expert to a class of confounded students. It is instead the beginning of a dialogue with the text that can intrigue parishioners throughout the week.

Nothing less than the biblical literacy of the Christian church is at stake.

One final brief comment before we leave this topic of biblical interpretation: postmodern thinkers have tended to dismiss the Bible as simply another metanarrative that oversimplifies and abstracts reality. Language, they insist, is simply too complex to allow single dominant ideas to explain everything, and purveyors of metanarratives have once more set up an arrogant subject/object perspective on events. But one insight recently has questioned whether indeed the Bible is a metanarrative. The contribution of Gina Hens-Piazza to *Handbook of Postmodern Biblical Interpretation* is a commentary on Jean-Francois Lyotard, one of the most significant poststructuralists. At the end of her article, Hens-Piazza offers a different perspective on scripture.

> Insofar as the Bible is represented and enlisted as a unified vision prescribing what is good, right, and true for all humanity and its destiny, it would qualify as a 'metanarrative'. However, recent studies of the biblical writings would assert otherwise. This so-called canon of writings is actually a motley collation of culturally constructed stories. The tales, characters, and lessons that make up the biblical traditions overlap, interweave, contradict, and complement one another.... Amid this diversity and complexity, no meta-discourse, meta-narrative or meta-language presides here. They are culturally constrained and generate different responses to the same inquiry. (166)

The point of this extended quote is to recognize a different way of looking at scripture, one that may add the virtue of diversity to previously monolithic, uniform views of the Bible's message, either fundamentalist or historical critical. This perspective helps us recover the Bible's ability to speak a fresh, ever-relevant word to widely different audiences, and calls disciples of Jesus Christ to reclaim the richness of a biblical heritage they have too often overlooked.

Returning to Dialogue: Science, Nature, and Technology

Earlier sections of this volume have lamented what today is called the "fact/value distinction" that describes a separation between empirically verifiable observations and faith-based declarations of what is good, true, and beautiful. The implication of this separation is that one can neither base ethical principles upon nor defend them by empirical facts. The employment of this principle in the past prompted a prolonged battle between religion and science, and in the present has left a confused populace wondering how to connect what they believe to what they see. Certain developments in the postmodern era, however, including some from explicit poststructuralists, now offer at least a window to see through that separation, although not necessarily an open door. Results of this new perspective include:

- A return to dialogue between science and religion
- Attempts to develop a new theology of nature
- Greater scrutiny of how technology endangers nature by treating it primarily as a resource for manipulation

These three themes form the substance of this final section on prospects for cooperation between postmodernism and theology. The wide boundaries of these fields necessitate at best a quick insight into them here rather than extensive treatment.

Returning to Dialogue

Of the primary components of postmodernism listed in the previous chapters, the two most applicable to the scientific enterprise are the immanence of norms (i.e., the fallacy of objectivity) and the insistence that signs and language establish meaning by separation and exclusion of other alternatives. We see especially how these apply to the gradually ascending dialogue between science and religion. The dichotomy between faith and scientific reason played out over the prior three centuries, usually granting scientific objectivity steady victories over what it exposed as superstition.

Postmodern suspicion of foundationalism and universal objectivity in the last decades led some to question science's hidden presuppositions. Commenting on the debate, Robert Bellah's essay for *Postmodern Theology* stresses that modernity "...claimed to offer a new metalanguage which is really true, and to which all the particular languages of culture and religion must be reduced. The new metalanguage is the language of facts, proven by scientific method to be truly, objectively there" (75). However, as metalanguages or metanarratives of all sorts, including religious ones, come under scrutiny, the comprehensive strategy of objective rationality implied in science will itself lose some luster. From this and other recent critiques, Bellah draws this conclusion, "The actual practice of science does not warrant the claim...to be a universal language superior in its validity to all the beliefs and practices of mankind", and thus "...science turns out to be just one more 'tribal tradition'" (78).

Research scientists would prickle at being termed part of a *tribal tradition*. Yet, a certain freedom arises from such emerging awareness. It prompts, among other things, new efforts to connect recent fields of scientific research to theological doctrines. Professor Thomas

Torrance of Edinburgh, a prominent translator of Karl Barth, in his later career dedicated his life to the intersection of theology and science. Torrance offers scientists perhaps a more palatable explanation of the new situation. Especially he studied the late works of Albert Einstein and how new theories of relativity affect both presuppositions of science and principles of theology. In *Christian Theology and Scientific Culture*, Torrance emphasizes that Einstein's view of general relativity

> ...which defines the universe as a continuous whole, considerably reinforces the conviction deriving from the Christian doctrine of the creation of all things by one God, that the universe is characterized throughout by a unitary rational order. (31f.)

Torrance then takes his case further. Connecting Einstein to later works like Thomas Kuhn's *The Structure of Scientific Revolutions* or Michael Polanyi's *Personal Knowledge*, Torrance believes that a better trend is now emerging in the "epistemology" of science, as it were. That direction allows us

> ... to recover the epistemic process in which, as historic Christian theology has so often claimed, we believe in order to understand, while in the course of developing our understanding we test and clarify our beliefs and thereby strengthen the hold of authentic belief upon our minds. (69,70)

This definition of process can rightly describe both the scientific method in the laboratory and a committed Christian belief, a belief mature enough to know that merely believing it does not make it so, that it must be tested against the realities of life. Surely, this similarity can form one bridge for cooperation between two hesitant partners.

If the dialogue between science and religion bears fruit, it is also indebted to works by the following authors (among many others) who have contributed to the dialogue over the last 50 years. Ian Barbour, former professor of physics and religion at Carleton College, compiled his Gifford Lectures of 1989-1991 into two volumes: *Religion in an Age of Science* and *Ethics in an Age of Technology*. He also provides an excellent set of categories that reveal alternative approaches to the relationship in *When Science Meets Religion*.

John Polkinghorne, former professor of mathematical physics at Cambridge, is a fellow of The Royal Society who is also an ordained priest of the Church of England. He follows the Nicene Creed to testify to his own belief in the compatibility of science and religion in *The Faith of a Physicist*. Polkinghorne combines cosmological theory and eschatology in *The End of the World and the Ends of God*. Assisted by Nicholas Beale, Polkinghorne offers laypeople a very useful set of answers to key inquiries about science in *Questions of Truth*. Nancey Murphy and Warren Brown are primary contributors to, and editors of, *Whatever Happened to the Soul?*. The book presents the emerging idea of "nonreductive physicalism" as a way to overcome the dualism of body and soul. These are but a sampling of writers who have engaged in the contemporary attempt to carry the relationship between science and religion beyond an uneasy truce toward fuller cooperation.

The science/religion dialogue, broad in its own right, gains an even wider perspective when seen as part of an intermittent 20th century attempt to restate the relationship of humanity toward physical nature. Within the last half-century, two writers among many within the Reformed Protestant tradition (doubtless mirrored in other denominations) have proposed that it is time to gather multiple postmodern insights, connect them to Christian doctrines, and develop a new theology of nature.

A Theology of Nature

What would a theology of nature look like? George Hendry, the first of our two guides for the next few pages, hopes that such a theology would answer the following question: "What is the place, meaning, and purpose of the world of nature in the overall plan of God in creation and redemption?" (*Theology of Nature*, 11). Before trying to provide that answer, Hendry reminds us that it is wise to distinguish "theology of nature" from "natural theology". Readers will remember the earlier pages in this volume that treated 18th century natural theology, a view based in Newtonian mechanistic physics, and its resultant deism. This is not what Hendry and others wish to reclaim. Too much has happened in the interim, including the theory of evolution, quantum physics and relativity, to name but a few. A theology of nature must not make the same mistakes as the natural theology that led to a crisis of faith in 19th century England when confronted with evolution.

Instead, Hendry would have us start by interpreting nature in light of creation. He reminds us that nowhere in the Old Testament does the word "nature" appear. It is a Greek word, and though it is used occasionally in the New Testament, even there it usually implies a tendency within us rather than referring to the whole realm of physical reality. Hendry does recognize that the objectifying of nature that occurs in modern science permits accurate observation and engineering toward many beneficial uses. Nonetheless, because nature is now unmoored from the intentions of a creator God, it also lies open to abuse. "The ruthless exploitation of nature and its resources...is in fact the result of a substitution of nature for creation, which made the world the property of man and not of God" (196,7). He also points to a second factor affecting a revised theology of nature, *viz.* the effect of evolution upon humanity's approach to physical reality. "Our perception of ourselves in the context of an evolving nature may also be integrated with our faith as it brings us to a deeper recognition of the fact that we and nature are involved in a common history" (186,187).

It is impossible here to do justice to Hendry's full contribution to a new theology of nature; however, the last pages of his book do summarize his approach. Employing the themes above and using Paul's guidance in Romans 8:18-23, Hendry proposes three key elements:

- First, a Christian perception of nature will include "...sympathy, community with nature in its suffering" (214). He connects Christian sympathy for the suffering of all living creatures to the recognition by redeemed believers that they "...owe their being as Christians to the suffering of Christ for them."
- The second element is to perceive nature always in the light of the gospel. "The groanings of creation...are heard as the travail pangs of the new creation. Christians, therefore, perceive the world around them under the sign of hope" (215,216). This element connects not to the crucifixion, but to the resurrection and second coming; the source of our own hope brings hope also to nature.
- Thirdly, the Christian perception of nature recognizes "...the responsibility that rests upon us for the fulfillment of God's purpose with nature" (216).

Hendry expounds this with reference to how prayer and worship engage us. These activities allow us "...to become engaged in the transcendent purpose of God" (217). We learn to view the world sacramentally, using the example of the Eucharist as our guide. In other words:

> All natural objects continue to be what they are, and they are to be used according to their natural properties, but to those who perceive them in the light of the incarnation they become charged with the promise of something more than what they are, and they will be treated accordingly. (218)

Through sympathy with creation, the hopeful perspective of the gospel, and learning to see nature sacramentally, humanity gains a completely new relationship to nature, signaling a much more beneficial future for our place in the created world.

Our second guide in the incipient statement of a new theology of nature is the German theologian Wolfhart Pannenberg. The significance of Pannenberg's work is that he does not just respond to the modernist view of nature by accommodating doctrines to it, but by challenging the very presuppositions of scientific observation and its resultant laws. In two works, *Theology and the Philosophy of Science*, and a collection of essays titled *Toward a Theology of Nature*, Pannenberg repeatedly expresses dissatisfaction with the easy separation that has existed between religion and science over the last centuries. At least since Kant's effective arguments against proofs for the existence of God, theology has allowed itself to be squeezed into an "anthropological" footing, with an emphasis on moral or historical questions, while allowing rationalist, empirical science free rein in epistemology and investigation of the natural world. The usual bromide that science answers questions of how and religion answers questions of why is a false dichotomy, Pannenberg claims. It has allowed the fact/value distinction to harden into absolutes.

Here is the substance of the problem. In his essay "Theological Questions to Scientists" (*Toward...*), Pannenberg is blunt.

> If the God of the Bible is the creator of the universe, then it is not possible to understand fully or even appropriately the process of nature without any reference to that God. If, on the contrary, nature can be appropriately understood without reference to the God of the Bible, then that God cannot be the creator of the universe, and consequently he cannot be truly God and be trusted as a source of moral teaching either. (16)

Any attempt to get around that dilemma is little more than prevarication and accommodation. Pannenberg tries to face it head on. He will do so from several perspectives.

First, Pannenberg criticizes the scientific view of nature, saying that it is incomplete, that only when God is considered will science be able to understand nature adequately. This means, among other things, that science must re-examine the significant fact that the world is contingent, as are the natural events that are then incorporated, via persistent observation, into the laws that science uses. He contends that "...laws of nature are not eternal or atemporal because the fields of their application, the regularities of natural process, originate in the course of time" (21). Things that originate within time are contingent, and a contingent world points beyond itself and allows openness to other influences.

> When natural science, in seeking laws and especially the origin of the present world with its forms and laws, comes upon

contingent conditions and events, it opens nature up in such a way that the Christian can discover the expression of a creative act of God. ("Contingency and Natural Law", in *Toward...*, 98)

The laws of nature, then, that have for so long been seen as the key to understanding physical reality, are themselves located within an even more comprehensive framework when contingency receives its rightful consideration.

Pannenberg also employs the idea of *field theory*, originated by Michael Faraday and Clerk Maxwell, and furthered in the work of Einstein, to challenge the materialist presuppositions of modern science. The essay "The Doctrine of Creation and Modern Science" addresses "The tendency on a certain line of the development of modern physics to reduce all forces to bodies or 'masses...'" (*Toward...*, 38). This means that the understanding of nature becomes completely separated from God, who of course is not and has not a "body". Field theory, however, regards the interaction of things quite differently. As Pannenberg observes, "The main point of the field concept was to turn around the relation between force and body. To Faraday, the body was but a manifestation of the force that he conceived as an independent reality prior to the body, and he did so in conceiving forces in terms of fields" (38). Body and mass, in Faraday's theory, are "...secondary phenomena, a concentration of force at particular places and points of the field" (38). This new way of regarding entities, which is compatible with much recent physics, also has the possibility of reconnecting God to the overall picture of nature. God, as an invisible force, is not automatically excluded from the field.

A third point of Pannenberg worth mentioning is his recommendation that only if a theology of nature is based on the Trinity will it adequately capture God's role in creation. Newton, it will be recalled, embraced a form of Christianity without accepting the doctrine of the Trinity. That perhaps kept him from seeing that his picture of God would so easily become mechanistic and deistic.

> Today's Christian theology of creation will use, in distinction from Newton, the possibilities of the doctrine of the Trinity in order to describe the relationship of God's transcendence and immanence in creation and in the history of salvation. ("God and Nature", in *Toward...*, 65)

The Christological, almost *christomonistic*, emphasis of the Reformation, according to Pannenberg, will need to be balanced by a recovery of the doctrines of Creator and Holy Spirit. Only then will the line of separation between the "religious" sphere of moral decisions and the "scientific" sphere of empirical observation begin to fade. Wolfhart Pannenberg deserves public thanks for offering this and the two previous promising pathways toward a completely honest and effective theology of nature.

Re-examining Technology

Both the renewed science/religion dialogue and the search for a satisfactory theology of nature have been inspired in part by a vague, increasing fear that humanity is rushing headlong toward destruction of the planet's ecological balance. In the postmodern era, this has prompted a re-examination of technology and our use of it. In 1954, two foundational writings raised the question of whether we control technology or it controls us. Jacques Ellul's *The Technological Society* appeared in France. Martin Heidegger penned his lecture "The Question Concerning Techne (Technology)" in Germany.

Neither document appeared in English until at least a decade later. Both writers insist that technology ("Technique" to Ellul and "Techne" to Heidegger) is not merely machines and tools employed by humans as we see fit. Ellul, in an initial note to the reader, clarifies his meaning. "In our technological society, technique is the totality of methods rationally arrived at and having absolute efficiency ... in every field of human activity" (xxv). Heidegger states his definition this way, "Technology is therefore no mere means. Technology is a way of revealing" (11).

Although Ellul's work preceded the emergence of specific post-structuralist authors, he would recognize the final characteristic of postmodernism noted in the previous chapters, namely that for one sign or meaning to become dominant it represses and sidelines other possible meanings. In effect, that is how Ellul describes the march of technique toward its dominant position. "We can be confident that the final result will be that technique will assimilate everything to the machine; the ideal for which technique strives is the mechanization of everything it encounters" (12). Again:

> Technique has become autonomous: it has fashioned an omnivorous world which obeys its own laws and which has renounced all tradition. Technique no longer rests on tradition, but rather on previous technical procedures; and its evolution is too rapid, too upsetting, to integrate the older traditions. (14)

This leads Ellul to a slogan that appears frequently in his work: "A technical problem demands a technical solution (429).

This is the difficulty. We are caught, he contends, in a perpetual circle that makes it practically impossible to think outside of *technique*. Everyday examples of this dilemma abound. The manufacture of paper grocery bags created toxic wastewater from processing mills. Science discovered a technical solution, plastic bags, but they in turn deteriorate slowly into micropebbles that kill fish and pollute the ocean. Will the next technical solution also create problems, problems needing technical solutions? This dynamic operates in fields from economics to medicine and everything in between.

The value of Ellul's stark assessment is how it forces society to reevaluate, in his view, the naïve assumption that humanity can simply use technology as we see fit, and stop using it where and when we want. As long as that misconception prevails, we will be unable to act toward any end other than what the technical process directs us.

Heidegger approaches the question of technology with the postmodern awareness that it employs the subject/object dualism. Ever since the Greeks, *techne* was the act of making, of bringing something new into existence. Heidegger registers criticism even of this more ancient manner of grasping and mastering what it wished to shape, but that ancient tendency has taken a more destructive turn in modernity. He describes how, after the breakdown of the medieval religious forms of security, a concentrated inward turn began. As the translator/editor of this lecture, William Lovitt, expresses it, "In the *ego cogito (ergo) sum* of Descartes, man found his self-certainty *within himself*... Man could *represent* reality to himself, that is, he could set it up over against himself, as it *appeared* to him, as an object of thought" (xxv). This means that, in Heidegger's own unique wording:

> ... the revealing that holds sway throughout modern technology does not unfold into a bringing-forth in the sense of poiesis. The revealing that rules in modern technology is a challenging, which

puts to nature the unreasonable demand that it supply energy that can be extracted and stored as such. (14)

Heidegger arrives, therefore, at the belief that modern technology treats nature as resource, or in his own phrase, as "standing reserve" (17). He clarifies what he means through examining the energy that can be given by a windmill. The windmill operates only because and when the wind blows. In contrast, coal can be mined and stored, a standing reserve awaiting our command to use it. It becomes a symbol of the human relationship to nature in a technological society.

Like Ellul, Heidegger worries that modernity eventually will see all things through the prism of technology. When technology sees everything in the light of a

> ...cause-effect coherence, even God can, for representational thinking, lose all that is exalted and holy, the mysteriousness of his distance. In the light of causality, God can sink to the level of a cause.... He then becomes, even in theology, the god of the philosophers, namely of those who define the unconcealed and the concealed in terms of the causality of making, without ever considering the essential origin of this causality. (26)

If it is the very nature of techne to regard nature as a standing reserve, a resource only, and if technology does not stop until it sees everything in light of subject/object, cause/effect categories, then perhaps the time has come, for the future of the planet, to question seriously the direction of modern technology. This then is one arena where postmodern resistance to Enlightenment technical reason should be heeded promptly, both by the Christian church and by society as a whole. Indeed, this effort demands cooperation among all partners, religious or secular, premodern, modern or post.

Whether in a greater connection between scientific method and theological ends, the re-envisioning or nature within creation, or a reevaluation of technology, certain insights from postmodern writers can spur new, promising developments that reverse some of the mistakes of modernity regarding science and religion. If we combine those benefits with a cautious use of deconstructionism to dismantle the "isms" of social inequity and a cultural-linguistic model for cooperative debate, we will find there are at least some avenues down which Christian faith can walk side by side with postmodern ideas. Let us regard this as an optimistic final result of the encounter between our faith and our current cultural context.

| eight |

A Concluding Postscript

The paragraphs that follow are a conclusion only in a very limited sense. I have stated in the preceding pages all that I have come to understand about two key eras in the theology/philosophy dialogue. My intention from the start has been to relate "how we got to where we are" to the best of my abilities. That is done, so there is no option but to stop.

I have no wish, however, to presume a conclusion to the debates mentioned, as though they were settled, as if we had resolved them. This book has been primarily a descriptive rather than a prescriptive effort. The influences of modernity continue to surround us both consciously and unconsciously. The new directions of postmodernism will unfold for decades, accelerating as a once-hesitant minority voice grows confident and popular. The dynamics of both eras call for continuous, lasting attention in church and society.

Still, what we can do in these final few pages, this postscript, is reiterate the central descriptions within this book. As the objective here is to narrow our broad scope of study toward a few memorable ideas, we hope the reader can benefit from the following summary.

The most overarching organizing idea emphasized that epistemology, how we know what we know, has occupied both philosophy and theology in the 500-year period covered. From Luther's insistence in the Heidelberg Disputation that a theology of the cross leads one much closer to God's ultimate reality than does a theology of glory, to Ferdinand de Saussure's insistence on a new way of regarding language, epistemology has taken center stage in the theology/philosophy debate.

For instance, that emphasis provided a centering principle for chapter two of Part I, which traced the relationship between reason and revelation from the Reformation to the mid-20th century. Whether the topic be the rise and fall of natural religion, Locke's and Hume's interpretations of the "human understanding", or Schleiermacher's definition of religion as immediate self-consciousness of dependence on God, the ways we know God and other entities has been the underlying question prompting responses.

Explicitly within Part One on modernity, three guiding themes received treatment. Over the course of the 17th-19th centuries, definitions of freedom, history and happiness underwent significant change.

Freedom, as understood within Christian scripture and doctrine, had to consider and either adapt or reject developments such as the social contract theory of government, the emerging desire for individual autonomy, and capitalism's insistence that self-interest can produce wealth. Whether stated by John Locke or Thomas Hobbes, the social contract theory insists that government arises from a mutual agreement among its members to set aside certain native liberties in order to gain more overall security and greater ultimate liberty. Therefore, neither the security of a stable state nor moderate political freedom is still regarded as a gift from God. They are, instead, seen as largely self-created by contractual agreement.

Secondly, Immanuel Kant declares that Enlightenment frees us from our self-incurred tutelage, tutelage being our inability to reason without direction from another. He elsewhere insists that we should partake of no happiness unless we have created it by our own reason. This has often resulted in isolation of the individual from the community and in making autonomous decision-making a central tenet of freedom.

Finally, as capitalism receives clarity in Smith's *The Wealth of Nations*, citizens gradually discover their purchasing power. When generations of material progress ensue, citizens sense, rightly or wrongly, that their freedom has increased because they have more ability to buy tools that liberate them from manual labor and restrictions on their mobility. Moreover, they are assuaged by the belief that their self-interest brings benefits to society at large.

It is little wonder, given these three strong components of modern freedom, that few people can maintain a Christian conception of freedom rooted in divine acts of liberation into a covenant of obedience, or salvation from self-centered sin, or empowerment to serve God. That core belief can only succeed if they have been trained thoroughly within a caring community that emphasizes personal sacrifice for the sake of others. As we should remember, however, to allow God freedom to transcend our expectations, it just might also occur through an unexpected act of grace.

The new interpretation of history assumed two primary forms, as stated by a subtitle in chapter three, "History as Fact and Progress".

Thinking about the past in terms of "facts" and impartial observation in some respects began for western civilization as early as Thucydides' account of the Peloponnesian wars. In the modern era, though, the clearest turn toward seeing history as purely an objective recounting of circumstances and events arises in the late 18th and early19th centuries, with a few pioneers like Spinoza writing even earlier. It is this turn that heavily influenced what has been termed the historical-critical method, and this method, when directed toward the Bible, has aroused substantial controversy. Our treatment of this issue attempted to show not only how the critical investigation of scripture brings clarity and insight into historical situations faced by biblical figures, but also how it distorts the narrative intention of biblical authors and, if followed strictly, blocks the connection between biblical figures and relevant concerns of the current reader.

Regarding history as progress can be obliquely connected to a Christian belief in the eschatological fulfillment of God's plan. Yet, Hegel's view of history as the inevitable unfolding of *geist*, i.e., "mind", through dialectic movement is the predominant meaning of progress in the modern world. The prominence of Hegel's view leads humanity to look for a fuller revelation of God in idealist visions of the future rather than seeking that revelation within a book written thousands of years in the past. It has also led, for good or for ill, to a critical reevaluation of the idea of an omniscient, immutable God of divine sovereignty.

The modern view of happiness, or what we have called "the good life", presents a particular dilemma for Christianity today, slightly reminiscent of the early patristic attempts to distinguish heresy from orthodoxy. Why this reminiscence? It is because much of the modern view of happiness coalesces with Christian views of basic human equality before God and the full development of our divine gifts. Yet, like heresies of the past, too often the modern view of happiness takes partial truths and declares them to be the whole truth. The results can end up far away from initial good intentions.

We can recognize this tendency in all three declared objectives of the modern view of the good life, *viz.* to move from custom and tradition to education and innovation, from superstition to science, and from hierarchical authority to liberty and equality. Regarding the first of these three, despite the significant benefits that education and innovation bring, there also arises a sense of radical doubt that instills skepticism and an historicist perspective that diminishes awareness of spiritual and emotional influences. The desired movement from superstition to science has largely undervalued the Christian faith of many prominent scientists ancient and modern, leading to a public perception of antagonism between religious doctrine and scientific advancement. It also reveals the need for greater dialogue between those who develop new scientific inventions and ethicists who would guide the use of those inventions. The movement from hierarchical authority to liberty and equality, the third goal of the good life, has led to wondrous events like the rejection of human slavery in all its forms, whether race or gender based. Yet, genuine Christian discipleship recognizes an even higher view of happiness than what civic freedom and equality can bring, *viz.* the need to set aside our own self-realization, our own comfort and rights, for the sake of obedience to God and service to others.

These realizations about freedom, history, and happiness prompt the final chapter of Part One to insist that Christian faith can serve as both a complement and a counterbalance to the direction of modern society. The specific suggestions made there, I hope, will have been especially pertinent to Christian pastors and students of the faith.

Part Two on postmodernism describes a gnawing lack of confidence in the presuppositions of modernity, intensified by the calamities of two world wars and a devastating depression in the early 20th century. In combination with startling discoveries in science that challenged stable theories of empirical measurement and Newtonian physics, this search for a new framework of thought led to increased attention to language. The five central themes of postmodernism noted in the first chapter of Part Two stress the complexity of meaning, the illusion of objectivity, and the extent to which language reflects and entrenches power. The next chapter in Part II attempted to provide a basis for dialogue between postmodern themes and traditional Christian beliefs, despite obvious points of conflict. It therefore tracks different responses to the questions raised by postmodernism, including challenges to ontological realism, Nietzschean "death of God" assertions, and ways for Christian disciples to be freed from defensive, protective attitudes within institutional religion.

Three brief topics in a chapter at the end of Part Two expressed hope for collaboration between postmodern insights and foremost Christian goals for the 21st century. Does not poststructuralist "deconstruction" aid in dismantling racism, classism and sexism? Could not a greater appreciation for literary narrative and a less ontological approach to doctrine reduce interfaith and intra-faith quarrels? If the new physics opens windows to greater religious dialogue, could both forces combine to reverse technology's misuse of natural resources? These potential arenas of cooperation offer hope that Christian faith can remain a vital, respected voice in the decades ahead.

HOW WE GOT TO WHERE WE ARE - 323

These, then, are the broad themes that have guided the organization of this work. Hopefully, this review has captured the high points and general movement of the ideas and rendered an overall clarity to an admittedly ambitious project.

As these final remarks move toward their end, however, it is helpful to remind the reader that neither modernity nor postmodernism is a monolithic, unified presentation of thought. For example, the Kantian turn to deontological, categorical-imperative ethics in the 1790s clashes with the enlightened self-interest approach of Bentham and Mill's utilitarianism only a few decades later. It is equally hard to see how Descartes' deductive rationalism and Bacon's inductive research could have wandered side by side through the centuries, but they did, and they ultimately linked into the scientific method. Likewise with postmodernism, the general sense of disillusionment and the new scientific discoveries of the early 20th century which triggered a turn away from modernity need not lead inevitably to the revolutionary insights of the Parisian poststructuralists. Many thinkers in the postmodern period would have recoiled from certain extreme conclusions of Foucault, Lyotard, or Irigaray. The later radical insights are adopted with more or less stringency depending on the viewer.

Such wide-ranging diversity of thought prompts a call to wisdom, discernment, prudence. It also reiterates the postmodern prediction that 21st century citizens will need to learn to live with less certainty and more humility about their decisions, however necessary those decisions are. Wisdom, and an awareness of unique situations, might tell us that we can best address one public ethical choice by employing a utilitarian framework, i.e., what is the greatest good for the greatest number. Yet, the immense complexity of a different ethical choice might require a categorical imperative approach, asking whether our decision could be a universal law for all such situations and ensuring that no one involved be treated merely as a means to an end. Within the church, a Good Friday sermon that focuses on the crucifixion and the importance of personal sacrifice does indeed emphasize an indispensable, traditional doctrine of the faith. But no preacher should be unaware that a woman of color, upon hearing such a message, might sound a protest against how it has been misused to continue a patriarchal, racist oppressive system that threatens her future. Biblical teachings are diverse enough to support both the traditional doctrine and the protest, so wisdom and discernment must intervene to speak the truth in love and to make sure the "correct" word is also a timely word. That will be a fruitful practice, whether the issues we face arise from modern or postmodern principles, or from new discoveries in whatever era lies ahead.

PHILOSOPHERS AND THEOLOGIANS

This appendix has biographical briefs and chronological settings about prominent philosophers and theologians regularly considered in this book.

Aquinas, Thomas (c. 1225-1274). This Dominican friar first incorporated Aristotelian ideas into Christianity. His primary works, *Summa Theologica* and *Summa Contra Gentiles*, synthesize theology and philosophy, explain virtues and vices, and provided Roman Catholicism a lasting framework for doctrine.

Aristotle (384-322 BC). Along with his teacher, Plato, Aristotle was among the most significant of ancient Greek philosophers. Aristotle published treatises on topics from physics to ethics to politics. Disputing Plato's theory of forms, he develops a theory of substance and change that heavily influenced subsequent metaphysics. His theory of the four causes provides a holistic view of how and why something is made.

Augustine of Hippo (354-430). The most prominent of the Latin church patriarchs. His *Confessions* are a theological autobiography on his journey through less adequate philosophies toward his conversion. His emphasis on grace as the only basis for salvation, his explanation of the Trinity, and his interpretation of history in *The City of God*, provided central doctrines of early Christianity.

Bacon, Francis (1561-1626). This British philosopher, once Lord Chancellor of England, initiated the empiricist school with works like *The Advancement of Learning* and *Novum Organum*. He emphasized precise concrete examination of the physical properties of something. He believed if reason could be separated from the strictures of revelation humankind could advance remarkably.

Barth, Karl (1886-1968). As a pastor in Switzerland, he reacted against the dominance of theological liberalism, calling for greater awareness of the transcendence of God. His commentary on Romans and the multivolume *Church Dogmatics* shaped a new direction for 20th c. theology. His opposition to Nazism and key role in founding the Confessing Church led to his exile from Germany.

Calvin, Jean (1509-1554). As the Reformation began, Calvin escaped France to lead Geneva's new Protestants. Calvin's *Institutes of the Christian Religion* and extensive biblical commentaries provided a consistent theological foundation for the Reformed tradition. His social reforms made Geneva a leading city in Europe.

Derrida, Jacques (1930-2004). Born in Algeria, schooled in France, Derrida was among the first explicit postmodern authors. Using themes from Saussure and Heidegger, he promoted poststructuralism, and encouraged the "deconstruction" of complex systems. His primary books were *Speech and Phenomena, Writing and Difference,* and *The Margins of Philosophy.*

Descartes, Rene (1591-1650). Educated in France but resident mostly in Holland, Descartes wanted to place philosophy upon a whole new foundation. His works *Discourse on Method* and *Meditations on First Philosophies* sought an unshakeable basis for thought. Relying on nothing but logical and mathematical truths, he separated body from mind and argued rationally from complete doubt to certainty.

Fichte, Johann G. (1762-1814). His greatest contribution to philosophy was to explain the move from Kant's epistemology to Hegel's idealism. A student of Kant, he broke away and wrote *Wissenschaftslehre* to show that ultimately the human ego constructs the objective world from the appearances that surround it.

Foucault, Michel (1926-1984). This postmodern philosopher began work as a French diplomat but soon analyzed society from a deconstructionist perspective. Titles such as *The History of Madness, The Archaeology of Knowledge, Discipline and Punish,* and *The History of Sexuality* demonstrate his approach to institutions.

Hegel, George W.F. (1770-1831). Possibly the most influential philosopher on 19th and 20th century thought, Hegel interpreted reality as a movement of Being through history. He separated from Kant by believing that "things in themselves" can be intelligible if all reality is mental. His process includes progressive movement of Being according to a dialectic relationship. This affects the nature of truth.

Heidegger, Martin (1889-1976). Influenced by Kierkegaard and his teacher Edmund Husserl, Heidegger sought to examine experiences by removing all preconceived frameworks separating consciousness from the external world it viewed. His major work, *Being and Time*, reinterprets time, action, and knowledge, reducing divisions in order to break through to authentic existence.

Hobbes, Thomas (1588-1679). Only later in his long life did this translator of early Greek authors turn his attention to political matters. His *De Cive* and later *Leviathan* articulated a new science of government. He believed in a materialist philosophy and used that as a presupposition for his political theory, often called the social contract.

Hume, David (1711-1776). Beginning as an historian, this Scottish thinker produced influential works on topics from human nature and human understanding to the principles of morals and challenges to natural religion. He furthered Locke's views that knowledge of the external world is unreliable, saying we only are examining our beliefs about that world. Even causation may be doubted.

Kant, Immanuel (1724-1804). Few people influenced western civilization and western religion as much as Kant. His early work was in geophysics, but his later three *Critiques*, of Pure Reason (metaphysics and epistemology), Practical Reason (morality) and Judgment (aesthetics), restructured how we look at the world. He served as a transition figure from the Enlightenment to the philosophy of Idealism.

Kierkegaard, Soren (1813-1855). This Danish philosopher/theologian challenged the Hegelian model of God, stressing the importance of individual choice, insisting that truth is subjective. His writings are autobiographical, exploring the many aspects of humanity's personality, aesthetic, moral, and religious. His awareness of despair, dread, opened the way for existentialism.

Locke, John (1632-1704). This highly-influential English philosopher started his career as a physician to nobility, but soon left his mark in fields of political theory, epistemology and religion. His empiricist leanings put him in conflict with Descartes' rationalism. His treatises on government influenced movement toward democracy, and he interpreted religious revelation within reason's bounds.

Luther, Martin (1483-1546). Founder of the German Reformation, Luther was an Augustinian monk trained in Bible. After decades of struggling to win God's favor, he discovered the doctrine of justification by grace through faith. His opposition to Rome, writings on Christian freedom, and defiant leadership launched European Protestantism and affected the birth of separate nations.

Mill, John Stuart (1806-1873). This brilliant English thinker, son of philosopher James Mill, produced a landmark system of logic. However, he is remembered more for his promotion and refinement of utilitarianism and for his superb summary of Enlightenment freedom in *On Liberty*. His social reforms sought to improve life in education and sanitation.

Niebuhr, Reinhold (1892-1971). Coming from a devout, educated German family, Niebuhr wrote convincingly of how Christian concepts could keep government and society from committing dangerous mistakes. His *The Nature and Destiny of Man* summarized his teachings, including an understanding of history and the ongoing struggles between power and principle.

Nietzsche, Friedrich (1844-1900). Adjectives ranging from brilliant, poetic and revolutionary to atheist, chauvinist, and fascist describe the range of emotions stirred by Nietzsche. *The Genealogy of Morals* and *Beyond Good and Evil* reveal his critique of liberal Christianity. *The Birth of Tragedy* shows his preference of vital energy over rational thought. His impact on postmodernism is substantial.

Plato (c.428-348 B.C.). Along with his student Aristotle, the greatest of ancient Greek philosophers. His accounts of the dialogues between Socrates and students has shaped western thought on metaphysics, morality, and politics. His most famous writings include *Symposium, The Republic, Meno, Apology*, and *Laws*. The parable of the cave and his theory of forms memorably exhibit his contributions.

Ritschl, Albrecht (1822-1889). German professor and Protestant theologian, Ritschl's main contribution was to articulate clearly the concept of God as love. His *The Christian Doctrine of Justification and Reconciliation* reinforces the liberal

Protestant view that Christ has come not just to free the individual sinner but also the launch the reformation of the world's institutions toward justice and peace.

Rousseau, Jean Jacques (1712-1778). This French political and educational philosopher originally allied with the revolutionary Encyclopaedists of France. His *The Social Contract*, proposing a government based on the general will, incurred royal disfavor. Other works, *Discourse on Inequality, La Nouvelle Heloise*, and *Emile*, made lasting impact by encouraging naturalist and romanticist ideals.

Saussure, Ferdinand de (1857-1913). As the 20th c. dawned, the turn toward more study of language was cemented by Saussure's *Course in General Linguistics*. He emphasized that each element in language is based more on its relationship to other elements than on its relationship to an outside object. This opened the door to structuralism and poststructuralism.

Schleiermacher, Friedrich (1768-1834). Often called the father of liberal theology, Schleiermacher recognized that religion could not be the same after the Enlightenment. In *On Religion: Speeches to its Cultured Despisers*, and later in *The Christian Faith*, he encouraged a Christianity based on the immediate consciousness of God, less constrained by rationalist doctrine.

Smith, Adam (1723-1790). Though often regarded as only an economist, Smith's work affected moral and religious concepts. In the *Theory of Moral Sentiments* and also in *The Wealth of Nations*, he affirmed there is a natural law underlying how laissez-faire capitalism works, and that it is under the guidance of a divine hand.

Spinoza, Baruch (Benedict) (1632-1677). This Jewish rationalist philosopher crafted an elaborate system involving pantheism, Euclidean geometry, and determinism. One spinoff of that, explained in his *Tractatus Theologico-Politicus*, was his reinterpretation of the Bible according to strict categories of reason. This reinterpretation led to him being called the early father of historical criticism.

Voltaire (Francois-Marie Arouet) (1694-1778). Voltaire embodies many characteristics of the French Enlightenment. His famous novel, *Candide*, parodied optimistic rationalism, while his *Philosophical Dictionary* presented deist, anti-church, and anti-royal attitudes. His voice helped inspire the French Revolution.

Whitehead, Alfred North (1861-1947). This English philosopher is renowned for his partnership with Bertrand Russell on the *Principia Mathematica*. His religious impact arose from his system that repudiated the mind-body split and saw reality as a series of events rather than accumulations of matter. His key works in this area include *Science and the Modern World* and *Process and Reality*.

WORKS CITED

Adler, Mortimer J. *The Great Ideas: A Lexicon of Western Thought.* New York: Macmillan, 1992.
Allen, Diogenes. *Christian Belief in a Postmodern World.* Louisville: Westminster/John Knox Press, 1989.
--- "Christian Values in a Post-Christian Context." *Postmodern Theology: Christian Faith in a Pluralist World.* Ed. Frederic Burnham. San Francisco: Harper and Row, 1989 20-36.
--- and Springsted, Eric. *Philosophy for Understanding Theology.* 2nd Ed. Louisville: Westminster/John Knox Press, 2007.
--- *Spiritual Theology: The Theology of Yesterday for Spiritual Help Today.* Boston: Cowley, 1997.
Allitt, Patrick. *The Industrial Revolution: Course Guidebook.* Chantilly, Va.: The Great Courses, 2014.
Altizer, Thomas. "History as Apocalypse." *Sources of Christian Theology in America.* Eds. Mark Toulouse and James Duke. Nashville: Abingdon, 1999. 578-585.
Aquinas, Thomas. *Introduction to St. Thomas Aquinas: Summa Theologica and Summa Contra Gentiles.* Ed and intro. Anton Pegis. New York: Random House, 1948.
Augustine of Hippo. *The City of God.* Ed. and intro. Vernon Bourke. Garden City: Image Books, 1958.
--- "Enchiridion to Laurentius." *Seventeen Short Treatises.* Oxford: University Press, 1847.
--- "Homilies on the Gospel according to St. John." *Augustine: Later Works.* Oxford: University Press, 1954.

WORKS CITED

Bacon, Francis. *Novum Organum* (New Engine). Ed. and notes. Thomas Fowler. Oxford: Clarendon Press, 1878.

Barbour, Ian. *Ethics in an Age of Technology*. New York: Harper Collins, 1993.

--- *Religion in an Age of Science*. New York: Harper and Row, 1990.

--- *When Science Meets Religion*. San Francisco: Harper, 2000.

Barclay, William. *Introducing the Bible*. 1972. Nashville: Abington, 1997.

Barth, Karl. *Church Dogmatics*, Vol.1-4. Edinburgh: T.&T. Clark, 1936-1956.

--- *Epistle to the Romans*. Trans. Edwyn Hoskyns. New York, Oxford University Press, 1976.

--- *The Humanity of God*. Atlanta: John Knox Press, 1974.

--- *The Word of God and the Word of Man*. Trans. Douglas Horton. New York: Harper and Row, 1957.

Beardslee, William. "Process". *Handbook of Postmodern Biblical Interpretation*. Ed. A.K.M. Adam. St. Louis: Chalice Press, 2000.

Beck, Lewis White. Introduction. *Kant. On History*. Indianapolis: Bobbs-Merrill, 1963, vii-xxviii.

Becker, Carl. *The Heavenly City of the Eighteenth-Century Philosophers*. New Haven: Yale University Press, 1979.

Bellah, Robert. "Christian Faithfulness in a Pluralist World". *Postmodern Theology: Christian Faith in a Pluralist World.* 74-91.

Berger, Peter. *The Sacred Canopy*. New York: Anchor Books, 1990.

Boff, Leonardo. *Ecclesiogenesis: The Base Communities Reinvent the Church*. Maryknoll, N.Y.: Orbis Books, 1997.

Bonhoeffer, Dietrich. *Christ the Center*. Trans. John Bowden. New York: Harper and Row, 1966.

--- *The Cost of Discipleship*. Revised and Unabridged ed. New York: Macmillan, 1961.

--- *Creation and Fall/Temptation*. New York: Macmillan, 1971.

--- *Ethics*. Ed. Eberhard Bethge. New York: Macmillan, 1965.

--- *Gesammelte Schriften*. Vol. III. Munich: Christian Kaiser Verlag, 1966.

--- *Letters and Papers from Prison*. Ed. Eberhard Bethge. Enlarged ed. New York: Macmillan, 1972.

--- *Life Together.* Trans. and Intro. John Doberstein. New York: Harper and Row, 1954.

Bordo, Susan. "The Cartesian Masculinization of Thought and the Seventeenth-Century Flight from the Feminine". In *From Modernism to Postmodernism: An Anthology.* Ed. and Intro. Lawrence Cahoone. Expanded Second Ed. Oxford: Blackwell, 2003.

Breisach, Ernst. *Historiography: Ancient, Medieval and Modern.* 2nd ed. Chicago: Univ. of Chicago Press, 1994.

Brown, Warren, Malony, H. Newton, and Murphy, Nancy, Eds. *Whatever Happened to the Soul?: Scientific and Theological Portraits of Human Nature.* Minneapolis: Augsburg Fortress Press, 1998.

Brueggemann, Walter. *Theology of the Old Testament.* Minneapolis: Fortress Press, 1997.

Burnham, Frederic. Ed and Intro. *Postmodern Theology: Christian Faith in a Pluralist World.* San Francisco: Harper and Row, 1989.

Bury, J.B. *The Idea of Progress.* Dover ed. New York: Dover Publications, 1955.

Bushnell, Horace. *Christian Nurture.* New York: Scribner, Armstrong & Co, 1876. Facsimile ed. 1975.

Butterfield, Herbert. *The Origins of Modern Science: 1300-1800.* Rev. ed. New York: Free Press, 1965.

Cahoone, Lawrence. *From Modernism to Postmodernism.* Ed. and Intro. Expanded Second Ed. Oxford: Blackwell Publishing, 2003.

--- The Modern Intellectual Tradition: From Descartes to Derrida. Chantilly, Va.: The Great Courses, 2010.

Calvin, Jean. *Institutes of the Christian Religion.* Ed J.T. McNeill. Trans. Ford Lewis Battle. Vols 1&2. Philadelphia: Westminster Press, 1960.

Campbell, Charles. "Hans Frei." *A New Handbook of Christian Theologians.* Eds Donald Musser and Joseph Price. Nashville: Abingdon Press, 1996. 151-157.

Carlyle, Thomas. "Expositor." *Mistaken Identity.* Collected Works. Centennial Ed., 1896-1899.

Carr, Anne E. *Transforming Grace: Christian Tradition and Women's Experience.* San Francisco: Harper and Row, 1990.

Chadwick, Owen. *The Secularization of the European Mind in the Nineteenth Century.* Cambridge: Cambridge University Press, 1975.

Chambers, Robert. *Vestiges of the Natural History of Creation*. 1844. Cited in Vidler, Alec R. *The Church in an Age of Revolution*. Harmondsworth, Middlesex: Penguin Books, 1971.

Christian, C.W. *Friedrich Schleiermacher*. Waco, Texas: Word Books, 1979. Makers of the Modern Theological Mind series.

Christian History Institute. "Stories Behind Great Scientists." *Glimpses*. Issues 67-72. Worcester, Pa.: Christian History Institute Press, 1995.

Cobb, John and Herman Daly. *For the Common Good: Redirecting the Economy Toward Community*. 1989.

--- *Is It Too Late? A Theology of Ecology*. 1972

--- *Process Theology as Political Theology*. 1982

Cragg, Gerald R. *The Church and the Age of Reason: 1648-1789*. Revised ed. Harmondsworth, Middlesex: Penguin Books, 1970.

Darwin, Charles. *The Origin of Species By Means of Natural Selection*. Sixth ed. Garden City: Doubleday and Company, 1872.

Dawson, Christopher. *Progress and Religion: An Historical Inquiry*. Washington, D.C.: Catholic University of America Press, 2001 Edition.

Derrida, Jacques. "Differance" in *Speech and Phenomena and Other Essays on Husserl's Theory of Signs*. Trans. David B. Allison. Evanston: Northwestern University Press, 1973. Included in Cahoone, *From Modernism....* 225-240.

Descartes, Rene. *Discourse on Method*. Trans. and intro by Arthur Wollaston. Baltimore: Penguin Books, 1960.

--- *Meditations on First Philosophy*. Trans. Laurence J. Lafleur. Second, Revised Edition. Indianapolis: Bobbs-Merrill, 1960. The Library of Liberal Arts series.

Diderot, Denis, with Jean d'Alembert. *Encyclopédie, ou dictionnaire raisonné des sciences, des arts et des métiers*. 1751-1772.

Dillenberger, John and Claude Welch. *Protestant Christianity Interpreted Through Its Development*. New York: Charles Scribner's Sons, 1954.

Donahue, John. "Guidelines for Reading and Interpretation". *New Interpreter's Study Bible: NRSV with the Apocrypha*. Nashville: Abingdon Press, 2003. 2261-2267.

Dostoevsky, Fyodor. *The Brothers Karamazov*. Trans. Constance Garnett, Intro. and notes Maire Jaanus. New York: Barnes & Noble Classics, 2004.

Dulles, Avery. *Models of Revelation*. Maryknoll, N.Y.: Orbis Books, 1992.

Ellul, Jacques. *The Technological Society*. Trans. John Wilkinson. Intro. Robert K. Merton. New York, Vintage Books, 1964.

Engels, Friedrich and Karl Marx. *The Communist Manifesto*. Trans. Samuel Moore. London: Worker's Educational Association, 1848. Current edition, from Marxists Internet Archive, 2004.

Foster, A. Durwood. "Albrecht Ritschl." *A Handbook of Christian Theologians*. Eds. Dean Peerman and Martin Marty. Cleveland: World Publishing Co., 1965. 49-67.

Foucault, Michel. "Nietzsche, Genealogy, History". *Language, Counter-Memory, Practice: Selected Essays and Interviews*. Ed. Donald Bouchard, Ithaca, NY: Cornell University Press, 1977. Also, Excerpt from "Truth and Power". Both are in Cahoone, *From Modernism to Postmodernism*. 241-253.

Frei, Hans. *The Eclipse of Biblical Narrative: A Study in Eighteenth and Nineteenth Century Hermeneutics*. New Haven: Yale University Press, 1974.

Galbraith, John Kenneth. Introductory preface to Thorstein Veblen. *The Theory of the Leisure Class*. Boston: Houghton Mifflin, 1973 ed.

George, Timothy. *Theology of the Reformers*. Nashville: Broadman Press, 1988.

Gilkey, Langdon. "Four Traits of Modernity." *Theology Today*. Vol. 49 #3, 1982.

Goizueta, Roberto. "Juan Luis Segundo." *A New Handbook*.... 419-426.

Griffin, David Ray. "Charles Hartshorne" *A New Handbook*.... 200-213.

Gutierrez, Gustavo. *The Power of the Poor in History*. Maryknoll: Orbis Books, 1983.

--- *A Theology of Liberation: History, Politics, and Salvation*. Maryknoll: Orbis, 1973.

Hall, Douglas John. *The Steward: A Biblical Symbol Come of Age*. Revised Edition. Grand Rapids and New York: Eerdmans and Friendship Press, 1990.

Harding, Sandra. "From Feminist Empiricism to Feminist Standpoint Epistemologies". Cahoone, *From Modernism to Postmodernism*. 354-369.

Hauerwas, Stanley. *After Christendom?* Nashville: Abingdon, 1991.

--- with William Willimon. *Resident Aliens*. 25th Anniversary Ed. Nashville: Abingdon, 2014.

Hegel, George Wilhelm Friedrich. "Lectures on the Philosophy of Religion". *G.W.F. Hegel on Art, Religion, Philosophy*. Trans. E.B. Speirs and J.B. Sanderson.

Ed. J. Glenn Gray. Torchbook ed. New York: Harper and Row, 1970. 128-206.

--- *The Phenomenology of Mind.* Trans. J.B. Baillie. London: Harper and Row, 1967. Original German publication 1807 as *Phanomenologie des Geistes.*

Heidegger, Martin. "The Question Concerning Technology". *The Question Concerning Technology and Other Essays.* Trans. and intro. William Lovitt. New York: Harper Perennial Books, 1977.

Hendry, George. *Theology of Nature.* Philadelphia: Westminster Press, 1980.

Hens-Piazza, Gina. "Lyotard". *Handbook of Postmodern Biblical Interpretation.* Ed. A.K.M Adam. St. Louis: Chalice Press, 2000. 160-166.

Herbert of Cherbury. *De Religione Gentilium.* Quoted in Cragg. *The Church and the Age of Reason 1648-1789.* P. 77.

Hobbes, Thomas. *Leviathan: Or the Matter, Forme, and Power of a Commonwealth Ecclesiastical and Civil.* Ed. Michael Oakeshott. Selected and intro. Richard Peters. New York: Collier Books, 1962.

Hugh of St. Victor. *Didascalicon.* Quoted in Allen, *Spiritual Theology.* 119-120.

Hume, David. *Dialogues Concerning Natural Religion.* Ed. & Intro. Norman Kemp Smith. Library of Liberal Arts ed. Indianapolis: Bobbs-Merrill, 1947.

--- *Inquiry Concerning Human Understanding.* Ed. & Intro. Charles Hendel. Library of Liberal Arts ed. Indianapolis: Bobbs-Merrill, 1955.

Jaki, Stanley. *The Limits of a Limitless Science and Other Essays.* Wilmington: ISI Books, 2000. 1-23.

Jameson, Frederic. "The Cultural Logic of Late Capitalism". Cahoone, *From Modernism to Postmodernism.* 564-574.

Jones, Sheilah. "Womanist Theologians". *A New Handbook of Christian Theologians.* 513-519.

Kant, Immanuel. "Conjectural Beginning of Human History" Trans. Emil Fackenheim. *Kant on History.* Ed. & Intro. Lewis White Beck. Library of Liberal Arts ed. Indianapolis: Bobbs-Merrill, 1963. 53-68.

--- *Critique of Practical Reason.* Trans. & Intro. Lewis White Beck. Liberal Arts Press ed. Indianapolis: Bobbs-Merrill, 1956.

--- *Critique of Pure Reason.* Trans. Norman Kemp Smith. Unabridged ed. New York: St. Martin's Press, 1965.

--- *Groundwork of the Metaphysic of Morals*. Trans. & Intro. H.J. Paton. Harper Torchbook ed. New York: Harper and Row, 1964.

--- "Idea for a Universal History from a Cosmopolitan Point of View". *Kant on History*. 3-10.

--- "What Is Enlightenment?" *Kant on History*. 11-26.

Kierkegaard, Soren. *Concluding Unscientific Postscript*. Intro. Walter Lowrie. Trans. David Swenson and Walter Lowrie. Princeton: Princeton University Press, 1968 ed.

Krentz, Edgar. *The Historical-Critical Method*. Philadelphia: Fortress Press, 1975.

Kugel, James. *How to Read the Bible: A Guide to Scripture, Then and Now*. New York: Simon and Schuster, 2007.

Kuhn, Thomas. *The Structure of Scientific Revolutions*. Second, enlarged ed. International Encyclopedia of Unified Science Vol. 2 Number 2. Chicago: Univ. of Chicago Press, 1970.

Lindbeck, George. "The Church's Mission to a Postmodern Culture". *Postmodern Theology*. 37-55.

--- *The Nature of Doctrine: Religion and Theology in a Postliberal Age*. Philadelphia: Westminster Press, 1984.

Locke, John. *An Essay Concerning Human Understanding*. Oxford: Clarendon Press, 1894 ed.

--- *The Reasonableness of Christianity*. Stanford: Stanford Univ. Press, 1958.

--- *The Second Treatise on Civil Government*. In *John Locke on Politics and Education*. Intro. Howard Penniman. Roslyn, N.Y.: Walter J. Black, Inc. 1947.

Lorenzen, Thorwald. "Jürgen Moltmann". *A New Handbook....* 304-316.

Lovitt, William. Introduction. *The Question of Technology....* xvi-xxxiii.

Luther, Martin. "The Freedom of a Christian". *Martin Luther: Selections from His Writings*. Ed. & intro. John Dillenberger. Garden City: Anchor Books, 1961. 42-85.

--- "The Heidelberg Disputation". *Selected Writings of Martin Luther: 1517-1520*. Ed. Theodore Tappert. Philadelphia: Fortress Press, 1967.

Machinist, Peter. "The Voice of the Historian in the ANE and Mediterranean". *Interpretation.* Vol. 57, #2. 119ff.

Machiavelli, Niccolo. *The Prince.* Trans. & intro. George Bull. Harmondsworth, Middlesex: Penguin Books, 1961.

Marx, Karl. *Das Kapital: A Critique of Political Economy.* Ed. Friedrich Engels. Chicago: Henry Regnery Co. Gateway Edition, 1967.

McNeill, J.T. *The History and Character of Calvinism.* New York: Oxford University Press, 1954.

Metz, Johann Baptist. *Theology of the World.* Trans. William Glen-Doepel. New York: Seabury, 1969.

Mill, John Stuart. *On Liberty.* Ed. Alburey Castell. New York: Appleton-Century-Crofts, 1947.

Moltmann, Jürgen. *The Crucified God: The Cross of Christ as the Foundation and Criticism of Christian Theology.* Trans. R.A. Wilson and John Bowden. New York: Harper and Row, 1972.

--- *Theology of Hope: On the Ground and Implication of a Christian Eschatology.* Trans. James W. Leitch. New York: Harper and Row, 1964.

Momigliano, Armaldo. "Historiography". *Encyclopedia of Religion.* Ed. Mircea Eliade. Vol. 6, 383.

Newbigin, Lesslie. *Foolishness to the Greeks: The Gospel and Western Culture.* Grand Rapids: Eerdmans, 1986.

--- *The Gospel in a Pluralist Society.* Grand Rapids: Eerdmans, 1989.

Newton, Isaac. *Mathematical Principles of Natural Philosophy.* Ed. N.W. Chittenden. Wikisource, American Edition 1846.

Niebuhr, Helmut Richard. *The Meaning of Revelation.* New York: Macmillan, 1960.

Niebuhr, Reinhold. *Children of Light and the Children of Darkness.* New York: Charles Scribner's Sons, 1944.

--- *Does Civilization Need Religion?* New York: MacMillan, 1927.

--- *Faith and History.* New York: Charles Scribner's Sons, 1949.

--- *An Interpretation of Christian Ethics.* New York: Harper and Brothers, 1935.

--- *The Irony of American History.* New York: Charles Scribner's Sons, 1952.

\--- *Moral Man and Immoral Society: A Study in Ethics and Politics.* New York: Charles Scribner's Sons, 1934.
\--- *The Nature and Destiny of Man.* 2 vols. New York: Charles Scribner's Sons, 1943.

Nietzsche, Friedrich. *The Genealogy of Morals. In The Birth of Tragedy and The Genealogy of Morals.* Trans. Francis Golffing. Garden City: Doubleday & Company, 1956.
\--- *Thus Spoke Zarathustra. The Portable Nietzsche.* Translated, edited, and introduction, Walter Kaufman. New York: Viking Press, 1968.
\--- "On Truth and Lies in a Nonmoral Sense". Cahoone. *From Modernism....* 109-116.

Packard, Vance. *The Hidden Persuaders.* Intro. Mark Miller. Ig Publishers: 2007 Paperback edition.
Paley, William. *Natural Theology or Evidences of the Existence and Attributes of the Deity.* 12th edition. London: J. Faulder, 1809.
Pannenberg, Wolfhart. *Toward a Theology of Nature: Essays on Science and Faith.* Ed. & Intro. Ted Peters. Louisville: Westminster/John Knox Press, 1993.
Pascal, Blaise. *Pensees: Notes on Religion and Other Subjects.* Ed. & Intro. Louis Lafuma. Trans. John Warrington. London: J.M. Dent & Sons, 1960.
Pelikan, Jaroslav. *Jesus Through the Centuries: His Place in the History of Culture.* New York: Harper and Row, 1985.
Pellauer, David. "Paul Ricoeur". *A New Handbook of Christian Theologians.* 387-398.
Placher, William. "Hans Frei and the Meaning of Biblical Narrative". Christian Century. Dec.13, 2006. religion-online.org/showarticle.asp?title=15
Polanyi, Michael. *Personal Knowledge.* New York: Harper Torchbooks, 1964.
\--- *The Tacit Dimension.* Garden City: Anchor Books Edition, 1967.

Presbyterian Church (U.S.A.). *Book of Confessions.* Louisville: Office of the General Assembly, 2014.
Principe, Lawrence. *Science and Religion. Course Guidebook,* Great Courses series. Chantilly, Va.: The Teaching Company, 2006.
Ramsey, Paul. *Basic Christian Ethics.* Chicago: University of Chicago Press, Paperback ed.,1980.

Ricoeur, Paul. *Time and Narrative*. 3 volumes. Trans. Kathleen McLaughlin and David Pellauer. Chicago: Univ. of Chicago Press, 1988.

Ritschl, Albrecht. *The Christian Doctrine of Justification and Reconciliation*. Edinburgh: T. & T. Clark, 1900.

Rousseau, Jean Jacques. *Discourse on the Arts and Sciences. The Social Contract and Discourses*. Trans. & Intro. G.D.H. Cole. London: J.M. Dent & Sons, 1968. 117-142.

--- *Discourse on the Origin of Inequality. The Social Contract....* 143-229.

--- *Emile*. Trans. Barbara Foxley. Intro. Andre Boutet de Monvel. London: J.M. Dent & Sons, 1969.

Ruether, Rosemary Radford. "Feminist Theology in the Academy" *Sources of Christian Theology in America*. 534-543.

Russell, Bertrand, and Whitehead, Alfred North. *Principia Mathematica*. Cambridge: University Press, 1910-1913.

Ryle, Gilbert. *The Concept of Mind*. Chicago: Univ. of Chicago Press, 2002 ed.

Sartre, Jean Paul. *Existentialism is a Humanism*. Ed. John Kulka, trans. Carol Macomber. New Haven: Yale Univ. Press, 2007.

--- *Existentialism*. Cahoone, From Modernism..., 169-173.

Saussure, Ferdinand de. "Sign, Signified, Signifier". Course in General Linguistics. Cahoone, *From Modernism...*, 122-126.

Schleiermacher, Friedrich. *The Christian Faith*. Ed. H.R. Mackintosh and J.S. Stewart. Philadelphia: Fortress Press, 1976.

--- *On Religion: Speeches to Its Cultured Despisers*. Trans. John Oman. Intro. Rudolf Otto. New York: Harper Torchbooks, 1958.

Schneiders, Sandra. "Does the Bible Have a Postmodern Message?" *Postmodern Theology*. 56-73.

Smith, Adam. *An Inquiry into the Nature and Causes of the Wealth of Nations*. London: Methuen and Co., Ltd., ed. Edwin Cannan, 1904. Fifth edition.

--- *Theory of Moral Sentiments*. Vol. 1 &2. Ed. D.D. Raphael and A.L. Macfie. Sixth ed. Oxford: Liberty Classics, 1976.

Spener, P.J. Pia Desideria. Noted in Cragg, *The Church and the Age of Reason*. 101. Originally 1675.

Spinoza, Baruch (Benedict). *Theological-Political Treatise*. Trans. E. Curley. Princeton: Princeton University Press, 1985. Originally 1670.

Suchocki, Marjorie Hewitt. "John B. Cobb, Jr." *New Handbook*.... 106-117.

Swift, Johnathan. *The Battle of the Books. A Tale of a Tub, The Battle of the Books, and Other Satires*. Everyman Paperback ed. Intro. Lewis Melvin. London: J.M. Dent & Sons, 1968.

Tawney, R.H. *The Sickness of an Acquisitive Society*. London: Broadway Press, 1920.

Taylor, Mark McClain. "Gustavo Gutierrez". *A New Handbook*.... 189-199.

Tindal, Matthew. *Christianity As Old as the Creation*. Noted in Cragg, *The Church and the Age of Reason*. 159-161. Originally 1730.

Toland, John. *Christianity Not Mysterious*. Noted in Cragg, *The Church*.... 78. Originally 1696.

Tolstoy, Leo. "A Confession". *A Confession, The Gospel in Brief, and What I Believe*. Trans. & Intro. Aylmer Maude. London: Oxford University Press, 1974.

Torrance, Thomas. *Christian Theology and Scientific Culture*. New York: Oxford University Press, 1981.

Tyson, Timothy. *Blood Done Sign My Name*. New York, Three Rivers Press, 2004.

Veblen, Thorstein. *The Theory of the Leisure Class*. Boston: Houghton Mifflin Co., 1973 ed.

Vidler, Alec. *The Church in an Age of Revolution*. Harmondsworth, Middlesex: Penguin Books, 1974 revised ed.

Von Drehle, David. Editorial, *The Washington Post*, January 8, 2021.

West, Cornel, "A Genealogy of Modern Racism". Cahoone, *From Modernism*.... 298-309.

--- *Race Matters*. Boston: Beacon Press, 1993.

White, Andrew D. *A History of the Warfare of Science with Theology in Christendom*. Buffalo: Prometheus Books, 1993.

Whitehead, Alfred North. *Process and Reality*. Ed. David Ray Griffin and Donald W. Sherburne. New York: Free Press, 1979 corrected edition.

--- *Science and the Modern World*. New York: MacMillan, 1925.

Williams, Delores. "A Womanist Notion of Sin". *Sources of Christian Theology in America*. 556-561.

Williams, Rowan. "Postmodern Theology and the Judgment of the World". *Postmodern Theology*. 92-112.

Wolpe, David. *The Raleigh News and Observer*. Editorial column. Rabbi Mark Gelman, January 19, 2012.

Young, Iris Marion. "The Scaling of Bodies and the Politics of Identity." Cahoone, *From Modernism....* 370-382.

All biblical passages quoted herein come from *The New Interpreter's Study Bible: New Revised Standard Version with the Apocrypha*. Nashville: Abingdon Press, 2003.

INDEX

Allen, Diogenes – 96, 156, 184, 224-230
Altizer, Thomas – 247-252, 272
Aquinas, St. Thomas – 7, 38-40
Aristotle – 12, 15-17, 35, 87, 131, 144, 184
Augustine of Hippo, St. – 25, 35, 102, 157, 162, 266

Bacon, Francis – 7,12,16,42,46,120, 131, 133, 195,221,233
Barth, Karl – 1, 79-85, 89,92,196, 252, 255, 263, 272, 276, 305
Bonhoeffer, Dietrich – 79, 85, 244, 272-282

Calvin, Jean – 1, 11, 36-40, 78, 81-82, 89, 102-103, 150

Darwin, Charles (evolution) – 64-66, 76, 138, 159-165, 203, 257
Derrida, Jacques – 204-210, 221, 224, 230-234, 249, 288, 297
Descartes, Rene – 12-16, 41-46, 53, 88, 120, 131-133, 145, 150-152, 178, 180, 184-185, 194, 195, 204, 211, 219, 314
Diderot, Denis – 52, 156, 166, 188
Doubt – 42-43, 150-152

Ecology – 241-242, 263-264, 312
Ellul, Jacques – 166, 312-315
Existentialism (J.P. Sartre) – 198, 211-212

Feminist Critiques (Bordo, Harding, Reuther, Young, Carr) – 218-220, 292-293
Fichte, Johann – 26, 132, 146, 208, 210, 212, 238
Foucault, Michel – 214-216, 224, 230, 231, 235-240

Galileo, Galilei – 7, 12-16, 42, 46, 150-159, 165, 184-185

Hegel, George W.F. – 26-28, 36, 63-69, 131-133, 146, 160, 178, 180, 188, 196, 200, 212, 227, 235, 248, 250, 257
Heidegger, Martin – 83, 232, 236, 238, 312-315
Herder, Johann – 26, 64, 70, 131-133, 180
Historical-Critical Method – 76, 128-135, 180
Historicism – 150, 152-155
Hobbes, Thomas (*Leviathan*) – 18-19, 61, 104-105, 120
Hume, David – 21-23, 33, 55-59, 67, 106, 308

Idealism, Philosophical – 22, 26, 133, 143-148, 178

Kant, Immanuel – 22-26, 59, 70, 77, 83, 96, 106-110, 146-148, 170, 179, 183-184, 209-212, 225-226, 240, 309
Kierkegaard, Soren – 84, 154, 196
Kugel, James (*How To Read the Bible*) – 126-139

Liberalism – 34, 69-79, 214
Liberation Theology (Gutierrez et al.) 265-272
Lindbeck, George – 257, 293-303
Locke, John – 18-19, 45-51, 104-106, 112, 120, 145, 195, 200
Luther, Martin – 8, 10-11, 17, 36-40, 81-82, 102-103, 149, 272-273, 279
Lyotard, Jean-Francois – 203, 211, 224, 302

Marx, Karl and Engels, F. – 64, 110, 161, 196-197, 210, 236, 270-271
Metanarratives – 198, 201, 207, 228, 232, 238, 240, 252, 258, 302-304
Mill, John Stuart (*On Liberty*), Utilitarianism – 19-21, 148, 167-175, 181, 190, 227
Moltmann, Jürgen – 265, 289-290

Narrative Theology (Ricoeur, Frei) – 252-257
Natural Religion (Deism, natural theology) – 31, 45-53, 55-60, 162, 263, 307
Nature, Theology of (Hendry, Pannenberg) – 303, 307-312
Newton, Sir Isaac – 16, 45-53, 112, 158, 161-163, 200, 211, 214, 233, 258, 309, 312
Niebuhr, Reinhold – 81, 87-93, 189-191
Nietzsche, Friedrich – 198, 214-218, 237-243, 250-253, 255

Plato – 89, 147, 213, 238-240
Poststructuralism – 206, 232, 241, 248
Process Theology – (Hartshorne, Cobb) – 259-266

Protestant Reformation – 11, 31, 152, 253

Ramsey, Paul (*Basic Christian Ethics*) – 145, 146, 187, 188, 199
Ritschl, Albrecht – 77-82, 92
Romanticism – 36, 62, 64-66, 72, 134
Rousseau, Jean-Jacques – 35, 62-65, 90

Saussure, Ferdinand de – 203-208, 218, 233, 255, 299
Schelling, Friedrich – 28, 66, 148
Schleiermacher, Friedrich – 36, 61, 65, 71-81, 216, 259
Smith, Adam – 106, 112-121, 182
Social Contract Theory – 19-22, 26, 106-108, 112, 181
Spener, Jakob (Pietism) – 55, 56
Spinoza, Benedict – 66, 130-136, 182,
Structuralism (Cassirer, Levi-Strauss) – 206-210, 217

Tawney, R.H. – 119-121
Thirty Years War – 43, 135
Torrance, Thomas – 167, 307

Veblen, Thorstein – 117-119
Voltaire – 54, 150, 158, 220

Wesley, John and Charles – 56-57, 72, 73
West, Cornel – 219-220, 290
Whitehead, Lord Alfred – 246, 259-263

www.ingramcontent.com/pod-product-compliance
Lightning Source LLC
Chambersburg PA
CBHW060349080526
44583CB00012B/238